GEORGE
BUSH'S
WAR

GEORGE
BUSH'S
WAR

JEAN EDWARD SMITH

HENRY HOLT AND COMPANY   NEW YORK

Published by Henry Holt and Company, Inc.,
115 West 18th Street, New York, New York 10011.
Published in Canada by Fitzhenry & Whiteside Limited,
91 Granton Drive, Richmond Hill, Ontario L4B 2N5

Library of Congress Cataloging-in-Publication Data

Smith, Jean Edward.
George Bush's war / by Jean Edward Smith.—1st ed.
p.   cm.
Includes bibliographical references and index.
1. Persian Gulf War, 1991—United States.   2. Bush, George.
I. Title.
DS79.72.S65   1992
956.704′3—dc20   91-31059
CIP

ISBN 0-8050-1388-1

Henry Holt books are available at special discounts
for bulk purchases for sales promotions, premiums,
fund-raising, or educational use. Special editions
or book excerpts can also be created to specification.
For details contact: Special Sales Director,
Henry Holt and Company, Inc., 115 West 18th Street,
New York, New York 10011

First Edition—1992

Book Design by Claire Naylon Vaccaro
Printed in the United States of America
Recognizing the importance of preserving
the written word, Henry Holt and Company, Inc.,
by policy, prints all of its first editions
on acid-free paper. ∞

3   5   7   9   10   8   6   4

CONTENTS

It has been a splendid little war; begun with the highest motives, carried on with magnificent intelligence and spirit, favored by Fortune which loves the brave. It is now concluded, I hope, with that fine good nature, which is, after all, the distinguishing trait of the American character.

—John Hay to Theodore Roosevelt
July 27, 1898

GEORGE
BUSH'S
WAR

INTRODUCTION

To be a great president, you have to have a
war. All the great presidents have had their
wars.
—Admiral William J. Crowe
November 22, 1990

For George Bush, the war against Iraq was fought for high
principle. Aggression must be punished. "No nation should
rape, pillage, and brutalize its neighbor," said the president. "No nation should be able to wipe a member state of
the United Nations and the Arab League off the face of the
earth."[1]

For the president, the war was a personal crusade: a black-
and-white struggle between good and evil; an opportunity "to
stand up for what's right and condemn what's wrong."[2] Bush's
certitude provided resolute direction for American policy.
When some sought compromise, Bush held firm. When some
sought delay, Bush pressed ahead. When some cautioned restraint, the president went all out. No deals, no negotiations,
no face-saving exit. Iraq must withdraw from Kuwait, and Saddam Hussein must be humiliated.

Bush personalized the crisis. Past presidents—FDR, Eisenhower, Nixon, even Lyndon Johnson—usually spoke of the United States, or the government, when describing national policy. For George Bush, it was invariably first-person singular. "I've had it";[3] "I am getting increasingly frustrated";[4] "Consider me provoked";[5] "I am not ruling out further options";[6] "I don't want to say what I will or will not do";[7] "I am more determined than ever in my life";[8] "I have not ruled out the use of force";[9] "I have no specific deadline";[10] "I will never—ever—agree to a halfway effort."[11] It was as if foreign policy had become presidential autobiography. The crisis became a struggle of will between George Bush in Washington and Saddam Hussein in Baghdad. Each consistently misjudged the other. Neither was prepared to back down.

Much like Saddam, Bush directed policy with a small coterie of subordinates: his national security adviser, Brent Scowcroft; Secretary of State James Baker; Secretary of Defense Dick Cheney; and, as the occasion required, General Colin Powell, chairman of the joint chiefs of staff. The National Security Council* lapsed into an informal men's club, "boys sitting around shooting the shit before the weekend," according to one participant.[12] On the one hand, such informality facilitated the president's personal direction of the crisis. These were his men. They carried out his bidding—and they did that very effectively. On the other hand, such intimacy screened out contrary opinions and deprived the president of expert advice. Professional experience in the area, usually a cautionary influence, counted for little in the decision-making structure of the Bush White House.

At times, American policy seemed to be based on the mood swings of a president who substituted Martin Gilbert's *The Second World War*[13] for reasoned position papers, and who fortified his resolve with tales of atrocities committed by SS Death's

---

*Pursuant to the National Security Act of 1947, as amended, the NSC consists of the president, the vice president, and the secretaries of state and defense. The president's national security adviser, the director of central intelligence, and the chairman of the joint chiefs of staff attend in an advisory capacity.

Head regiments marching into Poland. The fact is, Bush read little and reflected less. But what he did read made an indelible impression. He got hooked on Gilbert's book in early August, and from that point on, Iraq's invasion of Kuwait was identified with the Holocaust, and Saddam equated with Hitler.

The war revealed the strengths and weaknesses of the American system. The United States responded quickly and decisively to an international crisis halfway around the globe. The military performed miraculously. Never in the history of warfare, saving perhaps Eisenhower's landing on D-Day, have a nation's armed forces served with greater efficiency, or been more responsive to political necessity. The requirements of our allies were never lost sight of. The coalition grew tighter as the struggle evolved. If Lawrence of Arabia is alive, his name is Schwarzkopf.

At the tactical level, the doctrine of AirLand Battle, developed over the past twenty years, was executed with flawless precision. America's high-tech weaponry, communications equipment, and intelligence-gathering facilities proved themselves many times over, often under the most adverse conditions. Never before have so many soldiers, and so much equipment, been transported so far, so quickly, and with so little advance notice. Karl von Clausewitz, the Prussian military strategist, said that war is logistics. It is also esprit, bravery, and professionalism: the routine performance of hazardous duty. The United States provided the world with an awesome display of military prowess.

Once hostilities began, the home front, if one can call it that, did not waver. And, perhaps most importantly, when the enemy was beaten, the dogs of war were leashed and recalled. The military quietly resumed its role as defender of the State, slightly over the horizon from public view.

The weaknesses of the war were not military. They were political. And they go to the core of our constitutional scheme of government. Was the war necessary? What did it accomplish? And how was the decision made to initiate hostilities in the first place? Would lesser means have sufficed? Would the results be less burdensome and heart-wrenching? Were America's vital interests at stake? Was sufficient thought given to the consequences of victory? Did American involvement reflect concerted national policy, as, say, the decision to defend Western Europe after World War II, or was it a by-product of presidential whim—a visceral hiccup of executive emotion? It may have been a just war, but was it a wise one?

The Constitution posits a system of checks and balances. But in foreign affairs, they are often short-circuited. George Bush maintains that foreign policy is a personal prerogative. "I have an obligation as president to conduct the foreign policy of this country the way I see fit," he said in August, shortly after Saddam's troops took over Kuwait.[14] Bush claims that the framers of the Constitution intended it that way.[15] He is fond of quoting John Marshall to the effect that the president is "the sole organ of the nation in its external affairs."[16]

Not only is the president responsible for foreign policy, but in Bush's view he is also free to take the country into war. Speaking at a campaign rally in October, Bush insisted that he had the authority to initiate hostilities unilaterally.[17] Baker and Cheney agreed. Baker testified to that effect at length before Congress in October.[18] Cheney told the Senate Armed Services Committee on December 3 that "there is no question that the president, as commander in chief, can order the forces to engage in offensive action, and they will properly obey his command."[19] As late as January 9, 1991, one week before Desert Storm, Bush continued to proclaim unlimited power to make war. "I think Secretary Cheney expressed it very well," he said. "I feel that I have the constitutional authority" to go to war, and "Saddam Hussein should be under no question on this."[20]

Bush's assertion of arbitrary presidential power is a throwback to the days of the English crown. It is unsupported in usage, precedent, or the text of the Constitution. George III may have enjoyed the power of determining war or peace. George Bush does not.

If the framers of the Constitution were clear on one point, it was that the president was not a king, and that he did not enjoy the royal prerogative. Alexander Hamilton, a friend of executive power if there ever was one, expressed it best when he explained why the Founding Fathers had divided the responsibility for foreign relations between the president and Congress. "The history of human conduct," he wrote, "does not warrant that exalted opinion of human virtue which would make it wise in a nation to commit interests of so delicate and momentous a kind as those which concern its intercourse with the rest of the world to the sole disposal of a magistrate, created and circumstanced as would be a president of the United States."[21] Hamilton went on to say in *Federalist* 69 that the power of the president as commander in chief was "much inferior" to "that of the British King," because the king could initiate war and the president could not.[22]

The framers of the Constitution were realists. They divided the war powers along functional lines. The president, as commander in chief, possessed the necessary authority to repel sudden attacks, but the power to initiate war rested with Congress. James Madison, the Constitution's principal architect, wrote that the power to commence war was "fully and exclusively vested in the legislature" and that the executive "has no right . . . to decide the question."[23] Later, he wrote to Thomas Jefferson that "the Constitution supposes what the history of all governments demonstrate, that the executive is the branch of power most interested in war, and most prone to it. It has accordingly, with studied care, vested the question of war in the legislature."[24]

Bush's history is also faulty. John Marshall, the great chief justice, was not one of the framers of the Constitution. His remarks about "sole organ" were made in 1800 while he was a member of the House of Representatives, and related exclusively to President Adams's authority to speak on behalf of the nation. For Marshall, "sole organ" meant that the president was the United States' sole vehicle for communications with foreign nations. It had nothing whatever to do with who formulated foreign policy.[25] As chief justice, Marshall consistently upheld Congress's war powers, often at the expense of the president.[26] In *Talbot v. Seeman*, he wrote, "The whole powers of war being, by the Constitution of the United States, vested in Congress, the acts of that body can alone be resorted to as our guide."[27]

Because the Gulf war was short and glorious, Bush's attitude counts for little. But the perils of presidential prerogative were evident in Bush's tendency to make policy on the spur of the moment. His watershed announcement that Iraq's occupation of Kuwait "will not stand" was delivered while stepping down from Marine Corps One onto the White House lawn.[28] Congress was not consulted. The State Department was not informed. The military was not prepared. Even his closest aides were caught by surprise at the president's statement. There had been no meeting of the National Security Council and no debate. General Powell reports that it was as if "the president had six-shooters and was blazing away."[29]

By the same token, Bush's abrupt decision on November 30 to invite Tariq Aziz, Iraq's foreign minister, to Washington (and send Baker to Baghdad) undercut the diplomatic pressure that was building on Saddam, and convinced him that Washington had blinked. Our allies were appalled, the State Department was surprised, and Congress was caught off base. The president's unanticipated order to the Navy on August 12 to interdict Iraqi shipping was cut from the same cloth. It sent the French and Russians running for cover, and required two frantic weeks of intense diplomatic activity to repair the damage. It was the scariest moment of the crisis, according to one White House aide. "I would sit on my bed looking out the window down the Kennebunk River and I could almost see those destroyers on the horizon."[30] A premature war was averted, but just barely.

Advocates of unrestrained presidential power must take the bitter with the sweet. If, as Bush suggests, the president makes foreign policy, then he must bear responsibility for the confusion that preceded Saddam's invasion of Kuwait. As the record makes clear, the United States sent mixed signals throughout the summer of 1990. On the one hand, the Kuwaitis were encouraged to hang tough in their negotiations with Iraq. On the other, the Iraqis were led to believe that the United States would not intervene if Kuwait were attacked. Ambassador April Glaspie was merely parroting official policy when she told Saddam that Washington had "no opinion on Arab-Arab conflicts, like your border disagreement with Kuwait."[31]

That position was not as foolish as it later appeared. Iraq had long and legitimate grievances against Kuwait, and the State Department understood that. In addition, Iraq, a secular, modernizing state, stood four-square against Khomeini-style Islamic fundamentalism. Saddam was an ugly piece of work, but he also served American purposes as a counter to Hafez Assad's terrorist regime in Syria. When all was said and done, Saddam had proved capable of governing the grab bag of nationalities that comprised Iraq—albeit with methods far removed from the Magna Carta and the Bill of Rights. Given the choice between a modicum of social progress in Iraq and the unrepentant feudalism of Kuwait, it was a tough call. The one variable unaccounted for in the State Department's analysis was Iraq's military strength and the menace it posed to the region, especially to Israel.

On August 2, when the invasion occurred, Bush was flummoxed. His instincts to resist aggression were aroused, but there appeared no urgency to intervene. The widespread assumption, especially among the Arab states, was that Saddam would take what he wanted and quickly withdraw. It was not until Bush met with British prime minister Margaret Thatcher later that day in Aspen, Colorado, that American policy reversed. Thatcher convinced the impressionable Bush that the loss of Kuwait was equivalent to the sellout of Czechoslovakia at Munich. She encouraged him to follow his instincts, to stand up to Saddam and force him to withdraw. The "Arab solution" fashioned by Jordan's King Hussein, Saudi Arabia's King Fahd, and Egyptian president Hosni Mubarak that would have rewarded Iraq with a slice of Kuwait was torpedoed, and the mobilization of American power followed in due course.

Initially, Bush dissembled. The original deployment of U.S. forces in the Gulf was egregiously misrepresented as necessary to defend Saudi Arabia from Iraqi attack. But the Saudis were not convinced they were threatened by Saddam, and, despite the elaborate spin control engineered by Washington, there is no evidence that they were. Certainly, when he had abundant opportunity in August to overrun Saudi Arabia, Saddam declined to do so. The massive augmentation of American forces, announced by Bush after the November elections, was concealed at first from Congress and the public. Its very size made its use inevitable. Either that or back down ignominiously and withdraw.

If Bush hid his hand at home, his diplomacy was masterly. He revitalized a dispirited and moribund United Nations, brought the Arabs and Israelis into tacit alliance, and worked hand in glove with the Soviets and Chinese to counter Saddam. The oil-rich Gulf states, the Germans, and the Japanese picked up most of the tab. The Syrians were brought back into the fold of accepted behavior. The Turks, the Egyptians, and the fractious French worked easily in tandem. No one but Bush could have built such an alliance, or held it together so tenaciously. His personal rapport with world leaders was unparalleled.

From that first day in Aspen with Margaret Thatcher, this was George Bush's war. The State Department did not press it. The military did not seek it. And, except for the Israeli lobby, there were no war hawks in Congress. Secretary of State Baker consistently sought compromise;[32] Colin Powell wanted to stick with sanctions;[33] and General H. Norman Schwarzkopf told the press in December that "if the alternative to dying is sitting out in the sun for another summer, that's not a bad alternative."[34]

George Bush was the architect of conflict, and the locomotive that drove it forward. Unless Saddam withdrew from Kuwait, there was no alternative. Time was slipping by. The longer the Iraqis held on, the more difficult they would be to dislodge. Kuwait was being dismantled, and the alliance was a transitory thing. Public opinion, here and abroad, was fickle. Traumatized by Vietnam and a succession of failed presidencies, Bush put his chips on military victory.

The war lasted 43 days. The ground assault, 100 hours. The United States deployed 540,000 troops. Our allies over 200,000. In the air bombardment phase, the pilots of Desert Storm dropped 142,000 tons of bombs on Iraq and Kuwait—about 5 percent of the total in the years of World War II. Iraq's infrastructure, its power and communications nets, and its armaments industry were laid waste. Its army was destroyed. More than 100,000 Iraqi troops have been reported killed. Three hundred thousand were wounded. Another 60,000 surrendered. Saddam lost 3,700 tanks, 2,400 armored vehicles, and 2,600 artillery pieces. American casualties were 148 killed in action, of whom 35 were struck by friendly fire. Fifty-seven U.S. planes and helicopters were lost. Not one American tank was destroyed.

Seldom, if ever, has a victory been so one-sided, or a defeat so massive. Aside from Henry V's devastating rout of the French at Agincourt in 1415 (English bowmen picked off more than 10,000 of the enemy while suffering scarcely a casualty), the closest parallel is Kitchener's defeat of the Dervish forces of the Kalifa Abdulla at Omdurman in 1898. As in Desert Storm, Kitchener relied on superior technology, supply, and transportation. By contrast, the Dervishes could not feed their outlying men and horses. They were a spent force militarily before the battle began. Kitchener lost 350 men; the Kalifa, 20,000. And the Egyptian treasury paid most of Kitchener's costs. The British public was elated. Kitchener and Lord Salisbury, the prime minister, won overwhelming acclaim. Kitchener was knighted and became chief of the imperial general staff. Salisbury won reelection.[35]

It is invariably true that after successful wars, generals become heroes and politicians benefit. Eisenhower and MacArthur after World War II. Pershing from World War I. Grant, Sherman, and Sheridan after the Civil War. Sometimes, even in defeat, our generals are paid homage, such as Lee and Stonewall Jackson. After Desert Storm, acclaim has gone to two contemporary military heroes: Colin Powell and H. Norman Schwarzkopf, battle-scarred veterans of the Army's tragic experience in Vietnam. As chairman of the joint chiefs of staff, Powell is rightfully credited for insisting that if force be used, it be used massively, and that the enemy be overwhelmed quickly. Schwarzkopf, the commander of Desert Storm, also deserves praise for insisting that he have the tools to do the job. If the president wanted an offensive option to drive Saddam from Kuwait, Schwarzkopf wanted the Army's best: the heavy armor of VII Corps from Germany—a unit that had been trained to take on the tanks of the Red Army. The Iraqis were equipped with Soviet tanks, had been trained by the Russians, and employed Red Army tactics. For VII Corps, it was like going into action against the B-team.

Schwarzkopf may have been a difficult subordinate, but he knew the requirements of his job, and he kept his potentially divisive coalition marching in cadence. America's forty years of multilateral experience in NATO provided a model for military cooperation, and the staff of Desert Storm utilized that experience effectively. Both Powell and Schwarzkopf merit accolades for the flanking tactics that were used, and Schwarzkopf for the precision with which they were executed. Secretary of Defense Cheney and President Bush let the generals do their job. And, like Salisbury, they have been rewarded handsomely.

The costs have been very high. As the euphoria of victory recedes, it has become increasingly apparent that the damage wrought by Desert Storm has been enormous. A United Nations survey called the bombing of Iraq "near-apocalyptic," threatening to reduce "a rather highly urbanized and mechanized society to a preindustrial age."[36] The *Washington Post* reports that 70 percent of the bombs dropped on Iraq missed their intended targets, and that civilian and military casualties numbered in the hundreds of thousands.[37] Because of oil spills related to the war, marine life in the upper Persian Gulf is unlikely to recover for at least forty years.

Kuwait has been liberated, and the emir has been returned to power. Despite their enforced exile, the al-Sabahs, like the Bourbons of France, appear to have learned nothing and forgotten nothing. The emir displays none of the ardor for democracy he proclaimed during the war, and the repressive feudal structure has been restored *en bloc*. That regime seems incapable of confronting the tasks of reconstruction. Were it not for the Army's Corps of Engineers, Kuwait City would still be without light, water, and telephone service. The last of the 750 oil-well fires were not extinguished until November. Six million barrels of oil, 10 percent of the world's daily supply, went up in smoke every day.[38] The ecological damage has been incalculable. Even worse, the *vae victus* arrogance of returning Kuwaitis ushered in a reign of terror directed against those persons who remained behind, especially the Palestinians.

In Iraq, Saddam Hussein remains in power, as firmly entrenched as ever. Having made the removal of Saddam an important adjunct of American strategy, Bush turned tail when civil war erupted. Iraq sits at that strategic juncture between the Persians, the Arabs, and the Turks. Its population is an unstable mixture, always threatening to unravel. Belatedly, the White House recognized that instability in Iraq is even more threatening to the region than the continuation of Saddam in power. Whether he was another Hitler or not, no one other than Saddam appeared capable of holding the country together. As a result, he was given virtual carte blanche to suppress the revolts that Bush had inspired. The Shiites were put down with fearsome brutality in the south. The fate of the

Kurds in northern Iraq has become an international tragedy. Throughout Iraq, the suffering brought on by the war has been appalling.

An unsettling parallel emerges between defeated Iraq and Germany of 1919. Like Germany, Iraq was compelled to comply with peace terms dictated by the victors. Like Germany, those peace terms require significant disarmament that the victors must police. In the 1920s and '30s, the Western allies failed in that responsibility, and the indications are that the current allies may be no more successful.

Iraq, like Germany after World War I, remains bitter and resentful. And like Germany, it retains the potential to do something about it. Whether Saddam remains in power or not, future Iraqi leaders can fan the flames of that resentment and seek revenge. If, today, peace in the Middle East is more secure, it may prove to be a transitory thing.

The war was fought to punish aggression. The sovereignty of every state, no matter how small, is fundamental. A noble principle was at stake. That principle lies at the root of the international system. But it does not exist in isolation. Was it applied selectively in the Gulf? Was American action vindictive? Did George Bush's judgment measure up to U.S. military proficiency?

1.

INVASION

The Assyrian came down
Like the wolf on the fold . . .
—Lord Byron

At 2 A.M., August 2 (7 P.M., August 1, Washington time), the lead tanks of two Iraqi armored divisions rolled past startled Kuwaiti customs guards and began a lightning dash toward Kuwait City, some sixty miles to the south. A third armored division crossed the frontier to the west. The thirty thousand troops in the initial assault wave were from Iraq's republican guards: decorated veterans of the war with Iran, and fiercely loyal to Saddam Hussein. Equipped with modern Soviet T-72 tanks, the Iraqi forces encountered only sporadic resistance as they rumbled down Kuwait's six-lane superhighway toward the capital. Within three hours, the guards divisions, supported by helicopter assault troops, were fanning out through the city. Within five hours, all effective opposition had ceased. Within twelve hours, all of Kuwait—an area approximately the size of New Jersey—was under Iraqi control. Seldom has an invasion been so swift, or a victory so complete.[1]

The Iraqi invasion reflected crisp military efficiency. The guards divisions enjoyed only a 3:2 numerical advantage over Kuwaiti armed forces,[2] but achieved total tactical surprise. Their momentum was overwhelming. In addition to the main crossings, flank units sliced across the desert to the east and to the west. The guards' assault was supported by self-propelled artillery and three motorized infantry divisions from the 3rd and 7th army corps stationed near Basra, forty miles north of the Kuwait border. While the main force advanced against Kuwait City, other units moved eastward toward the Persian Gulf. Simultaneously, troop-carrying helicopters headed for the two uninhabited Kuwaiti islands of Bubiyan and Warba. The islands (more like sandbars) dominate the approaches to Umm Qasr, Iraq's only port with direct access to the Gulf, and had long been a source of tension between the two countries. Air power was employed sparingly, its main purpose to intimidate the few Kuwaiti defenders.

The invasion was no contest. Casualties were extremely light. Fewer than one hundred persons were killed on both sides. Speaking of the Iraqi tactics shortly afterward, General Powell said that Iraq's generals "conducted the Kuwaiti operations in a very professional manner. It's an army that's very capable. They've had eight years' experience in war."[3]

What little fighting there was centered on two army barracks west of Kuwait City, the international airport, and Dasman Palace, the emir's seaside residence. Special Kuwaiti battalions, trained by British commandos to protect the emir and his family, put up a dogged defense until overwhelmed by superior Iraqi firepower. These were exceptions. For the most part, the Kuwaiti armed forces offered little resistance, surrendered quickly, or joined the panic flight of the royal family and others to neighboring Saudi Arabia. The emir, Sheik Jabir al-Ahmed al-Sabah, fled abruptly in a caravan of Mercedes 600s shortly after the Iraqi troops crossed the border.[4] The family's honor was saved by the emir's half-brother, Sheik Fahd al-Ahmed al-Sabah, who perished with a rifle in his hand defending the all-but-deserted palace. A brave man, Sheik Fahd was president of the Olympic Council of Asia, a well-known figure in international athletic circles, and was regarded by many as the driving force behind the 1988 Seoul Olympics. Often critical of the al-Sabah family's high style of living, he had served as a commando officer fighting with the Palestinians in the 1967 Arab-Israeli war, had been wounded, and taken prisoner. Alone among Kuwait's ruling dynasty, Sheik Fahd held his ground when the invader approached.[5]

For their part, the guards divisions were well disciplined. The London *Times* reported Iraqi troops mixing freely with the local population to assure them that "Baghdad bore no animosity toward the Kuwaiti people." Some went to barber shops for a morning shave; others knocked at residents' doors to ask for tea and coffee.[6] Americans in Kuwait City told *The New York Times* of watching Iraqi soldiers enter a cafeteria in a downtown hotel and have breakfast. "They talked to the Americans who were in the hotel. It was all very friendly."[7] At the nearby Sheraton hotel, scores of guardsmen wandered in and out like tourists.

Kuwaiti officials who offered no resistance were well treated. The Kuwaiti cabinet was trapped at the headquarters of the supreme defense council with telephone and telex links cut. Iraqi troops blockaded the building but soon allowed the ministers to go home. Seventy-one British military personnel stationed in Kuwait to provide technical advice and support for the aircraft and tanks supplied by Great Britain took no part in the fighting and were not harmed.[8]

In Baghdad, motorists honked their horns and flashed their lights to celebrate the invasion. Radio and television stations broadcast patriotic songs and mobilization orders for the military. According to Reuters, most Iraqis thought the attack was justified. There was widespread support for Saddam, and relief that victory had come so quickly. *The New York Times*, in its own sampling of Baghdad opinion, quoted college student Ahmed Khalis that "the Kuwaitis boast of their aid to Iraq [during the war with Iran], but it was Iraq that defended their thrones and wealth with blood. We sacrificed our brothers, fathers, and sons to let them enjoy life."[9]

Somewhat belatedly, Iraqi radio announced that the invasion was launched in response to an appeal from "young revolutionaries [inside Kuwait] who sought support in a coup to install a new free government."[10] But the "young revolutionaries" were not identified, and few took the claim seriously. As U.S. Ambassador Thomas Pickering told the U.N. Security Council immediately afterward, the Iraqis "got it the wrong way around. They invaded Kuwait and then staged the coup d'état in a blatant and deceitful effort to try to justify their action."[11] Quite clearly, Iraq's slipshod political preparation for the invasion in no way matched the effectiveness of its battle-tested war machine. Either that, or Saddam's decision to invade was taken so quickly that insufficient time was left to organize a coup.

The latter explanation may be the most plausible. Like virtually all other observers, the White House, the State Department, and most of the intelligence community believed that Saddam's massing of troops on the Kuwaiti border—clearly visible to motorists driving between Basra and Kuwait City for a week preceding the invasion—was simply saber rattling to improve Iraq's bargaining position in negotiations with the emir. Even if Saddam's forces did cross the frontier, only a minor incursion was anticipated—again, to exert leverage on Kuwait. No one foresaw that Iraq would occupy the entire country.

As if to underscore the lack of concern, April Glaspie, the American ambassador to Iraq, left Baghdad two days before the invasion for a brief vacation in London before returning to Washington for consultations. Her Soviet counterpart left the same day for the Black Sea. Harold "Hooky" Walker, the British ambassador, was on holiday in Woking. Even the chief of Israeli intelligence was caught flatfooted, enjoying his own wedding party in Tel Aviv, when Saddam's forces invaded.[12]

News of the invasion did not reach Washington until nine

o'clock in the evening, two hours after the first Iraqi tanks crossed the border. Brent Scowcroft, the national security adviser, was summoned from his home in nearby Maryland and informed President Bush shortly thereafter. Just before midnight, the White House issued a brief statement condemning the invasion and calling for the Iraqi forces to withdraw.[13]

At the same time, Assistant Secretary of State John H. Kelly summoned the Iraqi ambassador, Mohammed Sadig al-Mashat, to the State Department, where he was given a strenuous protest.[14] But to judge from the initial soundings, there was no great alarm in Washington, and no suggestion of an attempt to roll back the Iraqi assault.

At the Pentagon, officials said they were monitoring the situation, but had "no plans for a U.S. military response."[15] Defense Secretary Dick Cheney remained at home and did not return to work. "There is no decision for him to make," said a Pentagon spokesman. "This ain't our show."[16] General Powell also remained in his quarters.[17]

Several times that night, President Bush was awakened by Scowcroft with additional details of the invasion. At 5 A.M., the president signed an executive order freezing Iraqi assets in the United States and shutting off all trade between the two countries. At 8 A.M., Bush met with Scowcroft, Cheney, Powell, Judge William Webster of the CIA, White House Chief of Staff John Sununu, and other members of the National Security Council. The prevailing attitude among the group, according to one participant, was "Hey, too bad about Kuwait, but it's just a gas station, and who cares whether the sign says Sinclair or Exxon?"[18] At a brief press conference, the president said that American military intervention was not under consideration. "I am not contemplating such action," Bush said.[19] Certainly, the situation was not deemed sufficiently critical to keep the president in Washington. He left immediately for Aspen, Colorado, where he and Prime Minister Margaret Thatcher had speaking engagements at the Aspen Institute.

Later that day, Bush's advisers once again played down the

possibility of a military response. The *Washington Post* reported that the administration's military experts believed "it would be difficult, if not impossible, to do more than put on a limited display of military muscle . . . without a major mobilization." Instead, spokesmen said the United States "would attempt to put the economic screws to Iraq."[20]

Admiral William Crowe, the recently retired chairman of the joint chiefs of staff, appeared on "Nightline" with Ted Koppel that evening and cautioned that Iraq was "a long ways away and it's a harsh climate. . . . We can dominate the Gulf from a naval standpoint. We can keep Iraq off the water. We can dominate them in the air. But the question of ground troops in that vast desert, that's another matter altogether."[21]

On Capitol Hill the response was similar. While those legislators who were interviewed deplored the invasion, the tone was set by Senator Sam Nunn of Georgia, the powerful chairman of the Senate Armed Services Committee. "I don't think we have a military obligation at this moment," said Nunn. "I believe our primary recourse should be to very intensive diplomatic activity."[22]

Secretary of State James Baker, meeting in the Siberian city of Irkutsk with Soviet foreign minister Eduard Shevardnadze, spoke with President Bush by telephone, and then made plans to return to Washington. The following day, at the airport in Moscow, Baker and Shevardnadze issued a joint statement criticizing "the brutal and illegal invasion of Kuwait. Today, we take the unusual step of jointly calling upon the rest of the international community to join us in an international cutoff of all arms supplies to Iraq."

Shevardnadze added that "as for military intervention, the Soviet Union does not have any plans for such operations and I understand the United States has no such plans at this time."[23]

At the United Nations, the Security Council convened in special session to condemn the invasion, and called on Iraq to withdraw. There was no suggestion that force be employed.[24] The NATO allies, meeting in Brussels, joined the call for an unconditional Iraqi withdrawal and agreed to consider an American request to ban all trade with Iraq and to freeze Iraqi assets. Again, there was no discussion of military action, and diplomats said that NATO was planning no initiatives.[25]

In Cairo, the Arab League's council held an emergency meeting and agreed to call an Arab summit. But the League issued no statement, and the London *Times* reported that "not one Arab government even went so far as a formal condemnation of the attack." A majority of the Arab countries wanted a resolution mildly disapproving of Iraq's action, said the *Times*, but a significant minority was expected to remain silent.[26] A senior Arab cabinet minister from a country that had been friendly to Kuwait was quoted as saying "I am afraid that we may have to sacrifice Kuwait as we knew it to get out of this," meaning that the al-Sabahs' days of rule were likely over.[27]

Even Saudi Arabia, Kuwait's closest ally in the region and founder of the Gulf Cooperation Council, the alliance to which both Kuwait and the United Arab Emirates belonged, appeared content with giving refuge to the emir and his family.[28] In effect, the world greeted Saddam's lightning takeover of Kuwait with surprise, consternation, and disapproval—the degree of that disapproval increasing in direct proportion to the critic's distance from Kuwait. The fact that casualties had been light, and that the Iraqi army had behaved itself initially, caused the neighboring Arab states to hope that a formula could be found to effect a quick Iraqi withdrawal. Saddam might be rewarded, but the damage would be minimal. There was no discussion of military intervention to reverse the takeover. In the United States, where support for Kuwait seemed greatest, the Bush administration restricted its moves to the economic sphere.

Decision to Invade

Why Saddam had suddenly decided to invade Kuwait is not clear. Iraqi resentment against Kuwait and the other Gulf states had been building since the end of the war with Iran in 1988. In particular, and despite the fact that it was Saddam who began the war, the Iraqis resented that they had borne the full weight of resisting Iran. They complained that their sacrifices were not sufficiently recognized by their neighbors, and certainly were not adequately compensated. As William B. Quandt of the Brookings Institution observed, "Whatever one thinks of Saddam Hussein, it is indisputably true that in the 1980s no one other than Iraq was willing to stand up to an Iranian bid for hegemony in the Gulf."[29] Mr. Quandt had been in charge of Middle East affairs for the National Security Council under President Carter. His assessment was shared by Richard W. Murphy, assistant secretary of state for Near Eastern affairs under President Reagan. It was "a constant theme we heard from the Iraqis in 1988," said Murphy.[30]

Iraqi resentment centered on the dire financial plight into which their country had fallen, and the failure of other Gulf states to render assistance. According to American estimates, the war with Iran had cost Iraq $500 billion.[31] For most of the conflict, the Iraqis had devoted about 40 percent of their gross domestic product to military expenditures, choking off consumer spending and economic development.[32] When the war ended, pent-up demand stoked a raging inflation. By early summer 1990, the dinar had fallen to one-twelfth its official value.[33] Add to the inflation a significant unemployment problem created by demobilization, thousands of homeless and wounded to be housed and cared for, enormous war damage to be repaired, a crushing foreign debt estimated to be in the vicinity of $80 billion (before the war, Iraq enjoyed a $30 billion surplus in net foreign investment), and severely depressed oil prices flowing in large measure from the systematic overproduction by Kuwait and the United Arab Emirates.

For Iraq, seeking to recover from the war, oil prices meant everything. With an output of 3.14 million barrels a day,* every $1 drop in the price of oil cost Iraq about $1 billion a year in lost revenue. With such a huge piece of the action, it is not surprising that Saddam focused his efforts on raising oil prices, and starting in February 1990, began to lean heavily on his Gulf neighbors to reduce production. In fact, *Time* magazine, in its pre-invasion issue in August, concluded that "within OPEC, Saddam had an excuse for adopting a tough-cop role. In an organization filled with quota cheaters, Kuwait and the U[nited] A[rab] E[mirates] have been among the most incorrigible in exceeding their agreed-upon production limits . . . driving the average price . . . from $20.50 in early January to a mere $13 in June."[34] Iraq's foreign minister, Tariq Aziz, put the problem more succinctly when he said that Iraq's budget "is based on a price of $18 a barrel for oil, but since the Kuwaitis began flooding the world with oil, the price has gone down by a third."[35]

As the summer wore on, and as its economic condition worsened, Iraq escalated its demands against Kuwait. In addition to curtailing its massive overproduction,[36] Saddam insisted that Kuwait pay $2.4 billion in compensation for oil allegedly pumped from Iraqi territory along the countries' disputed one-hundred-mile frontier. He also demanded that Kuwait renounce whatever claims it might have to the disputed (Rumaila) oil field; pay Iraq a direct subsidy of $12 billion in compensation for the reduced oil prices triggered by Kuwait's overproduction; forgive Iraq's war debt of some $10 billion (the Saudis had already done so); and lease or cede to Baghdad the island of Bubiyan, which controls the approach to Iraq's port at Umm Qasr. Contemporary reports in the *Washington Post* and the London *Times* indicated that Kuwait was prepared to concede the Rumaila field and to pay Iraq "a large sum of money" in

---

*In 1990, Iraq was tied with Iran for the second highest quota in OPEC. Both trailed Saudi Arabia's output of 5.42 million barrels.

compensation. But the Kuwaiti royal family appeared determined not to yield to demands that it surrender or lease Bubiyan island to Iraq, because of anticipated tidewater drilling in the area.[37]

In an effort to resolve the crisis, King Fahd of Saudi Arabia, along with Egypt's Hosni Mubarak and King Hussein of Jordan, sponsored a meeting between the two countries in Jidda on July 31, with a second session scheduled for the following day. What happened on July 31 is unclear. The two sides met for two hours that evening, but the details are sketchy and each side asserts its own interpretation of what happened. According to Crown Prince Saad al-Sabah, the Kuwaiti negotiator, the Iraqis merely restated their demands and insisted that Kuwait comply immediately. The Iraqis, who were led by Izzat Ibrahim, Saddam's second-in-command, maintained that the Kuwaitis were unwilling to listen or negotiate seriously. "They were arrogant. They were conducting themselves like small-time grocery store owners. The gap was irreconcilable, so the meeting collapsed."[38] The meeting scheduled for the following day was not held.[39]

Since Saddam had been massing his troops at the border for well over a week, and since all parties were fully aware of Iraqi military movements, the July 31 meeting is difficult to decipher. On the one hand, it is possible that Saddam was giving the Kuwaitis a final opportunity to grant the concessions he sought before he attacked. On the other, it is equally possible that Saddam had already written off the al-Sabah dynasty, and that the meeting was window-dressing in prelude to the attack he had planned all along. King Hussein, one of Saddam's few defenders, reports that the Iraqi president decided "in late July" that military action was necessary. The Iraqis were bitter, said the king. "They recalled with fury, for example, that after Iranian-backed terrorists had tried to assassinate the Emir, 'Iraq had blasted Iran with everything [we] had—ground-to-ground missiles, the works.' Iran had retaliated, causing 1,500 civilian casualties, but Kuwait would not write off its debt, or end the border dispute, or stop stealing oil."[40]

If the Iraqi account is true, the Kuwaiti performance that evening is even more unfathomable. Since they had been warned by King Fahd, King Hussein, Mubarak, and Yasir Arafat that Saddam meant business, it is difficult to understand why they continued to stonewall. "When the lion is hungry, you don't tell it there is not going to be any dinner," said one U.S. official in retrospect.[41]

Tariq Aziz, in a postwar interview, said that Saddam's decision to invade was made at the last minute, after the collapse of the negotiations in Jidda. "President Saddam Hussein had no intention of invading. . . . It was never discussed at any level of government."[42] Aziz suggests that Saddam simply lost patience with the Kuwaitis, and ordered the troops to go in.

Once he decided to invade, it is not surprising that Saddam elected to occupy all of Kuwait. In the first place, as he later told King Hussein, he did not intend to stay, and "he believed he would be in a stronger position . . . if he eventually withdrew to a point that left Iraq with the disputed territory only."[43] In other words, it was a bargaining ploy against an uncertain future. Saddam believed that Iraq would appear magnanimous in Arab eyes when he pulled back, and that would help legitimize his taking of Rumaila and Bubiyan. Also, whatever government was installed in Kuwait would pay generously to secure an Iraqi withdrawal. That would solve Saddam's financial problems, and the cost to Iraq would have been slight.

Another reason stemmed from Saddam's 1980 experience when he attacked Iran. Instead of dealing a mortal blow to the Iranian army and trying to topple the revolutionary regime in Tehran, Saddam had opted for a quick, limited campaign, reasoning that it would bring the mullahs back to their senses without painting them into a corner. Accordingly, he calibrated his assault. When, after the first week of fighting, his army had achieved a decisive breakthrough, Saddam called a halt. The result was disastrous. The Iranian army was saved from certain defeat; Tehran made no effort to sue for peace, and instead, used the opportunity to regroup and reorganize. Even worse, by denying his army the victory it deserved, Saddam saw morale plummet and fighting efficiency deteriorate. He wanted no repeat of that when he entered Kuwait.

Finally, by punishing Kuwait for its fiscal arrogance, Saddam provided vicarious satisfaction to millions of impoverished Arabs from Mauritania to Yemen. Kuwaiti per capita income was among the highest in the world—estimated by the World Bank at $13,400 in 1988. In South Yemen, now reunited into the Republic of Yemen, the average person earned $430 a year; in Mauritania, $480; and in Egypt, $660. From Syria to Morocco, the figures were similar.[44] By striking at the petroeconomy of Kuwait, Saddam kindled hopes for a redistribution of the vast oil wealth that had benefited only a few. As he himself put it, "This is the only way to deal with these despicable Croesuses who relished stealing the part to damage the whole, who relished possessions to destroy devotion, and who were guided by foreigners instead of virtuous standards and the principles of pan-Arabism."[45]

It would be wishful thinking to believe that Saddam's words fell on deaf ears. The theme of pan-Arabism fit neatly into Saddam's move. By attacking Kuwait, Saddam was attacking the West's proxy—America's proxy. The latent hatred for the United States, the symbol of everything Western and alien— "civilization without culture," in a telling phrase of Princeton's Bernard Lewis[46]—ran deep in the Middle East. America, whose lifestyle Kuwait emulated, was the staunch supporter of Israel, which few Arabs could accept. More often than not, America was seen to be aligned with the repressive, feudal monarchies of the region, standing against social and economic change— and the instability that such change might bring to the oil market. More importantly perhaps, America symbolized the enemy in the millennial clash between Islam and the West: a struggle between rival systems that has lasted some fourteen centuries. Facts count for little in such eternal struggles, and Saddam easily tapped that vein. Having posed as the defender of secular values against fundamentalist Iran, he donned the mantle of the Koran to defend his annexation of Kuwait, "so that death might not prevail over life."

To many in the streets of Amman, Cairo, and Damascus, Saddam seemed to be a second Gamal Abdel Nasser. "A Nasser with teeth," said one Jordanian.[47] Saddam was the only Arab leader who could confront the West, and perhaps more significantly, the only one whom Israel genuinely feared. The support he engendered among the Arab masses reflected pride as much as anything. As Professor Fouad Ajami of Johns Hopkins, an astute observer of the Middle East, noted in *Foreign Affairs*, Saddam expressed the "hidden anguish of the Arab soul."[48] These latter reasons did not motivate Saddam directly, but they established the context for his decision to invade.

The World's Richest Nation

It is now forgotten that the Kuwait of August 1990 had few defenders in the Middle East.[49] "A boutique nation," as George Will scathingly described it, Kuwait engendered disapproval at best, and hatred at worst, among its less fortunate neighbors. "Envy is a plant you must not water," the Medici had proclaimed in Renaissance Florence, but the Kuwaitis took little heed. Instead, they flaunted their wealth and were notorious for avoiding the extremes of their arid desert environment (and the rigors of their Moslem faith) by spending as much time as possible in London, Paris, and the mountains of Switzerland. The holy month of Ramadan, with its dawn-to-dusk fasts, was a favorite time of travel for wealthy Kuwaitis.[50]

Before the oil boom, the Kuwaitis had been among the poorest of the poor: a Bedouin people whose desolate, sand-swept landscape offered little but hardship, and where temperatures frequently hovered above 115°F for months at a time. In

1939, the average per capita income in Kuwait amounted to $35 a year. The entire budget for the royal family, all of which was contributed by a few merchant families in Kuwait City, was $7,500. And total public revenues, two-thirds of which came from port duties, did not exceed $290,000.[51]

The history of Kuwait traces to the early eighteenth century when wandering Bedouins fled a lengthy drought and accompanying famine in central Arabia to settle on the coast of the Persian Gulf at a place they began to call Kuwait, the diminutive of the Arabic *kut*, a fortress built near the water. The area, nominally a part of the Ottoman Empire, was under the suzerainty of Sulaiman al Hamad, sheik of the powerful Bani Khalid tribe, whose dominion extended from Basra in the north to Qatar in the south.[52] The al-Sabah family exercised a mild form of leadership over the settlers with Sulaiman's approval, and upon his death in 1756, Sabah bin Jabir was chosen by the principal family elders as the first recorded sheik of Kuwait. It is from him that the present dynasty descends.

Throughout the latter eighteenth and early nineteenth centuries, Kuwait remained an undistinguished part of the Arabian holdings of the Ottoman Empire. In 1850, Kuwait City was recommended by Britain's General F. R. Chesney as the terminus of a proposed Euphrates Valley railway, and fifty years later it attracted attention as a desirable site for the terminus of the Berlin-Baghdad railway. Sheik Abdullah al-Sabah (1866–1892) implicitly recognized Turkish authority over Kuwait by his payment of tribute and his acceptance of the title of Qaimagam (commandant) under the Ottoman administration for the region, located at Basra. (This would become a critical link in Saddam's chain of evidence claiming Iraqi control of Kuwait.) But when the Turks sought to occupy Kuwait, Abdullah's successor, Mubarak al-Sabah (1896–1915), who came to the throne after killing two of his half-brothers,[53] sought British protection to fend off Constantinople. When the British appeared reluctant, Sheik Mubarak publicly mused about giving the rival Russians a coaling station in Kuwait. The British reconsidered, and in 1899, Mubarak signed an agreement pledging not to enter into any foreign relationship without British consent in return for an annual British subsidy. In effect, Kuwait became a British protectorate, secured by England's naval presence in the Gulf. That relationship was formalized in 1914 when His Majesty's Government declared that "the British Government does recognize and admit that the Shaykhdom of Kuwait is an independent Government under British protection."[54] Mubarak's successful diplomacy earned him the title of "Mubarak the Great." He established that future succession to the throne would pass exclusively through his heirs, and his example of playing the great powers against one another set a pattern for future Kuwaiti diplomacy.

In World War I, Mubarak, despite his pledge to Britain, traded freely with both sides, and his heirs—especially his second son, Salim—sided openly with the Turks. The British responded by blockading Kuwait, and after the war, in 1922, convened a conference at the Persian Gulf port of Uqair to fix the boundaries of Saudi Arabia, Iraq, and Kuwait—a conference at which Kuwait pointedly was not represented. Sir Percy Cox, the British high commissioner in Baghdad, presided. In keeping with the colonial style of the period, Sir Percy's decisions were final. To compensate Ibn Saud for territory ceded to Iraq, Kuwait's southern boundary was moved northward and a divided zone, or neutral zone, was established along the Gulf, which Kuwait and Saudi Arabia shared. For Kuwait's northern boundary with Iraq, Sir Percy selected an old line drawn in 1913 by the Turks and the British that had never been ratified. The Kuwaitis smarted over losing territory in the south to Saudi Arabia, and the Iraqis resented the narrow twenty-six-mile coastline with which they were left. Iraq was given minimal entrance to the Gulf through the shallow Shatt al-Arab waterway, while Kuwait retained 120 miles of shoreline as well as the largest natural harbor in the Gulf, at Kuwait City. Such were the wonders of imperial cartography, designed, among other things, to prevent Iraq from seriously challenging British naval power in the Gulf, but scarcely fashioned to bring accord to the region. "We protected our strategic interests rather successfully," said Sir Anthony Perkins, former British ambassador to the United Nations. "But in doing so we created a situation where the people living there felt they had been wronged."[55]

Ahmad al-Jabir al-Sabah, who had succeeded to the Kuwaiti throne in 1921, accepted Sir Percy's decision as a fait accompli, and ruled for the next thirty years—years that would bring incredible prosperity to Kuwait beginning with the discovery of oil in 1938. When the gigantic Burgan field south of Kuwait City was brought in with a massive gusher by the Kuwait Oil Company (jointly owned by British Petroleum and Gulf), the way of life in Kuwait began to change dramatically. Under the original concessions, all payments were made to the emir, but all Kuwaitis shared the wealth that flowed from the desert. The authoritative *Oil and Gas Journal* estimates the country's crude oil reserves at nearly 70 billion barrels—enough to last well into the twenty-second century.[56] Commercial production commenced in 1946. By the 1980s, Kuwait's wealth had become legendary.

When Iraq invaded, tiny Kuwait was the world's sixth largest producer of petroleum. Its assets abroad totaled $100 billion, not to mention another $50 billion that the ruling family and other wealthy Kuwaitis held privately. Because the Kuwaitis had chosen their investments and their investment counselors wisely, their revenues from investments actually surpassed those from oil by some $6 billion annually.[57] Thus, unlike Iraq, the Kuwaitis had little incentive to increase oil prices in 1990 because such increases would have depressed the stock, bond, and currency markets which had become Kuwait's main source of income. That rankled the Iraqis even more.

At home, Kuwaitis paid no income taxes but enjoyed free education through university level, free medical care, subsidized housing and transportation, as well as generous children's allowances and marriage bonuses. For students at all levels, the government absorbed the cost of books, clothing, meals, and transportation. With government help, some ten thousand Kuwaitis had studied at American universities, fifteen hundred of whom were in the United States when Saddam attacked.[58] Illiteracy, which is prevalent in the Middle East, is virtually unknown among Kuwaitis under forty. Kuwait's medical care also was among the world's best. In 1988, there was one doctor for every six hundred residents, and one nurse for every two hundred—ratios that no other country could match.

Except for medical care, most benefits were reserved for Kuwaiti citizens. Noncitizens and foreign workers fared less well. And Kuwait's citizenship law (like Switzerland's) was one of the world's most restrictive. One simply could not become a Kuwaiti citizen. There were no provisions for naturalization, and even birth in the country was not sufficient. Under Kuwait's 1960 citizenship law, one must be a descendant of someone living in Kuwait in 1920 (*jus sanguinis*). No others need apply. In addition, what limited suffrage there was in this feudal paradise was restricted to the sixty thousand or so male Kuwaitis with significant property holdings. And even that meant little. By tradition, all political power was held by the emir, sixty-four-year-old Sheik Jabir al-Ahmed al-Sabah. A withdrawn man unaccustomed to criticism,[59] Sheik Jabir had disbanded Kuwait's rudimentary parliament in 1986, imposed a rigid censorship on the press, and banished fifty or so of the country's leading writers and editors.[60]

At the time of Saddam's invasion, Kuwait's total population was estimated at 2.1 million, of whom less than 40 percent were Kuwaiti citizens. The other 60 percent were foreign workers. Kuwaitis comprised only 18 percent of the work force, mostly in the service industries and government. Filipino women cared for Kuwaiti children. Egyptians, Iranians, and Palestinians (the largest foreign contingent at more than 400,000) staffed its banks, offices, and hospitals. Some 10,000 Americans and Britons kept the oil fields running. In 1975, the Kuwaiti government had bought out all foreign interests, but the technical staff of the Kuwait Petroleum Corporation continued to be largely British and American.

The Kuwaitis were investors, traders, and gamblers—a heritage from their past as an entrepôt for British shipping from India and a reflection of the quick wealth that oil had provided. Unlike the conservative Saudis, the Kuwaitis were known as risk-takers. Professor Ajami called them reckless—a loose cannon on the deck of the Arab world.[61] The Middle East's first stock exchange, the Souk al Manakh, was founded in Kuwait, and by the early Eighties, stock trading had become a national pastime. Share dealings using post-dated checks, sometimes a year ahead, created a huge unregulated expansion of credit. The crash came in 1982, when a dealer presented a post-dated check for payment, but the issuer lacked the necessary funds. The house of cards collapsed. Official investigators revealed that the total of outstanding checks amounted to $94 billion, more than three times Kuwait's GNP, and involved some six thousand investors from all levels of the population. The largest debtor reportedly owed $10.5 billion; he was a former postal clerk and not known to be wealthy.[62]

The risk-taking endemic to the financial market was reflected in Kuwait's foreign policy. Beginning with Mubarak the Great, who had played the Russians against the British against the Turks, Kuwait's modern leaders often sought to work both sides of the street. Though the country depended heavily on American markets and expertise, and was among the Gulf's largest importers of American consumer goods, Kuwait's rhetoric was often the most stridently anti-American in the Arab world. In 1987, to protect their tankers from Iranian attack, the Kuwaitis approached Washington with a request to reflag eleven ships as American vessels. When the United States did not respond, Kuwaiti officials turned to Moscow. After the Soviets agreed to charter at least three tankers, Washington quickly announced that it would take the eleven vessels the Kuwaitis had initially proposed. Such hard-nosed self-interest won few friends for Kuwait, especially when Crown Prince Saad al-Sabah dissociated his country from any hostilities in which the United States might be involved while protecting Kuwaiti shipping. "These are now American vessels," Sheik Saad said, implying that Kuwait was no longer concerned.[63]

The Kuwaitis relied on the same tactics when dealing with Saddam. They assumed that Iraq's bluster could be offset by American support. They saw no reason to compromise. And in taking that position, they were tacitly supported by Washington. When Baghdad insisted that Kuwait curtail its oil production, Kuwaiti negotiators raised the issue of Iraq's unpaid war debt.[64] The Iraqis felt they could make no headway against such tactics, and as former Assistant Secretary of State Richard Murphy remarked, Saddam simply "blew his stack."[65]

Saddam Hussein

Since Iraq's invasion of Kuwait, Western media have described Saddam alternatively as the Butcher of Baghdad, or another Hitler, with variations in between. His actions and statements have often lent credibility to that view. The Middle East is not a gentle place, and Saddam's view of due process has a distinctly terrifying ring. Nevertheless, to call him another Hitler, as George Bush was fond of doing, not only overstates his importance, it trivializes the enormity of evil that flowed from the Third Reich. Like all villains of the moment, from Noriega, to Marcos, to the Ayatollah, Saddam has been depicted in the lurid colors of contemporary hyperbole. To ordinary Arabs, his authoritarian style and his ruthless treatment of dissidents are not that unusual. A more dispassionate assessment of his role in Iraq was provided by the Library of Congress in the spring of 1990, three months before his incursion into Kuwait. It described Saddam as follows:

> *Between the overthrow of the monarchy in 1958 and the emergence of Saddam Husayn in the mid-1970s, Iraqi history was a chronicle of conspiracies, coups, countercoups, and fierce Kurdish uprisings. Beginning in 1975, however, with the signing of the Algiers Agreement—an agreement between Saddam Husayn and the shah of Iran that effectively ended Iranian military support for the Kurds in Iraq—Saddam Husayn was able to bring Iraq an unprecedented period of stability. He effectively used rising oil revenues to fund large-scale development projects, to increase public sector employment, and significantly improve education and health care. This allied increasing numbers of Iraqis to the ruling Baath (Arab Socialist Reconstruction) Party. As a result, for the first time in contemporary Iraqi history, an Iraqi leader successfully forged a national identity out of Iraq's diverse social structure.[66]*

A similar view of Saddam was stated by Phoebe Marr, a leading Iraqi scholar who told a congressional committee shortly before the invasion that "he is a shrewd politician and tactician, has a canny understanding of the political dynamics of his own society, and is a survivor who kept himself and his regime in power for twenty-two years in a country notoriously difficult to govern."[67]

Immediately after the invasion, a Western diplomat who had observed Saddam at close quarters for four years in Baghdad was contacted for his assessment by the *Washington Post*. He told the *Post* that Saddam was "a consummate politician at the height of his power."[68]

The point is that Saddam Hussein is not the devil incarnate. At the height of the Cold War, when the threat of Communist takeover was real, a wise president named Dwight Eisenhower categorically refused to condemn or criticize Stalin in public. "I don't know when I may have to sit down and negotiate with the man," said Ike, "and it's not going to improve chances of coming to an agreement if I castigate him."[69] If George

Bush had followed Eisenhower's prescription, a different outcome to the Gulf crisis might have ensued. By describing Saddam as Hitler, negotiations with Iraq became impossible.

Saddam Hussein was born in 1937 into an illiterate peasant family living in the wrenching poverty of rural Iraq. He knew deprivation from infancy. At the age of ten, he fled from an abusive stepfather to live with his uncle, a cashiered army officer residing in Baghdad. There, Saddam entered school for the first time. Overage and untutored, he was a poor student. But fierce determination propelled him ahead. *The New York Times* has reported him to be "a voracious reader and student of revolutionary politics who has read the biographies of most great world leaders."[70] Like many young Iraqis, Saddam soon found himself swept up in a world of political action and intrigue. In 1956, he participated in an abortive coup against the monarchy. The next year, at the age of twenty, he joined the revolutionary Baath Party. The Baath were a minuscule movement at the time, dedicated to Arab unity and social egalitarianism, militantly anti-Western and anti-Communist, inspired by a vision of a glowing Arab future. They believed that all existing Arab regimes had to be swept away, and all borders eliminated. The movement possessed great appeal for young radicals like Saddam, for numerous disaffected intellectuals, and for dissident army officers chafing under the inefficiency of the old regime. It flourished first in Syria, where Baathist officers seized power in 1960, then in Iraq.

As a member of the party, Saddam courted notoriety. In 1958, at the age of twenty-one, he was briefly imprisoned for the murder of his uncle's Communist rival in a local election, a man who happened to be his own brother-in-law. Other terrorist assignments followed in due course. According to the London *Times*, Saddam quickly developed a reputation among the Baath as a meticulous and daring assassin.[71] The following year, he was chosen by party leaders to head a hit squad against Iraqi strongman Abdul Karim Qassim, apparently in collusion with the Egyptian government of Colonel Abdel Nasser and the CIA.[72] When the assassins bungled the job, Saddam fled briefly to Syria, then to Egypt, where he studied law intermittently. In 1963, after a second and successful attempt on Qassim's life, Saddam returned to Iraq and soon emerged as the Baath's enforcer. He rose quickly through party ranks by intimidating or eliminating his rivals, and helped organize the party's takeover of the government in 1968, when he became the effective strongman of the regime.[73] Ostensibly second in command to Baath leader Ahmad Hassan al-Bakr, Saddam was the moving force behind the party.[74] On July 16, 1979, when President Bakr resigned, Saddam officially replaced him as president of the republic, secretary general of the Baath Regional Party, chairman of the Revolutionary Command Council (RCC), and commander in chief of the armed forces.

Unlike affluent Kuwait, the Iraq that Saddam now headed had a troubled, violent history, and Saddam's formal acquisition of power merely seemed to confirm that. For some, he represented what Arab scholars have called the "just despot" who would revive ancient glories and gain the respect of an outside world that was largely hostile.[75] For others, he was just another tin-pot dictator in a long line of petty tyrants who strutted across the Middle East stage. Make no mistake about it, by Western standards Saddam is far beyond the pale of moral acceptability. His blatant use of force would be unacceptable in any well-ordered society. But in the rough-and-ready world of Arab politics, he is no worse than most, and as Edward Luttwak has pointed out, far better than some.[76]

Cradle of Civilization

Despite his brutality, Saddam is reported to have remained committed to the ideals of his youth. By comparison to other Middle East potentates, his lifestyle has never been opulent. Married for twenty-five years to his first-cousin, a former schoolteacher, he and his wife have five children. Under Saddam,

Iraq is the one country in the Gulf where women enjoy more-or-less equal status, and where income redistribution and social programs have been taken seriously. The country is secular and relatively open. Iraqi artists hang nudes in state-owned galleries and religious freedom is widely tolerated. Tariq Aziz, who was then Iraq's foreign minister, is Christian. But Iraq is also one of the most politically repressive regimes, perennially cited by Amnesty International and organizations such as Middle East Watch for vast human-rights violations, and it has been ruthless in suppressing dissent and separatism. To Saddam's credit, he has forged a single nation out of the patchwork of diverse and often antagonistic peoples that had been cobbled together in a fit of colonial absentmindedness following World War I. But the cost has been very high.

Somewhat larger than California, Iraq lacks the ethnic homogeneity of Egypt, Syria, or Saudi Arabia. Its population of 17 million is divided among Sunni and Shiite Arabs, Kurds, and Bedouin tribes living in the sparsely populated western desert. The Sunnis dominate politically, but constitute only 20 percent of the population. For years, Saddam was able to retain the support of the majority Shiites (60 percent), even while fighting Shiite Iran, and to keep the Kurds nominally pacified, all the while extending the authority of the central government in Baghdad. For better or worse, Iraq had become a dominant power in Middle East affairs.

Saddam's reassertion of Iraq's role in the region evoked the ancient history of the land between the Tigris and Euphrates rivers—the cradle of civilization. The Greeks gave the name "Mesopotamia" to the area, meaning land between the rivers, and it was here that the first civilization, that of the Sumerians, appeared in the Middle East. Using the fertile land and abundant water supply available, the ancient Sumerians developed sophisticated irrigation systems and the world's first urban culture. The first system of writing, cuneiform, evolved here. The Sumerians' successors, the Akkadians, created the first conscript army and the first successful administrative bureaucracy more than two thousand years before the birth of Christ. The Babylonians who followed developed an even more extensive civilization and the first comprehensive legal code, the Code of Hammurabi, designed "to cause justice to prevail in the country, to destroy the wicked and the evil, that the strong may not oppress the weak."[77] The Babylonians were gifted astronomers and developed the system of measuring time that we continue to use: sixty seconds to the minute; sixty minutes to the hour. The Babylonians were followed in turn by the warlike Assyrians, the Chaldeans—whose great king Nebuchadnezzar (605–562 B.C.) built the famous Hanging Gardens of Babylon—and the Persians. In 637 A.D., the Persians were in their turn defeated by the tribes of Arabia, newly converted to Islam, at the Battle of Qadissiyat. With the coming of Islam, Mesopotamia flourished, particularly when Baghdad was the seat of the Abbasid caliphate between 750 and 1258.

At the height of their power, the Abbasids ruled that vast area from Afghanistan to the Iberian peninsula, and among other things encouraged a rebirth of scientific knowledge and literary creativity. While Europe stumbled through the Dark Ages, the Abbasids established research libraries and pioneered in the study of geography and mathematics. In the thirteenth century, the Abbasid caliphate fell to the Mongols, who twice sacked Baghdad and swept away centuries of learning and culture. Political chaos, severe economic deprivation, and social disintegration followed in the wake of the Mongol invasions. Between the sixteenth and the twentieth centuries, the course of Iraqi history reflected a continuing struggle between the neighboring Turks and Persians. The Turks were Sunni Moslems, the Persians were Shiite. The impact of that struggle was to widen the rift between Shiite and Sunni in Iraq, as each side freely took vengeance on the other. For nearly six hundred years, from the collapse of the Abbasid caliphate through the waning days of the Ottoman Empire, political authority in Mesopotamia was tenuous. The disconnected and often antagonistic ethnic, religious, and tribal bands professed little or no allegiance to any central government.

Modern Iraq traces to the secret Sykes-Picot agreement of 1916, in which Britain and France divided the spoils of the Ottoman Empire. Britain got the Gulf, France the Levant, and the Turks were left to fend for themselves. Those arrangements were confirmed at the Paris Peace Conference, which, under Article 22 of the League of Nations Covenant, made Mesopotamia, now designated as Iraq, a British mandate. Britain imposed an Arabian prince of the Hashemite dynasty as a constitutional monarch, defined Iraq's territorial limits with little correspondence to natural frontiers or traditional tribal and ethnic settlements,[78] and established a British type of parliamentary government—none of which was conducive to future stability.

In 1932, Britain agreed to terminate its mandate. Iraq became an independent state and was admitted to the League of Nations. In return for independence, the Iraqi government agreed to accept the British-imposed boundaries of 1922. But the problems of political instability and economic retardation continued. The British-imposed monarch, King Feisal, died prematurely in 1933 (at the age of fifty-six) and was succeeded by his young son Ghazi, who died in a car crash six years later. The monarchy was finally overthrown in 1958 by a military coup led by General Qassim. Qassim ruled tumultuously for five years until he was overthrown by the combination of Baathist conspirators and pan-Arabist army officers that ultimately brought Saddam to power.

Claims Against Kuwait

Iraq's territorial claims against Kuwait grew out of its colonial past. The first dealt with the huge, banana-shaped Rumaila oil field that lies under the disputed border between the two countries, 10,200 feet below the desert sands. More than 90 percent of the fifty-mile-long formation lies under Iraq, yet most of the oil pumped from Rumaila in the last decade was pumped by the Kuwaitis. The oil in the Rumaila field flows easily. Pumps located inside Kuwait could, in theory, drain the entire field. In Saddam's view, the Kuwaitis were stealing Iraqi oil. This was not a minor issue. The Rumaila field is one of the world's largest, with reserves estimated at 30 billion barrels—three times the original size of Alaska's Prudhoe Bay formation. The field had been discovered in 1953, and roughly one-third of Iraq's wells were located there. But during the eight-year war with Iran, Iraq mined its share of the field to keep it from falling into Iranian hands. Kuwait stepped up its production, capturing some of Iraq's customers and pumping millions of barrels from the field. More importantly, Saddam maintained that the entire field belonged to Iraq.

Iraq's second territorial claim involved Bubiyan Island. This claim too was based on the view that the border between the two countries had been imposed on Iraq by the stroke of Sir Percy's pen in 1922 and lacked legitimacy. According to that view, Kuwait was a part of the Ottoman vilayet of Basra and was severed by the British to deny Iraq easy access to the Gulf. That ignored the fact that Kuwait was an autonomous area within the Turkish empire; that it had been ruled by the al-Sabah sheiks since the middle of the eighteenth century; and that it had been a British protectorate—unlike Basra itself—since 1899. It also ignored the fact that Iraq twice officially accepted the border with Kuwait: once in 1932 when it gained independence, and again in 1963 when the Baath came to power.

Nevertheless, Iraq's claim was not without merit. Unlike the Western world, boundaries in the Middle East often enjoy little legitimacy. Determined by-and-large during the period of colonialism, they frequently reflected the interests of Great Power diplomacy rather than regional reality. As former Under Secretary of State George Ball has pointed out, "Iraq's border with Kuwait . . . is but one of many such examples. The border between Mauritania and Morocco is a continuing source of tension, as is Morocco's border with Algeria; Libya and Egypt; Saudi Arabia and Yemen, Oman and the United Arab Emirates, and within the emirates themselves."[79] As if to substantiate that view, Bartholomew's, the legendary Edinburgh cartographers who prepare the maps for *The Times Atlas*, have consistently produced maps of Kuwait without boundaries.

Indeed, Iraqis were taught to regard Kuwait as rightfully part of their country long before the Baath came to power—much as the Argentines regard the Falklands; the Spanish regard Gibraltar; or the Chinese, Hong Kong. James Akins, a former U.S. ambassador to Saudi Arabia who served in both Baghdad and Kuwait, told *The New York Times* that "Every single Iraqi I know believes the border is unjust—that the British took [Bubiyan Island] away because they wanted Iraq to be landlocked."[80]

Iraq's recognition of its border with Kuwait in 1932 had been the price extracted by the British for independence. But after the death of King Feisal in 1933, Baghdad began a sustained effort to undermine that arrangement. Opposition groups, supported by Iraq, emerged in Kuwait, aided by growing tension between the al-Sabahs and prominent merchant families who wanted to limit the ruling family's power. In 1937, King Ghazi, the young son of Feisal, began broadcasting incendiary appeals to the Kuwaitis from a private radio station in the palace. Ghazi also denounced British influence in the Gulf. He depicted the emir as an outdated feudal monarch maintained in power by the British, and advocated Kuwait's absorption into Iraq.[81]

During the 1940s and '50s—throughout World War II and its aftermath—an uneasy truce prevailed. But in the early Sixties, Iraq's claims resurfaced. Kuwait became independent from Britain on June 19, 1961. Six days later, Iraqi president Abdul Karim Qassim claimed the emirate as an integral part of Iraq, citing the refrain that Kuwait had once belonged to the vilayet of Basra. Qassim said that he did not intend to use force, but he did not rule out the possibility, and there were rumors of Iraqi troop movements on the frontier. The British intervened once more, sending a detachment of regular troops to Kuwait City. Later that month, when Kuwait was admitted to the Arab League, Iraq abruptly withdrew from the League and recalled its ambassadors from those states that had recognized Kuwait. In September, League members added their own forces to the British military contingent and the crisis eventually passed. In 1963, the last of the foreign troops were withdrawn.

Qassim's quixotic gesture in 1961 proved to be an embarrassment for Iraq. His menacing words turned out to be empty threats and worsened Iraq's relations with its Arab neighbors. When Qassim was overthrown in 1963, the new Baathist regime recognized Kuwait's borders for a second time, apparently settling the dispute in return for a generous payment from the Kuwaitis.[82] Yet like most contentious subjects in the Middle East, the issue was not settled. In the late Sixties, Iraq again raised the issue of Bubiyan and Warba islands, seeking to improve access to its port at Umm Qasr. This time with British approval, Iraq offered to provide Kuwait with fresh water from the Shatt al-Arab in return for Warba and a portion of the coastline of Bubiyan. But the Kuwaitis demurred.

In 1969, Iraq placed its forces on Kuwaiti territory to defend Umm Qasr from possible Iranian attack. The episode closed without incident when the Iranians backed down and the Iraqis withdrew. Tensions escalated again in March 1973, when Iraqi troops occupied Kuwait's border outpost at al-Samitah, the closest Kuwaiti checkpoint to Bubiyan. Kuwait declared a state of emergency, recalled its ambassador from Baghdad, and asked the Arab League for support. When all of the Arab states backed Kuwait, Iraq grudgingly removed its troops, but not before its foreign minister, Murtadah Said Abdul-Baqi, restated the view that "the whole of Kuwait is a disputed area. There is a document saying that Kuwait is Iraqi territory [a reference to the Basra vilayet]. There is no document which says it is not Iraqi territory."[83]

Given the dire straits into which Iraq's economy had fallen in 1990, it is not surprising that Saddam should dust off these claims, particularly given the Baathist view that all borders in the Middle East were artificial to begin with. In 1988, at the end of the war with Iran, Saddam had signed nonaggression pacts with Saudi Arabia, Bahrain, and Jordan. The Saudis and Bahrain moved to forgive Iraq's war debt, and Jordan looked to Iraq as its ultimate defender against Israel. But Saddam pointedly ignored Kuwait. When Crown Prince Saad al-Sabah paid a much publicized visit to Baghdad in 1989 to sort out the border problem, he left empty-handed. According to Kuwaiti and Western diplomats in Baghdad, Saddam had refused to discuss the issue.[84] Saddam's refusal was noted in Kuwait City, but it scarcely made a ripple elsewhere. When Assistant Secretary of State John Kelly visited Baghdad in early February 1990, he found no cause for alarm. According to both Arab and American accounts, his meeting with Saddam was a success. Washington believed it had cemented its relationship with Iraq, and Kelly picked up no clue as to Saddam's intentions.[85]

Mixed Signals

To judge from the record, it is doubtful that Saddam would have leveled with Kelly in the first place. American policy toward Iraq has been confused and divided, a series of mixed signals and crossed messages. At the diplomatic level, commencing with the Carter administration in 1979, the United States sought to assist Saddam and encourage him to move from Moscow's orbit toward the West. Iraq was seen as a valuable bulwark against Iran and the Moslem fundamentalism represented by the Ayatollah Khomeini. With encouragement, it was hoped that Saddam's more distasteful traits could be ameliorated. This was the policy of the Reagan and Bush administrations as well. It was a policy strongly supported by the Commerce and Agriculture departments, whose officials reflected the interests of American businessmen and farmers.

Alongside this official tilt toward Iraq was a second stream of policy, focused in the intelligence agencies, sections of the Pentagon, and especially among Israel's supporters in Congress and the media. It emphasized the danger Iraq posed to the Middle East, and stressed the negative side of Saddam's regime, including its quest for chemical and nuclear weapons, as well as its links to wanted terrorists. The adherents to this stream of policy worked surreptitiously to destabilize Iraq. In these efforts, the voice of Israeli intelligence appeared to loom large, often with surprising results.

For example, two days after Kelly's visit to Baghdad, the Voice of America aired an editorial strongly critical of Iraqi police methods and calling for the overthrow of Saddam. Perhaps it was typical of Washington's bloated foreign affairs bureaucracy that one hand didn't know what the other was doing. But it was also a reflection of the two strands of policy at work. April Glaspie, the U.S. ambassador to Baghdad, attempted to reassure the Iraqis that the editorial did not reflect Washington's attitude, but it was difficult for Saddam to believe otherwise. Glaspie cabled Washington that Saddam "read the editorial as USG [United States Government] sanctioned mudslinging with the intent to incite revolution."[86] She then wrote to Tariq Aziz that the VOA editorial had been incorrectly interpreted in Baghdad. "It is absolutely not United States policy to question the legitimacy of the government of Iraq nor interfere in any way with the domestic concerns of the Iraqi people and government," said Glaspie.[87]

Such fits and starts typified American policy toward Iraq, and Baghdad responded in kind. Under General Qassim, Iraq had withdrawn from the U.S.-sponsored Baghdad Pact in 1959 and had moved toward Moscow. When Qassim was toppled in 1963, a brief period of cooperation set in, only to be terminated in 1967 with the Arab-Israeli Six-Day War. Iraq broke relations with Washington and in 1972 signed a fifteen-year friendship treaty with the Soviet Union. Washington responded with one of many attempts to destabilize Iraq, providing arms and equipment to the Kurdish rebels.[88] In 1979, with the taking of American hostages in Tehran, the United States reversed itself and began to woo Saddam. Zbigniew Brzezinski, President Carter's national security adviser, stated publicly that he would not object to "an Iraqi move against Iran,"[89] and the United States provided Baghdad with intelligence and satellite data prior to its invasion of Iran on September 22, 1980. Admiral Stansfield Turner, who was CIA director at the time, said that he had no evidence that Iraq had cleared the invasion with Washington, but he did know that the CIA was aware of it beforehand and had advised President Carter accordingly.[90]

The opening of direct diplomatic contact between Washington and Iraq occurred in April 1981, when Deputy Assistant Secretary of State Morris Draper met with Iraqi officials in Baghdad. From that point on, particularly as Iraq's military position deteriorated, American assistance increased significantly. According to Geoffrey Kemp, who headed the Middle East section in the Reagan White House, "It wasn't that we wanted Iraq to win the war; we did not want Iraq to lose. We really weren't naive. We knew he [Saddam] was an S.O.B., but he was our S.O.B."[91]

In March 1982, Iraq was removed from the list of terrorist countries maintained by the State Department, making it eligible for U.S. economic aid. "No one had any doubts about [Iraq's] continued involvement with terrorism," said Noel Koch, head of the Pentagon's counterterrorism unit. "The reason was to help them succeed in the war with Iran."[92] Late that year, the Department of Agriculture agreed to guarantee $300 million in credits for the purchase of American farm products. By 1990, Iraq had received about $3 billion in farm and other loans. It had become the world's largest importer of American rice and the fifth largest importer of American wheat. Full diplomatic relations were resumed in 1984, at which point the United States stepped up its assistance to Iraq, providing limited military equipment and intelligence information to Baghdad in its continuing struggle with Iran.

Relations deteriorated precipitously in 1986 when National Security Council staffers Robert "Bud" McFarlane and Oliver North turned up in Tehran with cake and Bible, pleading for the release of American hostages in Beirut. Official American policy notwithstanding, North told his hosts that "there is a need for a non-hostile regime in Baghdad," and suggested that "we can bring our influence to bear with certain friendly Arab nations," to get rid of Saddam.[93]

As if to complicate matters further, John Kelly, who was U.S. ambassador in Beirut at that time, was one of North's back-channel operatives. And it was April Glaspie, then Kelly's superior in Washington, who blew the whistle on Kelly's activities.[94] Glaspie informed Secretary of State George Shultz, who said it "made me sick to my stomach." Shultz disciplined Kelly (Kelly and Glaspie are less than friends) and the State Department apologized profusely to Baghdad.* The United States increased its assistance to Iraq and then looked the other way the following year when an errant Iraqi jet launched an Exocet missile into the U.S.S. *Stark*, killing thirty-seven seamen and coming within an inch of sinking the vessel. This time it was Saddam who apologized profusely and provided $27 million for the victims and their families.

When the war with Iran concluded with Iraq nominally victorious, Washington continued its official tilt toward Baghdad. When Saddam directed his attention to Iraq's Kurdish

---

*Like Kelly and Glaspie, James Baker and George Shultz are also less than friends. When Baker succeeded Shultz as secretary of state, Shultz's reprimand to Kelly became a badge of honor. Despite Kelly's lack of familiarity with the area, Baker promoted him to become assistant secretary for the Middle East, in which capacity he now supervised the work of Glaspie in Baghdad. To judge from the selective news leaks from the State Department since August 2, 1990, the tension between Glaspie and Kelly has not lessened.

minority, including the infamous gas attack at Halabja,* the United States more or less ignored it. The Bush administration, which took office in January 1989, reviewed America's pro-Iraqi orientation and decided that there was no reason to change. A national security directive to that effect was issued in October 1989.[95] In the meantime, American trade with Iraq had mushroomed to $3.6 billion annually, and the United States had become one of the principal purchasers of Iraqi oil. On January 17, 1990, President Bush signed an executive order certifying that to halt loan guarantees to Iraq by the government's Export-Import Bank would not be "in the national interest of the United States."[96] Bush believed that Washington should keep trying to use political and economic incentives to moderate Saddam's behavior and increase American influence.

Nevertheless, despite the renewed loan guarantees and Ambassador Glaspie's assurances to the contrary, the VOA's February editorial convinced Saddam of American duplicity. Later that month he lashed out at the United States during the first anniversary meeting of the Arab Cooperation Council (ACC) in Amman. The ACC (Egypt, Iraq, Jordan, and Yemen) was the brainchild of Saddam and King Hussein, and brought together Jordan's close allies in a loose-knit regional organization, primarily for Jordan's advantage. In his public statement, broadcast over Jordanian TV, Saddam noted the collapse of the Soviet Union as a superpower and said that in five years the United States would dominate the Middle East. According to Saddam:

---

*Conventional wisdom to the contrary, *The New York Times* reported on April 28, 1991, that responsibility for the gas attack at Halabja remains unclear. The *Times* cited recent studies by the Bush administration which suggest that the deaths occurred "during fierce border fighting in the final months of the Iran-Iraq war."

"The fact is that both sides used chemical weapons," said a Bush administration official who reviewed intelligence on the massacre. "There probably wasn't an attempt on either side to kill the villagers, but instead, they were fighting over territory."

According to the *Times*, an earlier study by the Army War College indicated "that it was the Iranian bombardment that had actually killed the Kurds."

The country that will have the greatest influence in the region, through the Arab Gulf and its oil, will maintain its superiority as a superpower without equal to compete with it. This means that if the Gulf people, along with all Arabs, are not careful, the Arab Gulf region will be governed by the wishes of the United States. . . .[97]

Saddam warned that the United States would be able to fix the price of oil to its own advantage—his first public hint that Iraq's economy might be suffering. Privately, he is said to have told King Hussein and Egypt's Hosni Mubarak that he needed $30 billion immediately, and that if the Gulf states didn't provide it, "I will know how to take it."[98]

Saddam's comments went largely unnoticed, especially in Washington, where President Bush, Secretary Baker, and the top echelons of the foreign-policy establishment were busy dealing with the unraveling of the Soviet empire and German unification. In March 1990, two separate but scarcely unrelated events punctuated the grim reality of the Middle East. On March 9, the Iraqis brought to trial and later executed an Iranian-born British journalist, accused of being a spy for Iranian and Israeli intelligence. Two weeks later, Dr. Gerald Bull, the Canadian artillery specialist working for Iraq, was murdered in Brussels. Reports at the time indicated that Mossad, the Israeli intelligence service, was involved.[99] Later in March, U.S. and British agents arrested several Iraqis attempting to smuggle sophisticated electronic equipment from the West without the required licenses. The devices could have been used to trigger nuclear weapons. Whether Israeli intelligence blew the whistle is unclear; Saddam believed they did. That, together with Bull's assassination, partially explains Saddam's tirade on April 2, when he announced that Iraq had developed powerful new chemical weapons. "By God," he said, "we will make the fire eat up half of Israel, if it tries to do anything against Iraq."[100]

In Washington, Saddam's remarks set off alarm bells in the State Department. It was agreed that Iraq should be sent a strong signal that Saddam's "menacing behavior would not be tolerated."[101] State Department spokesman Margaret Tutwiler called the remarks, "inflammatory, irresponsible, and outrageous."[102] The White House labeled them "deplorable and irresponsible."[103] With Secretary Baker's approval, State's proposal to discipline Saddam was referred to the so-called deputies committee—a second-tier body composed of the deputies to the members of the NSC—where it languished without action. Washington's policymakers simply had too much on their plates in the spring of 1990 to notice what seemed at the time to be a disagreeable sideshow in the Middle East. In addition, Saddam's comments, when placed in context, were not as menacing as subsequent commentators have suggested. His attack was couched with the proviso *"if Israel tries to do anything against Iraq."* Mubarak and King Hussein quickly came to Saddam's defense. The Jordanian monarch called Tutwiler's attack "vicious and harsh." He said, "We stand by Iraq and will always do so." Egypt tried to pour oil on the troubled waters. "We have made it very clear [to the United States] that any [verbal] attack against Iraq would be catastrophic," said a spokesman in Cairo. The need now, he said, "is to contain this whole affair and stop the escalation, which could be dangerous."[104]

Saddam himself sought to allay Washington's concern. He asked King Fahd to send an emissary to Baghdad who could speak authoritatively on his behalf to George Bush. Fahd sent the Saudi ambassador to the United States, Prince Bandar bin Sultan, who had previously acted as a middleman between Saddam and CIA Director William Casey during the war with Iran, and who was especially close to the president.[105] Bandar met with Saddam in Mosul on April 5. Saddam said that he wanted Bandar to assure President Bush that he wanted good relations with the West, but was worried that Israel might launch a preemptive attack. Since neither Iraq nor Saudi Arabia had diplomatic relations with Israel, Saddam wanted Bush to seek out Tel Aviv's intent. The White House eventually did so and sent word back to Saddam through Bandar that Israel would not launch anything against Iraq, if Iraq did not launch anything against them.[106] Bandar subsequently believed that Saddam sought assurance of Israeli intent to free himself to take action against Kuwait, although there was no indication of that at the time.

The week after Bandar's visit, Saddam received a delegation of five farm-belt senators, eager to restore harmony and fully aware of the importance of the Iraqi market for American grain and rice growers. The delegation was headed by the Senate's minority leader, Robert Dole of Kansas. Before flying to Iraq, Dole had called Bush from Cairo to be certain that the visit would be appropriate, given Saddam's recent threats against Israel.[107] When Saddam complained to the senators that the United States was intriguing against him, Dole replied that it was not coming from President Bush. Dole said that Bush had assured him personally only twelve hours earlier that he was pleased with their visit, that "he wants better relations, and the U.S. government wants better relations with Iraq."[108] Senator Alan Simpson of Wyoming, the Republican whip, told Saddam that his problem was not with the U.S. government, but with the Western media. "It is a haughty and pampered press," said Simpson. "They all consider themselves political geniuses. . . . They are very cynical."[109] Senator Howard Metzenbaum of Ohio, a liberal Democrat, suggested that Saddam could improve his image by talking more about peace. Reminding the Iraqi leader that he was Jewish, Metzenbaum said jokingly that "I am not the right person to be your public-relations man." The senators' impressions were summed up by Metzenbaum at the meeting's close. "I am now aware that you are a strong and intelligent man," the Ohio senator said, "and that you want peace."[110]

Nevertheless, Washington's policy continued its contradictory course. On April 14, the week after the senators' visit to Saddam, the White House suspended some $500 million in agricultural loan guarantees to Iraq after questions were raised about possible Iraqi kickbacks and malfeasance. Such practices are commonplace in the Middle East, and Saddam, who has an extraordinarily conspiratorial view of the world, could scarcely have been reassured as to the Bush administration's friendly intent. Again, he saw the hand of Israeli intelligence. At the same time, when Vice President Quayle proposed to give a speech taking a hard line against Saddam, the National Security Council asked him to tone it down.[111] The fact is, American policy toward Iraq was not coordinated, and, in the absence of firm direction from the top, various factions appeared to be freelancing.

Despite the zigs and zags in Washington, it was Iraq's economic condition that concerned Saddam most. In late May, at a specially convened Arab League summit in Baghdad, he complained to his fellow leaders that some of the Gulf states were keeping the price of oil too low by pumping too much of it. The ostensible purpose of the Baghdad summit had been to denounce the continued influx of Soviet Jews to Israel. Since the United States had just vetoed a Security Council resolution that U.N. observers be sent to the occupied territories, anti-American feelings ran high. Saddam made the expected attacks on the United States and Israel. According to *The Economist*, he was the hero of the hour. "Arabs everywhere were thrilled."[112] Once again, in the private sessions that followed, Saddam directed his sharpest attacks at Kuwait and the United Arab Emirates for exceeding OPEC production quotas. "This is economic war," he was quoted as saying.[113] "We cannot tolerate this type of economic warfare which is being waged against Iraq."[114] *The New York Times* reports that Saddam wanted $27 billion in compensation from Kuwait, a request that the Kuwaitis, as usual, deflected.[115]

Saddam was in earnest about his need for money. At the end of June, he dispatched the Iraqi deputy prime minister, Saadun Hammadi, to the Gulf states to press for lower production. According to a senior Arab official, Hammadi also pressed Saddam's demand for additional aid. For the benefit of the Kuwaitis, he produced a list of Kuwait's assets to prove that the country had sufficient funds to honor Iraq's request. When the Kuwaitis stonewalled, Hammadi came away empty-handed.

Saddam's pressure was preliminary to a meeting of OPEC scheduled for July 24 in Geneva. At a planning session in Jidda on July 10, his bluster had its effect. The Gulf emirates, including Kuwait, reluctantly agreed to abide by OPEC's production quotas. That sent the spot price for Brent crude up by two dollars, but the *Financial Times* of London reported that there was still a "credibility gap as to whether Kuwait and the UAE would actually comply."[116] Tariq Aziz said the agreement "was too good to be true."[117] In announcing the arrangement the next day, Kuwait added a stipulation that it would review and possibly reverse the decision in the fall. Aziz claims that "tipped off major buyers to wait for October, when the price would drop again."

In the face of Kuwait's duplicity, Aziz wrote to the Arab League on July 16, once more accusing Kuwait of exceeding its OPEC quota and stealing oil from the disputed Rumaila field. He accused Kuwait and the United Arab Emirates of participating in "an imperialist-zionist plot against the Arab nation."[118] Speaking before an Arab summit meeting in Tunis that same day, Aziz said, "We are sure some Arab states are involved in a conspiracy against us. We want you to know that our country will not kneel, our women will not become prostitutes, our children will not be deprived of food."[119] Even for those accustomed to the verbal excesses of the Middle East, Aziz's words had a chilling effect. *The Economist* reported that it sounded "alarmingly like a pretext for invasion."[120]

Aziz's words were merely preliminary to the fusillade launched the following day by Saddam himself. In what the *Financial Times* called "an unprecedented verbal attack on his Arab neighbours,"[121] Saddam threatened military action if the Gulf states continued to flout OPEC production quotas. Speaking on the twenty-second anniversary of the coup that brought the Baath to power, Saddam said that "The policies of some Arab rulers are American. They are inspired by America to undermine Arab interests and security." Iraq, he said, had been stabbed in the back "with a poisoned dagger." Without mentioning either Kuwait or the UAE by name, Saddam said that "we have warned them. If words fail to protect Iraqis, something effective must be done to return things to their natural course . . . Iraqis will not forget the maxim that cutting necks is better than cutting the means of living."[122]

When Kuwait's cabinet reviewed the situation on July 18, there was little agreement as to how to react. Justice Minister Dari al-Uthman believed that Saddam's demands "were just the beginning." Others believed that Iraq was simply intent on extorting money. Crown Prince Saad al-Sabah suggested that military action was possible. Some agreed; others did not. Even those who thought that an attack might come believed that Saddam would seize only the disputed territory. A brief military alert was ordered, but the forces were quietly ordered to stand down. In effect, Kuwait believed that Saddam was bluffing.[123]

From Washington, the mixed signals continued. In a belated reaction to Saddam's reported gassing of the Kurds, legislation was introduced in both Houses of Congress to cut off agricultural subsidies to Iraq, and, over the Commerce Department's objection, the administration blocked the export of several high-tech furnaces that could have contributed to Saddam's nuclear program. When asked about Iraq's threats against Kuwait and the UAE, a State Department spokesman said merely that the United States remains "strongly committed to supporting the individual and collective self-defense of our friends in the Gulf with whom we have longstanding ties." He declined to say, when asked, whether the United States would provide help if Kuwait were attacked.[124]

If the State Department was speaking in diplomatic code, it was deciphered differently in Kuwait City and Baghdad. Each side found encouragement to continue its present course. The reference of support for "our friends in the Gulf with whom we have longstanding ties" convinced the Kuwaitis to hang tough, while the reluctance to commit the United States in case of attack caused Saddam to believe that America would not intervene. A collision was inevitable. Tariq Aziz complained on

Iraqi TV that the American statements "were clear encouragement for the Kuwaiti government to go on with its deliberate policy of aggression against Iraq."[125]

The Defense Department conveyed equally garbled messages. At a press breakfast on July 19, Secretary Cheney said that an American commitment made during the Iran-Iraq war to come to Kuwait's defense was still valid. "Those commitments haven't changed," he was quoted as saying.[126] Under Secretary Paul Wolfowitz made the same point at a private lunch with Arab ambassadors.[127] But later that day, Defense Department spokesman Pete Williams tried to steer reporters away from Cheney's comments, adding that the secretary had been quoted "with some degree of liberty."[128] An administration official, identified only as "a former U.S. envoy in the Persian Gulf," said that America's commitment to Kuwait has always been stated as a protection "against the spillover from the Iran-Iraq war" and did not address aggression growing out of the current dispute with Baghdad.[129]

Saddam and the emir both felt encouraged. On July 21, the CIA reported the first of Iraqi troop movements near the border. The following day, Saddam met with Egyptian president Hosni Mubarak in Baghdad. Mubarak, King Hussein of Jordan, and King Fahd of Saudi Arabia were now trying to mediate the dispute, and Mubarak was shuttling between Baghdad, Kuwait City, and Saudi Arabia. Mubarak informed Washington that Saddam had assured him that he would not invade Kuwait so long as negotiations continued, and the Egyptian leader took that as a positive sign.[130]

The messages from Washington continued to be ambiguous. On July 23, the Bush administration dispatched two KC-135 aerial tankers and a C-141 cargo transport to the Gulf in response to a request from the United Arab Emirates, and ordered its six naval vessels in the area to put to sea for joint exercises with the emirates. One senior administration official was quoted by The New York Times as saying that the actions were intended to "bolster a friend and lay down a marker for Saddam Hussein."[131] But when Navy Secretary H. Laurence Garrett told the House Armed Services subcommittee on seapower that "our ships in the Persian Gulf were put on alert status," an aide later told the press that the navy secretary had misspoken.[132]

The following day, in an attempt to clarify American policy, reporters asked top State Department spokesman Margaret Tutwiler whether the United States had any commitment to defend Kuwait. Tutwiler replied that "we do not have any defense treaties with Kuwait, and there are no special defense or security commitments to Kuwait."[133] Asked directly whether the United States would help Kuwait if it were attacked, she added that "we also remain strongly committed to supporting the individual and collective self-defense of our friends in the gulf with whom we have deep and long-standing ties."[134] A nod toward Saddam, a wink for the emir.

The situation was further complicated when the *Washington Post* quoted a senior U.S. military official (a designation sometimes used for the chairman of the joint chiefs of staff) who said that if Iraq seized a small amount of Kuwaiti territory as a means of gaining additional leverage over Kuwait in OPEC, the United States *probably would not directly challenge the move*, but would join with all Arab governments in denouncing it and putting pressure on Iraq to back down. "We are not going to war," the official said. "But you are going to see exercises and you are going to see ships."[135]

At that point, Saddam must have decided to clarify United States policy himself. On the one hand, American warships were patrolling the Gulf in a joint exercise with the United Arab Emirates. On the other, spokesmen for both the State and Defense departments were signaling that the United States would not defend Kuwait in case of attack. As soon as the report of Margaret Tutwiler's comments arrived in Baghdad, Saddam summoned Ambassador Glaspie for an interview. That was an extraordinary move for the Iraqi president. Glaspie had been at her post in Baghdad for almost two years. Except on ceremonial occasions, she had not met with Saddam, and had never had a private conversation with him.[136] Now he wanted to see her within the hour.

Glaspie was a seasoned diplomat, with long experience in the Middle East. A Phi Beta Kappa at Mills College with a master's degree from Johns Hopkins, she had made a career in the Arab world—where few doors are open to women. Fluent in Arabic, and highly respected by her colleagues, she had served in Amman, Beirut, Cairo, Damascus, and Kuwait. Prior to taking up her duties in Baghdad, she had headed the State Department's section on Lebanon, Jordan, and Syria, and was thoroughly familiar with every nuance of American Middle East policy.

When Glaspie was ushered in, Saddam dispensed with the small talk. "I have summoned you today to hold comprehensive political discussions," he said. "This is a message for President Bush."[137]

For the next thirty minutes, the Iraqi president spoke without interruption. That was Saddam's style. He traced the bleak history of U.S.-Iraqi relations, pointing out that the two countries had not had much contact with each other and that mistakes were easy to make. "The worst of these was in 1986, only two years after establishing [diplomatic] relations, with what was known as Irangate. . . . We accepted the apology . . . of the American President . . . and we wiped the slate clean. And we shouldn't unearth the past except when new events remind us that old mistakes were not just a matter of coincidence." Saddam went on to complain about American attempts to undercut him, including efforts to convince the Gulf states not to provide the economic aid he needed. "I don't say the President himself—but certain parties who had links with the intelligence community and with the State Department."

Saddam then laid out Iraq's economic plight for Glaspie's benefit. He detailed Iraq's differences with Kuwait and then

asked about the recent statements from Washington about protecting its friends in the area. Such statements, he said, were
encouraging Kuwait and the emirates to take anti-Iraqi positions.

> *We clearly understand America's statement that it wants the
> easy flow of oil. We understand America saying that it seeks
> friendships with the states in the region, and to encourage
> their joint interests. But we cannot understand the attempt
> to encourage some parties to harm Iraq's interests.*

Then Saddam showed his teeth. If the United States pressured Iraq, he would strike back. He queried U.S. links with
Israel and mused about Israeli influence on American policy,
but ended his presentation with a general appeal for friendship
and understanding. As for the problem with Kuwait and the
UAE, "The solution must be found within an Arab framework
and through direct bilateral relations."

Ambassador Glaspie did her best to reassure Saddam that
the United States meant no harm. She identified herself with
Iraq's colonial past: "We studied history in school. They taught
us to say freedom or death. I think you know well that we as a
people have our own experience with the colonialists." She
lamented the hostile media coverage of Iraq in the United
States and told Saddam, "I have direct instructions from the
President to seek better relations with Iraq."

When Saddam mentioned the price of oil and suggested $25
a barrel, Glaspie replied that many Americans "would like to
see the price go above $25 because they come from oil-
producing states."

Saddam: The price at one stage dropped to $12 a
                   barrel and a reduction of $6 billion to $7
                   billion in the modest Iraqi budget is a
                   disaster.

Glaspie: I think I understand this. I have lived here
                for years. I admire your extraordinary efforts
                to rebuild your country. I know you need
                funds. We understand that and our opinion
                is that you should have the opportunity to
                rebuild your country. *But we have no opinion
                on the Arab-Arab conflicts, like your border
                disagreement with Kuwait.* [Emphasis added.]

Glaspie went on to say that she had served in Kuwait in
the 1960s, and at that time the embassy's instructions from the
State Department were that "we should express no opinion on
this issue." She said that Secretary Baker had recently reem-
phasized those instructions.* She then asked Saddam—"in the
spirit of friendship"—about his intentions concerning Kuwait.
In response, the Iraqi president detailed at some length the
fruitless course of negotiations that summer, but then told Glaspie that a meeting with the Kuwaitis would soon be held in
Jidda, with another session scheduled for Baghdad the following
week. He said that he had just told President Mubarak to "assure the Kuwaitis . . . that we are not going to do anything
until we meet with them. When we meet and we see that there
is hope, then nothing will happen. But if we are unable to find
a solution, then it will be natural that Iraq will not accept
death, even though wisdom is above everything else."

Glaspie interpreted that as good news. She overlooked Saddam's threat to take action if the negotiations soured. Glaspie
told Saddam that she was returning to Washington the following week and would try to deliver his message to President Bush
personally.[138]

In the weeks to follow, Ambassador Glaspie was made a

---

*On July 24, the State Department, over Baker's signature, explicitly instructed Glas-
pie to reiterate to the Iraqi government the standard phrase about the United States
having "no position" on Arab border disputes, but to remind Baghdad that the use
of force was "contrary to U.N. Charter principles." Scarcely a red light. See Leslie
Gelb, "Mr. Bush's Fateful Blunder," *The New York Times*, July 17, 1991.

scapegoat for American miscues because she had not been tough with Saddam; because she had not warned him of what might happen should he invade Kuwait. The fact is, Glaspie was faithfully executing the instructions given to her by the president and Secretary of State Baker. "April didn't invent the policy," said former Assistant Secretary Richard Murphy. "She inherited an effort of years' standing to try to mold a more sensible Iraq and develop commercial and industrial relationships so that there were a richer set of ties [between the two countries]."[139] Indeed, Glaspie's remarks to Saddam were almost exactly what State Department spokesman Margaret Tutwiler had said the day before and were fully consistent with the cabled instructions she had received from Washington that same day.

In her own defense, Ambassador Glaspie told *The New York Times*, "Obviously, I didn't think—and nobody else did—that the Iraqis were going to take all of Kuwait. Every Kuwaiti and Saudi, every analyst in the Western world was wrong too. That does not excuse me. But people who now claim that all was clear were not heard from at the time."[140]*

Immediately after meeting with Saddam, Glaspie cabled her account of the conversation to the State Department. She said that Saddam, "whose manner was cordial, reasonable and even warm," sought better relations with the United States. Glaspie thought Saddam's "emphasis that he wants [a] peaceful settlement [with Kuwait] is surely sincere. Iraqis are tired of war." Her recommendation was that Washington adopt a conciliatory attitude. "I believe we would now be well-advised to ease off on public criticism of Iraq until we see how the negotiations

---

*Táriq Aziz, who was present at the interview, discounts the impact of Glaspie's interview on Iraqi policy. As he told Milton Viorst after the war, "Having been a Foreign Minister, I understand the work of ambassadors, and I believe Miss Glaspie's behavior was correct. She was summoned suddenly. [Saddam] wanted to tell her that the situation was worsening and that our government would not waive its options, and he wanted to add that Iraq was not hostile to the United States. We knew she was acting on available instructions. She spoke in vague diplomatic language, and we knew the position she was in. Her behavior was a classic diplomatic response, and we were not influenced by it." *The New Yorker*, June 24, 1991, pp. 66–67.

develop."[141] Washington appeared satisfied, and on July 28, with a hundred thousand Iraqi troops massed at the frontier, the White House dispatched a cable from President Bush for Saddam that reiterated the American position along the lines laid out by Glaspie. America wanted better relations with Baghdad, and it had no opinion on Arab boundary questions, but it opposed the use of force and would "continue to support our friends in the region." Bush added that "my Administration continues to desire better relations with Iraq." No mention was made of the troop concentration at the border. The cable went through State Department channels, and Ambassador Glaspie delivered it to Iraqi foreign minister Tariq Aziz that day.[142]

Following a briefing by administration officials, the *Washington Post* reported that in his meeting with Glaspie, Saddam had sought "to allay U.S. concerns that American interests were at stake" in his quarrel with Kuwait. The *Post* said that while U.S. Central Command—the military structure headed by General H. Norman Schwarzkopf and responsible for the Middle East—sought a strong show of force to deter Saddam, "officials in the State Department, White House, and higher levels of the Pentagon cautioned that the United States should promote the free flow of oil through [the Persian Gulf] and avoid getting drawn into a military commitment to defend Kuwait."[143]

As it once was with *Pravda* in Moscow, all embassies in Washington read the *Washington Post* line by line for the latest nuances of American policy. That quasi-official rendition by the *Post* of American aims in the Gulf flashed a green light in Baghdad. And, in fact, the very day that Saddam had met with Glaspie, Assistant Secretary of State Kelly had killed a Voice of America editorial warning Iraq that the United States was "strongly committed to supporting its friends in the Gulf."[144] The *Financial Times* of London reported that some U.S. allies were already irritated at Washington's high profile in the crisis and that statements about defending its friends in the Gulf were "adding fuel to the flames."[145]

When the Senate voted 80–16 to cut off loan guarantees to Iraq (the House had passed a similar bill 234–175), State Department spokesman Richard Boucher condemned the action, saying that such measures would not help "in achieving the goals we want to achieve in our relationship with Iraq."[146] On July 31, Assistant Secretary of State Kelly went to Capitol Hill to testify against the upcoming conference report that would have reconciled the House and Senate versions of the loan cutoff. Kelly appeared before the Middle East subcommittee of the House Foreign Affairs Committee. Sitting in the committee's ornate hearing room in the Rayburn building, Kelly was interrogated by the subcommittee chairman, Democrat Lee Hamilton of Indiana. Hamilton asked Kelly whether Defense Secretary Cheney had been correct when he said (on July 19) that the United States had a commitment to come to Kuwait's defense if it was attacked.

Kelly:	. . . I'm not familiar with the quotation that you just referred to, but I am confident in the administration's policy on the issue. We have no defense relationship with any Gulf country. This is clear. We support the security and independence of our friends in the Gulf. . . .
Hamilton:	Now do we have a commitment to our friends in the Gulf in the event that they are engaged in oil or territorial disputes with their neighbors?
Kelly:	As I said, Mr. Chairman, we have no defense treaty relationships with any of the countries. *We have historically avoided taking positions on border disputes* or on internal OPEC deliberations, but we have certainly . . . called for the peaceful settlement of disputes and differences in the area. [Emphasis added.]

Hamilton: If there—if Iraq, for example, charged across
               the border into Kuwait . . . what would be
               our position with respect to the use of U.S.
               forces?

Kelly: That, Mr. Chairman, is a hypothetical or a
               contingency question, the kind of which I
               can't get into. Suffice it to say we would be
               extremely concerned, but I cannot get into
               the realm of "what if" answers.

Hamilton: In that circumstance, it is correct to say,
               however, that we do not have a treaty
               commitment which would obligate us to
               engage U.S. forces there?

Kelly: That is correct.[147]

Reports of Kelly's testimony were printed prominently on
August 1 in London's *Financial Times* and carried over the
BBC's World Service, both of which are monitored closely in
Baghdad. In addition, the Iraqi embassy in Washington filed its
own report. If Saddam was in doubt about possible American
intervention, Kelly's remarks certainly reassured him.

In retrospect, it is too easy to blame Glaspie and Kelly for
not having warned Saddam of the consequences of his action.
The fact is, both accurately portrayed administration policy,
and Washington itself is to blame for having signaled the go-
ahead to Iraq. What is less obvious, but more culpable, is the
encouragement the United States gave to the Kuwaitis at the
same time. In effect, the Bush administration, as Biblical scholars might say, spoke with forked tongue. By saying it would not
defend Kuwait, it encouraged Saddam to invade; by stressing
its continued support for "its longstanding friends in the area,"
the Kuwaitis were given no incentive to compromise.

It will be many years before the CIA and diplomatic cable
traffic between Washington and Kuwait City is made public.
Exactly what the United States was instructing its embassy to
tell the Kuwaitis in these top-secret transmissions cannot be

proved.* During an Arab summit meeting in Cairo in mid-August, Tariq Aziz threatened to reveal the contents of the messages from the CIA to the Kuwaitis. The *Washington Post* reports that the Kuwaiti foreign minister, Sabah al-Ahmed al-Sabah, fainted dead away.[148]

As if to confirm Washington's influence, both King Hussein and King Fahd placed the blame for the invasion squarely on the Kuwaitis, who were being exceptionally stubborn and difficult in their negotiations with Iraq. On July 30, King Hussein visited the emir in Kuwait City and warned him that the meeting scheduled for the next day in Jidda would be critical. "I pleaded with them," said the king. "They were warm and cordial, unusually so. But there was no commitment." Other Jordanian officials traveling with Hussein reported a similar response. The entire Kuwaiti leadership, it appeared, completely lacked any understanding of the danger they were in. "If the Iraqis attack us, we would call the Americans," Kuwait's foreign minister told his Jordanian counterpart. Kuwait's only concern was that relying on American military help might be embarrassing because of U.S. support for Israel.[149]

King Fahd also blamed the Kuwaitis. "It's all Kuwait's fault," he told King Hussein the morning after the invasion. "They would be this adamant. They've brought this about."[150]

The problem for the United States was that no one at a senior level was focused on the issue. No one quite realized how desperate Iraq was, or for that matter, how obstinate and

---

*Six months after the war, Sheikh Salim al-Sabah, the new foreign minister, told *The New Yorker* that "after the Iran-Iraq War, we had exchanges with the United States about the growing danger of Saddam Hussein. The United States knew something was going to happen . . . Schwarzkopf came here a few times and met with the Crown Prince and Minister of Defense. These became routine visits to discuss military cooperation and coordination. By the time the crisis with Iraq began last year, we knew we could rely on the Americans. There was an exchange of talks on the ambassadorial level just before the invasion. No explicit commitments were ever made, but it was like a marriage. Sometimes you don't say to your wife 'I love you,' but you know the relationship will lead to certain things." (Milton Viorst, "A Reporter At Large: After the Liberation," *The New Yorker*, September 30, 1991, p. 72.)

unforthcoming the Kuwaitis would be. It may also be true that there were those in Washington, below the top policy-making level, who feared Iraq's growing power in the Middle East, and who deliberately sought to provoke a confrontation. With Bush and Baker occupied with more pressing matters in Europe, those elements had relatively free play. And by encouraging the Kuwaitis to resist Saddam's claims, as the CIA apparently did, that confrontation became inevitable. Whether the motivation was deliberate or merely accidental, by giving encouragement to both sides, the United States bears substantial responsibility for what happened.

2.

THIS WILL NOT STAND

Remember, George, this is no time
to go wobbly.
—Margaret Thatcher
August 3, 1990

With Saddam in full control of Kuwait, the options for the United States were limited. Among America's European allies, only Britain appeared concerned. Elsewhere, the major powers—the Russians, the Chinese, and the Japanese—accepted the takeover more or less in stride. The Arabs shed scarcely a tear for the Kuwaitis. Saddam, it was assumed, would take the territory he wanted and quickly pull out. The Iraqis would install a new, much more pliant government in Kuwait, and that government would remedy Baghdad's economic distress. Such, at least, was the reasonable anticipation on August 2.

Immediately after meeting with the National Security Council, President Bush left Washington to keep a rendezvous with Margaret Thatcher in Aspen, Colorado. The renowned Aspen Institute had laid on a global conference dealing with the new world order following Communism's decline, and Bush and Thatcher were to be the keynote speakers. Mrs. Thatcher was slated to receive the institute's Statesman Award, while Bush's speech would deal with the military wind-down, the peace dividend, and the new, much reduced configuration of U.S. forces. (The president would announce that the American military would be reduced by 25 percent by 1995.) Just before boarding his helicopter on the South Lawn, the president told reporters that "we're not discussing intervention [in Kuwait]. I'm not contemplating such action."[1] And with that he took off.

Yet Bush brooded about the Iraqi takeover. "What happens if we do nothing?" he had asked, troubled that Saddam might not withdraw.[2] Aboard Air Force One, the president telephoned America's principal Arab allies in the Middle East: King Hussein of Jordan, Egypt's Hosni Mubarak, and King Fahd of Saudi Arabia. Fahd was unavailable,[3] but Mubarak and King Hussein were already seized of the issue and were actually meeting together at Mubarak's summer residence in Alexandria when the president's call arrived.[4] Both stressed the importance of finding an "Arab solution" to the invasion and urged Bush not to become involved.[5] King Hussein told the president that he had just spoken with Saddam by phone before leaving Amman and that the Iraqi leader had said he was planning to begin withdrawing from Kuwait within days. "Within a week we'll be gone," the king quoted Saddam as saying. King Hussein stressed to Bush that the situation was delicate and that Saddam was exceptionally touchy about his prerogatives. The king reported that Saddam had emphasized that he would "not respond positively to threats or intimidation." That meant it had to appear as if Iraq had made the decision to withdraw on its own and that it was not doing so under duress. Bush thereupon agreed to give King Hussein forty-eight hours to secure a commitment from Saddam.[6]

The president failed to honor that agreement. When Bush arrived in Aspen, he immediately met with Mrs. Thatcher to review the crisis. After eleven years in office, a record tenure for British prime ministers in this century, Thatcher had adopted an imperious mien that brooked no compromise. She was marvelously unassailed by self-doubt and absolutely convinced of the correctness of her opinion—much to the dismay of even her own party, it would soon become clear. But in Aspen she was at the top of her form and completely convinced that Saddam had to be slapped down.

For Thatcher, it was the Falkland Islands all over again. Reminiscent of what had been her finest hour, she was determined that Iraq's aggression be punished. For the British of Mrs. Thatcher's generation, and for her above all, the imagery of Munich has always loomed large: the sellout of innocent Czechoslovakia by unwitting Western statesmen, the reward of Hitler's aggression, and the penultimate step to World War II. The lesson was clear. Aggression had to be nipped in the bud, and the aggressor must be made to surrender his ill-gotten gains. The world must stand together and defeat Saddam.

Thatcher's views were colored by Britain's long ties to Kuwait. This was no remote desert sheikdom, but a British protectorate for over sixty years—or at least, a former British protectorate. The Kuwait Investment Office, the investment arm of the Kuwaiti government, was based in London, and much of the emirate's vast wealth was invested there. In addition, Britain had always nurtured a tutorial relationship with Kuwait. Kuwait's military forces were trained by the British, and most of their armament was British. Whereas Iraq had long rejected the colonial ties of the 1920s, Kuwait seemed to relish that relationship.

Thatcher also feared the long-term implications of Saddam's invasion. If the independence of Kuwait could be questioned by Iraq, the legitimacy of Britain's other creations in the Gulf was cast into doubt: Oman, Qatar, the United Arab Emirates, Bahrain, and even Saudi Arabia itself. Those countries, put in place by British imperialism and propped up by the West, controlled 34 percent of the world's oil reserves.

The electoral implications of a quick, popular war also did not elude Thatcher. In the spring of 1982, before the Falklands, the Tories trailed their two rival parties, garnering a mere 26 percent of the electorate. In July, after the Falklands, the Tories led the pack with 45 percent.[7] When she met Bush in Aspen, Thatcher's approval rating had sagged to a dismal 24 percent, lower than that of any prime minister since polling in Britain began.[8] For a politician of Thatcher's acumen, the electoral parallel to the Falklands was unmistakable.

In her many hours with Bush that day, Mrs. Thatcher precipitated the doubts that the president had had all along. In an expression that John le Carré might use, she turned him from grudging acceptance of what had happened in Kuwait to unremitting hostility. Thatcher insisted that long-term Western interests were at stake. Aggression had to be punished; there could be no compromise with Saddam.

"He must be stopped," she told Bush.[9] The two discussed possible military action to reverse the takeover, and Mrs. Thatcher pledged Britain's support. France could be counted on too, she said. "Mitterrand will give you trouble until the end, but when the ship sails, [France] will be there."[10] In a joint press conference that afternoon, Bush said that he and the prime minister had discussed a series of options concerning Kuwait, including military ones. "We're not ruling any options in, but we're not ruling any options out," the president said.[11] According to the Washington Post, Bush's statement "reopened the door to some kind of U.S. military operation, which the president appeared to close earlier in the day [in Washington] when he said he was 'not contemplating' military intervention, despite [a] Kuwaiti appeal." The Post said that no other Arab nation, including Saudi Arabia, had asked for U.S. military assistance.[12] The president was taking the lead.

Despite his pledge to King Hussein not to become involved

for at least forty-eight hours, and knowing full well of Saddam's sensibilities, Bush then lashed out at the Iraqi leader, stating that his behavior was "intolerable" and that the invasion was "totally unjustified." Bush urged all other nations to condemn what he termed the "naked aggression"[13] of Iraq, saying it was crucial that the "international community act together to ensure that Iraqi forces leave Kuwait immediately."[14] It was exactly the kind of statement King Hussein had warned Bush against earlier that day. The president added insult to injury when he said that he and his advisers were examining the "next steps needed to end the invasion," in effect, throwing down the gauntlet to Saddam.[15]

Thatcher was much more vehement. She called the Iraqi invasion a vivid example of "the evil in human nature."[16] The members of the United Nations, she said, "must stand up and be counted because a vital principle is at stake: An aggressor must never be allowed to get his way."[17] Throughout the press conference, America's chief executive deferred to Mrs. Thatcher. In what the London *Times* called a remarkably deprecating aside, "even for Mr. Bush," the president said he had been very comforted by the presence of the prime minister, who had provided the tough answers concerning Kuwait. According to the *Times*,

> The president was right. Mrs. Thatcher did articulate the toughest issues of the threat to small states from unopposed aggression, and the paramount need for international solidarity against President Saddam Hussein.

The *Times* said that Bush "was hesitant by comparison."[18]

The president may well have appeared hesitant: He had, after all, just welshed on his commitment to King Hussein. But by evening he was totally convinced that Saddam's aggression could not stand. In the words of a senior British official who was present, "The Rubicon between what happened and a much weaker response was crossed that afternoon."[19] Or as another senior Thatcher adviser somewhat more colloquially told the *Manchester Guardian*, "The Prime Minister performed a successful backbone transplant," and Bush resolved to take a much firmer line.[20]

Bush cut short his visit to Colorado and returned to Washington that night, rather than on Friday night as originally planned.[21] Whatever latent instincts the president may have had to deploy American forces anywhere in the world to resist aggression had been revitalized by Mrs. Thatcher. "She was a big influence on the basic decision he had to make," a White House official acknowledged.[22]

Brent Scowcroft, who had accompanied Bush to Aspen, added his counsel to that of Thatcher. Iraq's attack on Kuwait was a threat to the vital interests of the United States, argued Scowcroft, citing the Carter Doctrine of 1980.* A former Air Force general, Scowcroft looked on war in Clausewitzian terms: an extension of politics by other means. He deplored the American military's unwillingness to use force (the Vietnam Syndrome) and urged the president to respond vigorously to Saddam's assault.

The combination of Thatcher and Scowcroft, each speaking to Bush directly, convinced the president to take action. There was no debate, no formal consideration of policy alternatives, and no clear statement about goals and purposes. In George Bush's mind, and in his subsequent rhetoric, Saddam's action was equated with Hitler's invasion of Poland, the Japanese attack on Manchuria, and Mussolini's takeover of Ethiopia. According to *Newsweek*, the president became convinced that Saddam was so evil that any action would be justified to bring him down.[23] Bush reassembled his National Security Council the following morning and made clear his determination to intervene.[24] It was, in effect, a presidential directive. NATO

---

*As enunciated by President Carter in his State of the Union message, "An attempt by any outside force to gain control of the Persian Gulf region will be regarded as an assault on the vital interests of the United States of America. And such an assault will be repelled by any means necessary, including military force."

was alerted that the United States was preparing contingency plans for a military deployment in the Gulf.[25]

There are few countries in the world in which policy can turn on a dime. The United States, when it comes to foreign affairs, is one of those. And it reflects the power of the president. The vast national security structure that grew up in America during the Cold War was designed to carry into effect the president's singular decision to respond to nuclear attack. A national mind-set evolved that focused on the president as the country's sole decision-maker. That ability to decide quickly was essential when an instantaneous response was required. But the legacy of that mind-set, and the accompanying institutional apparatus, carried over into all other aspects of foreign policy. The president came to be regarded as the supreme decision-maker on all issues. On his word alone, the machinery of government was set in motion. Diplomats, the military, and the intelligence community looked to the president exclusively for direction. There was no built-in resistance, no vehicle for the articulation of policy alternatives. No Cabinet, as in a parliamentary system, where politicians of varying degrees of independence reconcile the government's policy. No loyal opposition to be confronted every day in the House of Commons—and to whom the government's policy must be explained. The president's command, even the president's whim, determined American policy. In the words of the Tower Commission (John Tower, Edmund Muskie, and Brent Scowcroft), which had investigated decision-making in the White House during Iran-Contra, "The President is the ultimate decision maker in national security."[26]

On Thursday, August 2, the United States was at peace. On Friday, after the president's meeting with Thatcher in Aspen, America was marching off to war. George Bush had changed his mind, and the executive branch fell into line. The United States had adopted what a critic of American foreign policy once called the "tar-baby option": Once stuck, one cannot turn loose.[27]

Bush's reversal can be pinpointed during those hours with Margaret Thatcher in Colorado. Before he left Washington that morning, Kuwait was just a gas station. Military involvement had been ruled out, and the National Security Council concurred completely. Speaking to Mubarak and King Hussein while en route to Aspen, the president had accepted the idea of an Arab solution and given Hussein the go-ahead. He agreed to a forty-eight-hour cooling-off period during which the United States would avoid any entanglement. The assumption was that a peaceful solution could be found and that Saddam would pull back, keeping only the disputed territory. After meeting with Thatcher, the president reneged. Predictability and consistency had always been problems for George Bush, but never with such momentous consequences. Steering without an ideological compass, with few underlying principles to guide his policy, the president had been savaged in the past by Washington's press corps for his unseemly willingness to adopt whatever momentary issue captured his fancy—"the momentum of shallow enthusiasm," in the chilling words of *The New Republic*'s Michael Kinsley.[28] Margaret Thatcher had urged Bush to be "Churchillian" in handling Saddam, and Bush eagerly accepted the challenge.

Time magazine, in naming Bush Man-of-the-Year for 1990, reported in awe that the president had made his decision after leafing through Martin Gilbert's *The Second World War*, citing Churchill's view that Hitler should have been stopped in the Rhineland in 1936.[29]

In 1961, another president, John F. Kennedy, was chosen Man-of-the-Year by *Time* for his successful handling of the Berlin crisis that year. Kennedy, reported Hugh Sidey, sat up nights when the Berlin Wall went up, reading Barbara Tuchman's *The Guns of August*, a classic treatment of how Europe stumbled into World War I.[30] One president kept the peace, another led the United States into war. Historical analogies sometimes fit; sometimes they don't. There are no hard and fast rules.

Unlike George Bush's pattern of selecting subordinates,

Kennedy surrounded himself with independent thinkers and men of experience. He heard the views of Schlesinger, Sorensen, and McNamara, but he also listened to Dean Acheson, Averell Harriman, John McCloy, and Lucius D. Clay. He steered a careful course between the extremes of too much and too little. He mastered the rule that collective security must be proportional: The benefits must be related to the costs, and there are few issues of black and white with which a president must deal. When Hitler marched into the Rhineland, Germany had only a hundred thousand men under arms and a much superior French army was two hours away. When Saddam entered Kuwait, Iraq's army numbered more than one million, and the United States was halfway around the globe.

George Bush not only lacked Kennedy's qualities of proportionality, but history would record that he was also surprisingly wilful, petulant, and "testy"—a word frequently used by his handlers. Thatcher had ignited his urge for greatness, and Bush caught fire. There were no Achesons or McCloys—no seasoned statesmen, no nay-sayers to warn of the dangers ahead; no Clays, no Harrimans to caution that the world was a complicated place and that America could not always have its way. George Bush had decided; the American chain of command responded.

King Hussein's Arab solution was the first casualty of that reversal in American policy. A close friend for many years of both President Bush and Saddam, King Hussein was uniquely positioned to bring about a settlement in Kuwait. The fifty-four-year-old monarch, who had ruled his fractious, refugee-filled country for thirty-eight years, had long enjoyed a reputation for political sagacity. Tossed between Israel and the PLO, he had kept Jordan intact: His long rule added a welcome dollop of stability to the volatile cauldron of Middle East politics. Like King Fahd, he blamed the incredible intransigence of the Kuwaitis for what happened on August 2.

After he talked to President Bush on the telephone, Hussein flew to Baghdad, where he found Saddam "fine and more relaxed than on my previous visit six days earlier."[31] Saddam reiterated that he was willing to leave Kuwait, provided that the Arab League, then meeting in Cairo, did not condemn Iraq or call for foreign intervention. (Thus far, only Syria's Hafez Assad, Saddam's longtime rival, had criticized the takeover.) Saddam agreed to attend an Arab summit that King Hussein, King Fahd, and President Mubarak were trying to organize for Jidda on Sunday, and said that he would be prepared to discuss whatever other grievances the nations of the region might have. The king reports that he left Baghdad "confident that agreement was possible."[32]

Later that day, as if to confirm King Hussein's impression, Iraq's Revolutionary Command Council, the country's top governing body, announced that it would start pulling its troops out of Kuwait on Sunday "unless something appears which would threaten the security of Kuwait and Iraq." But it barred any return to power of the al-Sabah family. Baghdad said there could be "no return to the extinct regime after the sun of dignity and honor has shone."[33]

In Kuwait City, the new, Iraqi-dominated government said that "after coordination with the leadership of brotherly Iraq, we have agreed that their brave forces which came to help their people and brothers, will start withdrawing according to a timetable on Sunday, August 5."[34]

But almost immediately the chances of an Arab solution began to evaporate. Reports of the Bush-Thatcher news conference were circulating widely, and the United States, now clearly hostile to any accord that might reward Saddam, began to exert maximum pressure on President Mubarak and King Fahd not to go along. Bush, who had not been able to contact Fahd aboard Air Force One, eventually reached him, and in a thirty-minute conversation, urged the Saudi leader to resist Saddam. "He won't stop," said Bush to Fahd, repeating what Thatcher had said to him.[35] The president said he and Mrs. Thatcher were "willing to offer air support and more," all of which came as a considerable surprise to Fahd, who did not believe Saudi Arabia was in any danger.[36] Nevertheless, the president's call had been effective. When King Hussein called Jidda later that day to report his conversation with Saddam, Fahd was unavailable. The sands of Saudi diplomacy, which for seventy years had shifted with the wind, were slowly beginning to move.

The White House was now working round the clock to derail King Hussein's Arab solution.[37] Washington's new position was expressed by an unidentified "administration policymaker," presumably National Security Adviser Scowcroft, who told The New York Times, "If the Iraqis withdraw and the Sabah family comes back to power, then Saddam has lost. If the Iraqis withdraw and they install a puppet regime, then Saddam has won. Aggression will have worked."[38] It was the Cold War dichotomy refurbished. The administration's thinking had not changed. Regardless of the issue, White House decision-making stayed in the same rut: we-they, win-lose, black-white, the president's men had sprung into action.

From that point on, the Arab solution proposed by King Hussein had little chance of success. Indeed, it was exactly such a compromise that the Bush administration was determined to abort. "We can already detect," said Scowcroft, "a strong impulse on the part of many Arabs to think that they can put Saddam back in his cage by tossing him Kuwait as a bone. They look at the Sabah family and say: 'Hey, they have plenty of money in Switzerland. They'll be okay. Why fight over them? Let's cut a deal.' "[39]

The first among the Arab leaders to fall in line was Egypt's Hosni Mubarak. When Bush spoke to Mubarak from Air Force One, the Egyptian leader had stressed the importance of the Arabs settling the dispute among themselves. "I think Arab leaders are capable of finding a solution to this problem without any foreign interference at all," he told Bush.[40] For the next thirty hours, Mubarak had remained publicly silent, hoping that King Hussein could put together an arrangement by which Saddam would withdraw.[41] But repeated phone calls from President Bush and Secretary of Defense Cheney, plus the personal in-

tervention of U.S. Ambassador Frank G. Wisner offering whatever blandishments the American government could put together, brought Mubarak around.[42] The United States provided
over $2 billion in economic and military assistance to Egypt
each year (only Israel received more), and that assistance did
not come without strings.[43] The personal chemistry was important as well. All heads of state in the Middle East regard one
another warily. But Bush and Mubarak were old friends. On his
most recent trip to Washington, Mubarak had attended a Bal-
timore Orioles game with the president.[44] The two communi-
cated easily and openly and had established more than a
modicum of trust.

Moreover, Mubarak was greatly annoyed with Saddam. The
Egyptian president had tried to mediate the dispute between
Iraq and Kuwait in late July, and he believed that Saddam had
been less than candid when he assured Mubarak that he would
not attack so long as negotiations continued. Mubarak considered that an ongoing commitment, not realizing that Saddam
might suddenly break off the talks as he did on July 31. "I
cannot say it was a stab in the back," said Mubarak, "because
if someone is planning an invasion, he would not tell the others
about it because this will spoil everything."[45] Nevertheless, especially in light of his efforts with King Hussein to resolve the
crisis peacefully, it is doubtful that Mubarak would have acted
against Saddam had Bush not intervened so forcefully.

Almost immediately, the Egyptian press—which until that
point had either supported Saddam or remained silent—attacked
the invasion. Al Ahram, the government-owned newspaper, assailed the takeover with a red banner headline: TERRIFYING ARAB
DISASTER. In the article that followed, Al Ahram said, "This is
indeed the blackest day in the history of the Arabs, which has
made them regress to the pre-Islamic days of barbarism, when
the sword was the master and bloodshed was the means of re-
solving problems."[46]

The public attack in Cairo was followed by Arab League

action Saturday that condemned "Iraqi aggression against Kuwait." Mubarak had spearheaded the League's move.[47] At Egypt's insistence, the League departed from its constitutional requirement that demanded unanimity before action could be taken. Instead, a simple majority of those present voted to condemn Iraq. That was unprecedented. It was designed to put the Arab League on record against Saddam and to block King Hussein's effort to resolve the crisis. After twelve hours of wrangling, the vote was 14 to 7. Egypt and Saudi Arabia had voted in favor of the resolution, Jordan against. American intervention had prevailed. Iraqi delegate Saadun Hammadi assailed the measure as "a grave precedent which will harm the Arab League and its credibility."[48] Tahseen Bashir, Egypt's former ambassador to the League, told the Washington Post that "the system was fractured deeply, beyond patching."[49]

It was at that point that Saddam balked at attending the proposed Jidda summit on Sunday. The scheduled Iraqi withdrawal from Kuwait slowed to a trickle. Saddam had not been bluffing. If pressed to withdraw, he was going to sit tight. The situation remained fluid, no irreconcilable positions had yet been taken, but the best efforts of King Hussein were already on the rocks.

Interviewed by British television immediately afterward, the Jordanian monarch sadly acknowledged that the League's action had scuttled the opportunity to resolve the crisis. Saddam, he said, was a hero to the Arab world, and "a patriotic man who believes in his nation and its future, and in establishing ties with others on the basis of mutual respect."[50] The following day, the king lashed out at the role the White House had played. Without mentioning Bush by name, and in a remarkably prescient observation, Hussein told NBC News that foreign intervention "could set the whole area ablaze. There is no need for that. There is no threat to Saudi Arabia, or any other Arab state."[51]

Jordan's prime minister, Mudar Badran, was more outspoken. He told Jordanian television that King Hussein and Mubarak had agreed to block any Arab League action critical of Iraq. According to Badran,

> The two leaders believed that a statement by the Arab League Council would hamper action, further complicate matters, and diminish the chance to hold a mini-summit. It would internationalize the crisis and encourage the interference of foreign forces and Israel. . . . Therefore, the two leaders instructed their foreign ministers to block the statement, in order to enable his majesty the king to mediate.

Badran said that "King Hussein's efforts were yielding fruit to contain the crisis," but that Jordan had been double-crossed. Despite the agreement that had been reached "with his excellency President Mubarak," the Arab League Council "insisted on issuing a resolution denouncing the Iraqi troops' crossing to Kuwait."[52] That made a settlement with Saddam impossible.

In subsequent interviews, King Hussein was especially critical of Mubarak and the Egyptians for torpedoing the summit. Hussein said he thought the Egyptian leader held a grudge against Iraq "for having led the campaign against Egypt" after its peace treaty with Israel in 1979, and that Mubarak was paying Saddam back.[53]

With the Arab League on record against Iraq, the United States now took the lead. Bush spent the next several days working the telephone. He not only lobbied Fahd and Mubarak, but eventually the president would place over sixty calls to government leaders and heads of state asking for support.[54] His immediate concerns were two-fold: to block what he saw as an Arab sellout to Saddam, and to convince the dubious Fahd and other Middle Eastern leaders that they needed U.S. military assistance. The confrontation with Iraq had become George Bush's show, and as one administration official put it, the president "had to muster all of his finesse on the telephone

to persuade the skittish Arab leaders that they would need—
and should accept—American help."[55]

From the beginning, Bush's aim was to punish Saddam and
deprive him of the fruits of his aggression. To a cranky WASP
of the president's persuasion, it was a matter of principle. The
stern teachings of a Puritan past now became public policy.
Ignore for a moment that those teachings might be selective or
capricious; ignore for a moment China's takeover of Tibet, In-
donesia's oppression of East Timor, Libya's invasion of Chad,
or, for that matter, Bush's own invasion of Panama—despite
explicit treaty obligations to the contrary.[56] For the president,
like Thatcher, the restoration of Kuwait had become a moral
crusade. There could be no compromise with Saddam, and the
president's tight-lipped certitude would insure that.*

For his entire political career, George Bush had been condemned as an opportunist devoid of purpose or principle: "the
vision thing." At last he had found one. Future critics might
suggest with some legitimacy that with the November congressional elections looming, the U.S. economy in the doldrums,
the S&L debacle worsening daily, and his son Neil fast becoming the Democrats' equivalent of Willie Horton, the president
seized on the Iraqi invasion of Kuwait as a needed diversion.
For Bush, like Thatcher, a short, popular war had a silver lin-
ing. Consciously or not, the president's vital interests had become America's vital interest.

The problem for Bush was that there were no significant
American forces in the Gulf and no way to enforce his will on
Saddam. The president scheduled another meeting of the National Security Council for late Friday afternoon, August 3, and
in the meantime instructed Cheney and Powell to put the hard-
sell on the Saudi ambassador to the United States, Prince Bandar bin Sultan, to accept American troops.[57]

---

*Martin Yant, in his recent book *Desert Mirage: The True Story of the Gulf War*
(Buffalo, N.Y.: Prometheus, 1991), points out that Bush also had a personal tie to the
region. Thirty years ago, the first oil well that had been drilled off Kuwait in the
Persian Gulf had been sunk by Bush's own Zapata Offshore Oil Company.

The forty-one-year-old Prince Bandar was widely known in Washington as a man one could steal horses with. A diplomatic colleague said he moved "with the enthusiasm of a terrier in the foreign-policy nether world of covert operations and clandestine deal-making."[58] His father was Saudi Arabia's defense minister, and King Fahd was his uncle. Trained as a jet fighter pilot by the United States, Prince Bandar had his thumbprints all over Iran-contra. Through Bandar, the Saudis had been the largest single contributor to Bud McFarlane and Oliver North's scheme, providing $32 million in covert aid for the contras in 1984–85.[59] Bandar avoided testifying before Congress, but in Newsweek's words, "Prince Bandar understands the game of not exactly lying, but not telling the whole truth either."[60]

By 1990, he was more than a diplomat; he was a member of the inner circle of the Bush administration. His ties to Bush went back to the early 1980s when he had enlisted the vice president's help to obtain a large arms sale package for Saudi Arabia. In 1985, when Bush was being widely criticized as ineffective, Bandar hosted a gala dinner for the vice president with singer Roberta Flack for entertainment. Bandar even went fishing with Bush. And his ties to Cheney, Powell, and Scowcroft were equally close. (He was Colin Powell's frequent squash partner.) If anyone would be receptive to the administration's case, it was Bandar.

The problem for Cheney and Powell was that there was no hard evidence that Saudi Arabia was threatened by Saddam.[61] To the contrary, the Iraqi Revolutionary Command Council had just announced its impending withdrawal from Kuwait. But the defense team showed the prince elaborate satellite photographs of Iraqi armor deployed near the neutral zone that separated Kuwait and Saudi Arabia. With three armored divisions in tiny Kuwait, and with no resistance remaining, it's not clear where else the Iraqi tanks should have been. There was no need for them in Kuwait City, and Saddam's generals, just as President Eisenhower had done with the Marines in Lebanon in 1958, ordered them into the countryside. Nevertheless, Cheney and Powell convinced Bandar that Iraq was poised for an assault on the Saudi oil fields near Dhahran, 175 miles to the south.[62] And in fairness to Prince Bandar, the photos could have proved anything. There was no way for him to know Saddam's intentions. In any event, the prince was soon convinced. Or perhaps more accurately, he was soon convinced of the importance of cooperating with his friends in the administration. He added his voice to those urging the reluctant Fahd to accept American forces in Saudi Arabia.[63]

Simultaneously with Cheney's and Powell's efforts, the administration began a concerted press campaign to emphasize the danger posed to Saudi Arabia by Saddam. Both *The New York Times* and the *Washington Post* carried front-page stories on Saturday, August 4, that Iraqi forces were massing at the frontier, ready to invade. Both articles were datelined in Washington. Both had been leaked by the administration. They were designed to help make the case for American involvement. Top White House officials were quoted by the *Times* as saying that "military intervention of some kind was rapidly rising to the top of their list of options."[64] The news had been deliberately doctored, despite the fact that at no time did either the Central Intelligence Agency or the Defense Intelligence Agency believe it probable that Iraq would invade Saudi Arabia.[65] The president had decided to intervene; the government's elaborate public-relations machinery was preparing the way.

In a companion article to its story on the Iraqi buildup, the *Washington Post* reported that "President Bush and senior administration policy makers have concluded that the United States must not acquiesce in Iraq's invasion of Kuwait and have begun examining options to restore Kuwait's sovereignty."[66] During what the *Post* described as "a very long conversation," Bush once more leaned on Fahd to accept American troops. Then he touched base with Margaret Thatcher, who was still in Colorado. If Bush needed any convincing, Thatcher more than provided it. She gently lectured the president on his duty as leader of the free world—the easy shorthand that was almost automatic for Thatcher in her dealings with Washington—and once again pledged Britain's support. For Bush, who was still under Ronald Reagan's shadow when it came to dealing with Mrs. Thatcher, the attention that she was devoting to him was doubly effective. A skeptic might observe, as Walter Lippmann did at the onset of the Cold War,[67] that the United States again had become the chosen instrument of British foreign policy.

When the National Security Council reconvened at 5 P.M. Friday afternoon, CIA Director Webster, who had been burned for missing Saddam's strike into Kuwait, stressed that Iraq had the capacity to move into Saudi Arabia almost unopposed— although there was no consensus that it planned to do so.[68] General Powell did not recommend a major deployment of ground troops. In fact, there was considerable daylight between Powell and Defense Secretary Cheney as to how to respond to Saddam. Powell stressed the impediments to intervention; Cheney was more eager to use force. As the president's ranking military adviser, Powell tried to contain the crisis. Cheney on the other hand sought military initiatives that Bush might employ. Powell rejected the idea that a few bombs or missiles would suffice. Cheney for a while appeared hooked on gimmickry. For Powell, the idea of a "surgical strike" was a contradiction in terms. He deplored the fantasies of civilian analysts who reduced the battlefield to an intellectual exercise and who made war look simple.[69] The *Washington Post* reported authoritatively that the Pentagon had no plans to alert airborne or light infantry divisions for possible deployment to the Gulf.[70] When President Bush was asked how much force he intended to send, he said, "I don't believe I have enough information to make those decisions right now."[71] He asked Powell to prepare a list of options, and ordered the NSC to reconvene at Camp David the next morning, Saturday, August 4. Given a direct order by the president, Powell instructed Schwarzkopf to stand by with Central Command's contingency plan for the defense of Saudi Arabia.

Before leaving for his Catoctin mountain retreat that eve-

ning, Bush told reporters, "I want to make very clear to everybody how strongly I feel about the nature of this uncalled for
invasion and our determination to see the matter resolved."[72]
In the days ahead, the administration would be criticized for its
failure to explain why America should be concerned about Kuwait, and why U.S. vital interests were at stake. For the president, it was simply a matter of principle: Aggression had to be
punished. That abstraction was hard to sell to the American
public, particularly as it related to a place so far away. The
president's spokesmen quickly began to tout other reasons: oil,
jobs, a New World Order, even the political science formula-
tion favored by General Scowcroft that this was "the first test
of our ability to maintain global or regional stability in the post
Cold War era."[73] For President Bush there was always only one
reason—to halt aggression—and for him that was sufficient.

At Camp David on Saturday the final touches were put on
Bush's policy. The meeting was devoted almost entirely to military options.[74] The defense of Saudi Arabia had become the
fig leaf for American intervention, but so far King Fahd had
refused to commit himself. Since Riyadh did not believe that
it was in any danger from Saddam, the king still declined to
accept Bush's offer of American forces. "The Saudis are being
Saudis," one White House official said in desperation,[75] referring to Fahd's traditional preference to compromise Arab disputes.

For two and a half hours Saturday morning, the nation's
top policymakers were closeted at Camp David's Aspen Lodge.
The name "Aspen" seemed appropriately symbolic since it was
in Aspen that the president had decided to challenge Saddam.
Those assembled were the same men who two days before had
called Kuwait a gas station, plus Secretary of State James Baker,
fresh in from Moscow. Now that the president had decided to
intervene—provided King Fahd could be convinced—the question they wrestled with was the shape that intervention would
take.

Sitting in his shirt-sleeves at the broad conference table in the rustic, pine-paneled conference room, Bush was flanked by the administration's chickenhawks: Vice President Dan Quayle, Defense Secretary Cheney, and White House Chief of Staff John Sununu. The expression "chickenhawk" was coined by Washington columnist Mark Shields.[76] It referred to men who were chicken during the Vietnam war when they might have had to serve in the Army but now, in positions of authority, were hawkish about the use of American military power in the Gulf. All three officials had avoided service in Vietnam: Quayle in the Indiana National Guard, Cheney and Sununu with college and hardship deferments that kept them out of harm's way. Cheney, in fact, had received seven successive deferments as he idled his time in graduate school, first at the University of Wyoming, then at the University of Wisconsin—from which he did not graduate.[77] Now, since the president had decided on military action, they were among the most bellicose.

Joining the chickenhawks was Judge Webster of Central Intelligence, damaged for not having provided an earlier warning of Saddam's intentions and rumored to be on his way out. Secretary Baker, whose State Department had also been guilty of following what now was considered a flawed policy toward Iraq, was the least enthusiastic about taking on the burdens of the Middle East. But Baker deferred to his longtime friend George Bush, and his concerns were muted. From the White House staff were two more of the president's men: National Security Adviser Brent Scowcroft and his assistant for the Middle East, Richard Haass. And finally, the military—the men who would be called on to carry out the president's policy: General Powell and General H. Norman Schwarzkopf, the burly four-star commander of Central Command, the military's joint headquarters responsible for the Gulf.

With the exception of Schwarzkopf, all were veteran operators in Washington's partisan political climate. As a team, they had proved remarkably effective in harnessing the government for the president's purposes. They shared the view that it was the president who determined American foreign policy. And for that matter, all had more than passing acquaintance with the back-channel operations of White House government—and the advantages that went with it. Bush had headed the CIA at the time of the assassination of Chile's President Allende and had been vice president during Iran-contra. Scowcroft had been a member of the Tower Commission, which investigated President Reagan's role in the affair. Webster had succeeded William Casey at CIA and had picked up the pieces of Iran-contra out of public view. Cheney had been the ranking House Republican on the congressional committee that investigated the matter, a committee that many observers believed had pulled its punches. Powell had come on as national security adviser shortly after John Poindexter was dumped. Having served as Poindexter's deputy, he too knew the terrain of White House deception. When interviewed by investigators probing Iran-contra, Powell was the only White House aide to pull out a tape recorder and make his own recording of the sessions.[78]

This was not a group prone to provide independent counsel or unpopular advice. Instead, they had demonstrated their dedication to serving the president's interests. They did not advocate alternative strategies. They saw their role as one of assisting the president to implement his strategy, and Bush now gave them the opportunity to follow through.

In retrospect, given the gravity of the decision to deploy troops, it is curious that with the possible exception of Schwarzkopf, none of those present could claim more than passing familiarity with the Middle East. Or with such intractable issues as the Arab-Israeli dispute. Or the residual anti-Americanism that flourished in much of the region. "Reading the Arab world is not one of our national skills," former Assistant Secretary of State Richard Murphy once said,[79] and the fact is, the United States simply could not muster in August 1990 a single senior official who possessed a firm grasp of the Middle East.* John Kelly, the current assistant secretary for the area, was primarily a European expert. He had served only a very brief tour in Beirut and neither read nor spoke Arabic. Richard Haass, who handled the Middle East for NSC, also did not speak Arabic, had recently joined the administration after several years at the John F. Kennedy School of Government at Harvard, and had devoted most of his career to academic work on arcane issues of conflict resolution. He had never been to Baghdad, or Kuwait, or Saudi Arabia, nor had any of his staff. In effect, the administration was flying blind, and George Bush was at the controls.

According to those present, the president was resolute in his determination that Kuwait be restored to its pre-invasion status and that the emir be returned to power. The meeting did not question whether that was a wise policy; it focused on how to accomplish it. There were no concerns expressed about the nature of medieval feudalism represented by Sheik Jabir al-Ahmed al-Sabah, about the lack of democracy in Kuwait, the suppression of representative institutions three years earlier, the absence of religious freedom or anything approaching gender equality, or what in Western eyes must surely rank as one of the world's most primitive legal systems. Nor were concerns expressed about the long-term consequences of a major deployment of American troops. For the president, the issue had been reduced to its simplest terms. Iraq's aggression must be punished. Were it not for the hum of air conditioners on a humid summer day, a listener might have thought he was in 10 Downing Street one hundred years earlier, listening to Lord Salisbury declaim upon the necessity of sending Kitchener up the Nile to avenge the death of Chinese Gordon at Khartoum and to punish the followers of the Mahdi. Except that the British had

---

*Robert C. Ames, the CIA's principal Middle East expert, had been killed in the Beirut embassy bombing in 1983 and had not been replaced. April Glaspie, the senior diplomatic professional, had blotted her copybook during her interview with Saddam and was rarely called on. Other State Department analysts were far too junior to have any impact on administration policy.

some familiarity with the area and knew what would be required.

General Schwarzkopf laid out the military contingency plans. Schwarzkopf, the Army's former deputy chief of staff for operations—the job Ike once held—had a firm grasp of the issue, or at least of the issue as it had been posed to him. Namely, the defense of Saudi Arabia. Earlier that summer, from his headquarters in Tampa, he had organized what the military calls a command-post exercise—a CPX—to determine what it required to protect Saudi Arabia's oil fields from a possible Iraqi attack. It was the type of drill that an alert commander runs constantly, and the fifty-six-year-old Schwarzkopf was one of the Army's best. His answer was that ships and planes would not suffice. To defend Saudi Arabia, the United States had to get "American boots on the sand." Schwarzkopf thought that four and a third divisions, supported by three Navy carriers and land-based aircraft, would be adequate. Based on the Army's contingency plans, he said it would take 120 days—seventeen weeks—to get all of the forces in place. General Powell upped the ante. Like Schwarzkopf, Powell, as a junior officer, had been seared by the Army's unhappy experience in Vietnam twenty years earlier. He urged the president not to repeat the mistake of deploying troops incrementally; not to ratchet up the level of conflict in the insanely logical scenario of desktop strategists, but, if force must be used, to do so decisively from the beginning. "If you want to deter, don't put up a phony defense, don't create a phony deterrence." Iraq had one of the largest armies in the world, said Powell, and it had to be met with land forces. "If you do it, do it real and do it right."[80]

The question of driving Iraq out of Kuwait was not discussed seriously. It simply "wasn't an option at the time," a key policymaker said.[81] When pressed, Schwarzkopf indicated that to take offensive action was a much, much larger undertaking than the defense of Saudi Arabia. He pointed out that ratios of 3 to 1, sometimes even 5 to 1, are the usual rule of thumb in the military. That would call for at least seven U.S. divisions and would take eight to twelve months to put in place. Both Powell and Schwarzkopf emphasized that merely to deter Iraq from invading Saudi Arabia required substantial forces. "You don't want to give up oil fields to deter them," said Powell. "You need defense in depth—you don't want to take on any more casualties than you have to."[82]

Neither Powell nor Schwarzkopf was convinced that Saddam intended to attack.[83] Neither offered advice on whether American troops should be sent to Saudi Arabia. That was a political decision. Both deferred to civilian authority. But if the president decided to intervene, they would insist on a massive deployment. Rightfully so. The military is not a plaything to be used flippantly or capriciously. It is not a spigot that can be turned on and off. The lives of thousands of men and women on both sides of a possible conflict are at stake. It doesn't require a Sherman, or an Eisenhower, or a Clausewitz to point out that war is messy and unpredictable. Its outcome can never be guaranteed. America's top soldiers, true to their professional calling, were insisting that the administration recognize that fact and not call on them unless it meant business.

From that point on, a saw-off prevailed. The military left control of the crisis to political authority: in this case, to Bush, Scowcroft, Cheney, and Baker. On their part, the president and his advisers left the military details to Powell and Schwarzkopf. One of the many mistakes of Vietnam—the micro-management of military strategy from the White House—was avoided from the outset. Whether American intervention was right or wrong will be debated for years to come. But in one important respect the system worked as it was intended. The military proved itself a reliable instrument of national policy. Future critics may argue that given the enormity of the destruction that followed, General Powell and General Schwarzkopf should have been even more outspoken about the potential costs of using military force. But on August 4, the military did not think beyond the defense of Saudi Arabia. No one vouchsafed to them that a larger purpose, the reconquest of Kuwait, was in the offing.[84]

Midway through the meeting, word was brought that President Mubarak had just reported that Fahd had decided to reject American troops.[85] The president left the meeting to call Jidda once again. Bush's ties to Fahd were of long standing. When Bush headed the CIA, Fahd, who had run Saudi intelligence for thirteen years, was directing Saudi foreign policy. The two had stayed in contact.[86] Nevertheless, his call to the king from Camp David was inconclusive. When he returned to the meeting, Bush reported that the Saudis were still shaky, but he thought that ultimately they would go along.[87]

King Fahd was not just being difficult. He valued the Saudi role as defender of Islam's two most sacred shrines, the birthplace of Mohammed at Mecca and his burial site at Medina. He was worried about the impact of American troops, both on the Arab world and on the unique and antiquated customs of Saudi Arabia itself. At that time, Fahd did not share Washington's desire for vengeance against Saddam. He knew full well that Iraq would not back down and that a war would be very costly. And he worried about the aftermath. In their repeated conversations, the king pressed Bush as to whether U.S. troops would definitely remain in Saudi Arabia until the situation was resolved. He wanted to be reassured that they would not cut and run, as they had in Beirut (and arguably in Vietnam). He also wanted assurance of the reverse: that once the crisis was over, the American troops would leave immediately. Finally, he wanted Bush's word that the United States would sell to Saudi Arabia the advanced warplanes and other weapons that often had been denied in the past—the high-tech sales that Israel strongly objected to.[88] On each count, the president agreed. Nevertheless, Fahd still held back.[89]

In the end, it was decided to go ahead with plans for the U.S. deployment and to hope that Fahd could be brought around. Bush felt that strongly. Powell rushed back to the Pentagon, ready to alert the necessary forces. Defense Secretary Cheney would be sent to Jidda to force Fahd's hand. Schwarzkopf would accompany him. Prince Bandar went ahead to prepare the way. If the Saudis didn't know what was best, Cheney, with Bandar's help, would try to convince them.

The initial configuration of the deployment conformed to the military's recommendation. A trip-wire force of lightly armed infantrymen from the 82nd Airborne Division at Fort Bragg, North Carolina, was placed on standby for immediate movement. Two Navy carrier groups, the *Independence* and its accompanying ships in the Indian Ocean, and the *Eisenhower* task force in the Mediterranean, were ordered to the area at flank speed. A third carrier group, with the USS *Saratoga* and the battleship *Wisconsin*, was readied to sail from Mayport, Florida. The Air Force was told to send two additional squadrons of F-15s to Bahrain immediately. Two Army divisions, the 101st Airborne at Fort Campbell, Kentucky, and the desert-trained 24th Mechanized Infantry Division at Fort Stewart, Georgia, were ordered to make ready. So too were the 16,500 men and women of the 7th Marine Amphibious Force from Twenty-nine Palms, California, and an equal number from the 1st Amphibious Brigade on Okinawa. In all, including support elements, the Pentagon alerted 125,000 troops for immediate deployment in the Gulf. Fahd had not yet agreed, but Powell and Schwarzkopf were making ready to move.

Sunday, August 5, was a time of testing for the United States. Bush arrived at the White House from Camp David that afternoon disgruntled and out of sorts. Except for Mubarak, no one in the Middle East seemed ready to go along with the president's wishes. King Hussein continued to snipe at U.S. policy (Bush had seen an advance tape of the king's interview scheduled to run on "60 Minutes" that evening), and the Saudis were no closer to agreement than two days before. To make matters worse, the news from Kuwait was unclear. Baghdad announced that the scheduled military pullout had begun at 8 A.M. that morning, and Iraqi television aired videotape of what it described as a "withdrawal operation."[90] Both *The New York Times* and the *Washington Post* reported that Kuwait City was calm. There were noticeably fewer Iraqi soldiers, and those that were there "appear to be in high spirits, waving at passersby," said the *Times*. "Even Americans can walk around the streets." The *Post* quoted a veteran American businessman as saying that "no one's panicking. . . . There's no real fear of immediate danger." The CIA discounted those reports and suggested that instead of withdrawing, the Iraqis were digging in.[91] As is frequently the case, the truth lies somewhere in between. Iraq undoubtedly began a tentative withdrawal, but coupled it with a warning to other nations not to interfere. The newly installed pro-Iraqi regime would remain in control of Kuwait. That was unacceptable to George Bush.

When he stepped down from Marine Corps One, the president barked at reporters, "This will not stand. This will not stand—this aggression against Kuwait."[92] He rattled off the names of world leaders to whom he had spoken (Kaifu, Kohl, Mitterrand, Mulroney, Thatcher), and boasted that "there seems to be a united front out there that says Iraq, having committed brutal, naked aggression, ought to get out and that this concept of their installing some puppet [government] will not be acceptable." Bush had prepared himself for battle. The *Washington Post* reported that the president had "ordered U.S. government agencies to begin a secret planning effort aimed at destabilizing and eventually toppling President Saddam Hussein from power."[93]

If, by beginning to withdraw his troops from Kuwait City, Saddam was signaling a willingness to compromise, Bush abruptly dismissed it. "Iraq has lied once again," he told reporters, and summarily rejected a suggestion that he talk to the Iraqi leader. It was obvious to those present that the president was spoiling for a fight.

General Powell watched the president's performance on television. He was struck by Bush's personalization of the crisis. The President of the United States was shooting from the hip,

Powell thought. With one offhand comment, Bush had set a new goal for the United States. The task was no longer to defend Saudi Arabia, but to evict Saddam from Kuwait. Powell had not been consulted. Neither had Baker or Cheney. Maybe Scowcroft had recommended it. Powell didn't know. But he did know that the United States now faced a much more difficult undertaking, and he was stunned that as the nation's ranking military officer he had been given no opportunity to offer his assessment.[94]

Baker shared Powell's concern. Like Powell, he realized that there had been no consultation and no debate. American policy had been decided unilaterally by George Bush. Later, Baker worried to aides that the White House was speeding. That Bush was not thinking through what he was doing.[95]

Sunday evening Bush gave General Powell the formal go-ahead. American troops began to move. The men of the 82nd's ready brigade boarded their planes for Germany. They could still be called back. But Bush's patience had worn thin. Rather than wait, he preferred to act. The contrast between George Bush and Dwight Eisenhower is striking. Eisenhower possessed enormous tactical patience. He refused to act until absolutely necessary, preferring to let his opponent move first so that he might take advantage of it. Sometimes he preferred not to act at all. In 1954, when pressed by America's allies, his own secretary of state, and the chairman of the joint chiefs of staff to intervene on behalf of the French at Dienbienphu, Ike stayed out. Bush was exactly the opposite. He was most comfortable doing something, even if it later proved wrong. Ike was reflective and reactive. George Bush was neither. Months later, after the president had been hospitalized for a heart flutter brought on by a hyperactive thyroid, New York Times columnist William Safire speculated about Bush's mental condition in the summer and fall of 1990. "To what extent was the president's uncharacteristically activist mindset after the Iraqi invasion affected by a hyper thyroid condition?" he asked.[96]

With American forces on the move, it was imperative that

Fahd be brought on-side. Bush had talked to him at length on Thursday, again on Friday, and twice on Saturday, but the wily Saudi monarch still dodged giving the president a commitment. Fahd knew there could be no turning back once American troops were deployed in the kingdom, and he lacked confidence that the United States had the will to destroy Saddam. In addition, he wasn't sure that was a good idea to begin with: In many Saudi eyes, a strong Iraq was necessary to balance a resurgent Iran, as well as to menace the common enemy in Tel Aviv. Fahd did not share Bush's messianic ardor that aggression had to be punished, and he knew that the Kuwaitis bore more than their share of responsibility for what had happened. Finally, there was the impact of Western forces on the Saudi way of life: Could it survive the onslaught? The combination of those reasons, any one of which would have been sufficient, caused Fahd to hang back.

Early Sunday morning, Bush had placed a fifth call to Fahd, this time asking him to accept a visit from Cheney, who Bush felt could convince the king of American resolve. Once more Fahd wavered, and suggested that the United States send a lower-level emissary "so it wouldn't look bad" if things went wrong.[97] For fourteen hours the deployment hung in the balance. Early Sunday evening, after the president had returned to the White House, he received a call from Fahd in Jidda. Cheney could come, said the king, but there was still no commitment.[98] As if to underline the point, Saudi spokesmen issued an emphatic denial that night of reports leaked in Washington that they had moved troops to their border with Kuwait to guard against an Iraqi attack. "All these reports are categorically untrue," said a government spokesman in Riyadh.[99]

Secretary Cheney's meeting with King Fahd on Monday was the critical moment on the road to war.[100] When Cheney arrived in Jidda, he found the Saudis divided. The younger members of the ruling family, such as Prince Bandar, favored American intervention and the overthrow of Saddam. They had been convinced by the sketchy evidence American intelligence had produced that Iraq was poised to invade and that the kingdom needed help. But the king's brothers—including Prince Bandar's father—were skeptical. Crown Prince Abdullah, another brother, maintained that the Saudis could handle Iraq as they always had by compromising their differences with Saddam. He pressed the Arab solution sponsored by King Hussein. In his view, a revived Kuwait with a pro-Iraqi government would be preferable to a war. Another official asked about American motives: Would the United States really leave once they had secured a foothold in the Gulf? That was difficult for many Saudis to believe.[101]

Cheney did his best to allay Saudi doubts. For Fahd's benefit, CIA officials produced elaborate mock-ups showing Iraqi armor deployed near the neutral zone with Kuwait. Clearly, the tanks were there. What Saddam planned to do with them was an open question. Eventually, to bring matters to a head, Cheney gave Fahd what was, in effect, an ultimatum. The United States would fight to defend Saudi Arabia, he implied, but it would not fight to liberate it. Only at that point did the king relent. Fahd's innate caution caused him to accept the American offer. It was always possible that Saddam might attack, and the insurance policy that Cheney offered seemed the safest way out. As Professor Eliot Cohen of Johns Hopkins observed, the king recognized that the House of Saud was "not likely to survive forever in a Persian Gulf whose dominant characteristic [was] Iraqi hegemony."[102]

In the end, Fahd extracted Cheney's assurance that if it came to a fight, Saddam "would not get up again."[103] With exceptional foresight, the king knew that an injured and resentful Iraq would be the worst of all possible solutions. He demanded a U.S. commitment to total war, and he got one.[104] Fahd prudently insisted that announcement of the deployment not be made until the first American troops were already in place.[105]

Monday afternoon, when Cheney called the White House to report Fahd's decision, Bush was meeting in the Oval Office with Margaret Thatcher. The British prime minister, determined as always to reinforce the president's resolve, had arranged a strategic refuelling stop in Washington on her return to London from Aspen. It was another vintage Thatcher performance: seeds of aggression, Munich, Hitler, Winston Churchill—the works. "She was very gung-ho," an aide recalled.[106] Within a short time, Scowcroft and General Powell joined the two in the Oval Office, and once again Powell laid out the military options. When Cheney's call came in, it was put on a speaker phone so that all could listen. While they were talking, Secretary of State Baker came in, as did Sununu and Quayle. With Cheney on the phone, it was the National Security Council with Mrs. Thatcher participating. The tone was euphoric. No one questioned whether the right decision had been made, or that Saddam ultimately would be forced to back down. Neither the impact of American troops on the Arab world nor the rifts within it were considered. Whether Congress would support the president's action was not an issue. The future, it was assumed, would take care of itself. Fahd and Mubarak had joined the team, and that was what counted. Offensive military action was not discussed.

Before the meeting broke up, word was brought that the United Nations Security Council had voted 13-0, with Cuba and Yemen abstaining, to impose economic sanctions on Iraq.[107] It was only the third time in its history that the Council had sought to discipline a country by ordering trade sanctions,* and it was obvious that Bush had pulled his coalition together. Both China and the Soviet Union supported the move.

If Sunday had been a day of testing, Monday was a day to rejoice. All of the pieces of Bush's grand strategy were falling into place. There was no reason to consider a compromise with Saddam. The point must be made, once and for all, that aggression did not pay. Speaking to the press, Bush praised the

---

*Earlier actions involved Rhodesia in 1967 and a ban of arms sales to South Africa in 1977.

U.N. action and called for "full and total implementation of these sanctions, ruling out nothing at all."[108] The implication was unmistakable. If sanctions did not work, the president was determined to drive the Iraqis out of Kuwait by force.

Not everyone in Washington shared Bush's enthusiasm for bearding Saddam. A senior military official—it is not clear whether it was General Powell—told the *Washington Post* that the assembly of forces from the great powers was moving "like a freight train going 100 miles per hour." He noted, as soldiers are prone to do, that there was "significant concern at high levels of the military that the growing confrontation with Saddam was not leaving him a face-saving 'out' from the crisis."[109]

In fact, that very day, Monday, August 6, Saddam had sought to communicate directly with Bush and had been summarily stiff-armed by the president's men. Symbolism is important in the Middle East. No one appreciated that more than the Iraqi president. Rather than summon Ambassador Glaspie's stand-in, chargé James Wilson, to the presidential palace, Saddam went to the foreign ministry to meet him. He gave Wilson an oral message for President Bush that explained Iraq's position on Kuwait, and stressed his interest in establishing normal relations with the United States.[110] According to generally accepted reports of the meeting, Saddam emphasized that Iraq had no designs on Saudi Arabia, and cited the nonaggression treaty between the two countries signed in 1989. "The security of Saudi Arabia is part of the security of Iraq," Saddam was quoted as saying.[111] Almost simultaneously, U.S. military officials reported that the first contingent of eighty Iraqi tanks was observed to be clearing Kuwait and returning to Iraq.[112]

But Saddam's overtures were rebuffed. "Why send him a message?" a senior administration official replied. "We don't have anything to say to him."[113] For George Bush, it was all or nothing. Saddam had to be struck down. The 101st and the 24th divisions were ordered to move. The Marines were already on the way. Schwarzkopf was ordered "to defend against an Iraqi attack on Saudi Arabia and be prepared to conduct other operations as directed."[114] This was not brinkmanship. A principle was at stake. Regardless of the cost—and Bush would subsequently make that point clear—aggression had to be punished.

3.

HAIL
TO THE CHIEF

The Constitution invests the President
with certain important political powers,
in the exercise of which he is to use his
own discretion, and is accountable only
to his country in his political character,
and to his own conscience.

—Chief Justice John Marshall
Marbury v. Madison (1803)

On Wednesday, August 8, with the men of the 82nd Airborne
already in Saudi Arabia, President Bush went on national television to announce his decision to intervene. The speech, art-
fully crafted by Brent Scowcroft and Richard Haass, complied
with established ground rules. The president told no falsehoods;
neither did he tell the whole truth. Viewers were left with the

impression that the United States was responding to an urgent request from a Saudi Arabia trembling before an Iraqi onslaught. The mission of U.S. forces would be wholly defensive.

Bush appeared nervous. His voice was scratchy and his rhythm off. His facial expression did not seem to match his words. And perhaps with good reason. The careful phrasings and deft shadings of the president's speech left an unmistakable impression that additional Iraqi aggression was in the offing. That, at best, was inaccurate. According to Bush:

> Iraq has massed an enormous war machine on the Saudi border, capable of initiating hostilities with little or no additional preparation. Given the Iraqi government's history of aggression against its own citizens as well as its neighbors, to assume that Iraq will not attack again would be unwise and unrealistic. And, therefore, after consulting with King Fahd, I sent Secretary of Defense Dick Cheney to discuss cooperative measures we could take. Following those meetings, the Saudi government requested our help, and I have responded to that request by ordering U.S. ground and air forces to deploy in the kingdom of Saudi Arabia.[1]

The president talked about Iraqi capabilities, but not about their intent. Impressions to the contrary, he offered no evidence of an imminent invasion. His reference to King Fahd suggested that the king was fearful of an attack and that it was he who sought to speak with Cheney. The president placed the onus of seeking American help on the Saudis. "I have responded to that request," he said. There was no mention that both the CIA and the Defense Intelligence Agency thought it unlikely that Iraq would invade.[2] In fact, the very next day, August 9, Pentagon spokesman Pete Williams told reporters that the Iraqi forces in Kuwait "seem to be in a defensive posture."[3] Another senior official told the *Washington*

Post that the Iraqis "were no longer in positions preparatory to an attack."[4]

It strains credulity to believe that a major army poised to sweep across the frontier one day should be dug in the next. It also does not explain why, if Saddam was intent on striking at the Saudi oil fields, he did not do so immediately before any sizable American deployment could take place. There was no reference in the president's speech to Saddam's repeated assurances that he had no designs on Saudi Arabia.[5] There was no allusion to King Fahd's own views—especially to his reluctance to accept American forces. Nor was anything said about the role of the United States in triggering Fahd's request.

Bush's presentation was effective. It galvanized America's impulse to stand up to a bully. The long years of Cold War confrontation had created a public attitude that made force a ready alternative to negotiation. For many, the horrors of Vietnam had faded. The role of world policeman beckoned once more. The peace dividend lapsed. Within Washington's beltway, strategic analysts discovered a new mission, as did those who worked in defense industries scheduled to be phased out. The possibility of another splendid little war, in John Hay's memorable phrase, loomed on the horizon.

The president was less than candid when he told viewers that he was ordering the deployment only after "exhausting every alternative." King Hussein's Arab solution, initially favored by Mubarak and Fahd, to say nothing of Bush himself, was totally ignored. Saddam's effort on Monday, August 6, to communicate directly with Bush through the American chargé in Baghdad was not mentioned. Neither were the continuing efforts, even at that late date, of King Hussein to bridge the gap between Saddam and Bush.

Equally disingenuous was Bush's reference to "elements of the 82nd Airborne Division," which he said "are arriving today to take up defensive positions in Saudi Arabia. I took this action to assist the Saudi Arabian government in the defense of its homeland." But the 82nd was already deployed when Bush spoke. For reasons of military security, that may have been a legitimate obfuscation. Nevertheless, in light of the president's avowed purpose of punishing Saddam, to stress, as Bush did, the defensive purpose of the deployment involved far more than literary license.

"*The mission of our troops is wholly defensive,*" said Bush. "Hopefully, they will not be there long. *They will not initiate hostilities*, but they will defend themselves, the kingdom of Saudi Arabia and other friends in the Persian Gulf." [Emphasis added.]

The president proclaimed that principle was involved. Aggression must be resisted. "Appeasement does not work," he said, citing the experience of the 1930s. "Standing up for our principles will not come easy. It may take time and possibly cost a great deal, but . . . America has never wavered when her purpose is driven by principle. . . ."

Bush specified not one but four principles that "guide our policy." All dealt with Kuwait and Iraq. None pertained to the defense of Saudi Arabia.

"First, we seek the immediate, unconditional and complete withdrawal of all Iraqi forces from Kuwait.

"Second, Kuwait's legitimate government must be restored to replace the puppet regime.

"And third, my administration . . . is committed to the security and stability of the Persian Gulf.

"And fourth, I am determined to protect the lives of American citizens abroad."

At the press conference that followed, Bush stressed the defensive nature of the deployment. "A line has been drawn in the sand," he said.[6] "My military objective is to see Saudi Arabia defended. That's the military objective."

Q: Are we at war?

Bush: We are not at war. We have sent forces to defend Saudi Arabia. . . .

Q: Is this an open ended commitment?

Bush: Nothing is open ended, but I'm not worried
            about that at all. I'm worried about getting
            them there and doing what I indicated in
            our speech in there as necessary, the
            defense of Saudi Arabia and trying, through
            concerted international means, to reverse
            out this aggression. . . .

Q: Was there any single thing that tipped your
            hand in deciding to send U.S. troops . . .
            into Saudi Arabia . . . ?

Bush: There was no single thing that I can think
            of. But when King Fahd requested such
            support we were prompt to respond. . . .

Q: How long will you keep American forces in
            Saudi Arabia, and why not use them to
            drive the Iraqi forces out of Kuwait?

Bush: Well, as you know, from what I said,
            they're there in a defensive mode right
            now, and therefore that's not the mission,
            to drive the Iraqis out of Kuwait.

The president was pressed repeatedly by correspondents as
to how he intended to reverse the Iraqi takeover of Kuwait if
the American deployment in Saudi Arabia was wholly defensive. Bush implied that sanctions would do the trick. "Economic sanctions, if fully enforced, can be very, very
effective. . . . [They] should begin to bite pretty soon. There
will be further steps to ensure that they are fully effective. And
then we'll wait and see where we go from there. But I have
no—we're not—I'm not beyond that in my thinking."

In light of the rapid shift in American policy that would
become obvious in the days ahead, an observer might question

whether Bush had more up his sleeve when he added, "There is obviously a lot of contingency planning that always goes on, and that should go on." Some reporters tried, unsuccessfully, to pin the president down.

Q: Could you share with us the precise military objective of this mission? Will the American troops remain there only until Saddam Hussein removes his tanks from the Saudi border?

Bush: I can't answer that because we have to—we have a major objective with those troops, which is the defense of the Soviet Union [sic] so I think it is beyond the defense of Saudi Arabia. So I think it's beyond that—I think it's beyond just the question of tanks along the border. . . .

Bush's confusing, inarticulate reply to what was the most penetrating question asked during the press conference suggests that the president intended to do more with the troops than merely defend Saudi Arabia. All options remained open, in the lingo of the White House, but no one picked up on it at the time. The New York Times did not even reprint the question in its transcript of the press conference.[7] The Washington Post drifted into ellipses.[8] Bush's halting answer was passed over. In effect, the administration was selling a bill of goods. The ostensible purpose of the deployment was to defend Saudi Arabia. Economic sanctions—the track record of which had been deplorable—would drive Saddam out of Kuwait. Since the Saudi government had not felt threatened by Saddam until convinced by Washington, the former reason was untrue, and the latter, if accepted at face value, was wishful thinking. American troops and planes were being whisked to Saudi Arabia to provide the administration with leverage to force Saddam out of Kuwait.

Bush was dissembling when he said their purpose was defensive, and it was tooth-fairy logic to assume that sanctions would, for the first time in recorded history, force an aggressor to heel. As commander in chief, Bush was determined to take whatever action was required to reverse ["reverse out"] the Iraqi takeover. But that purpose was concealed behind a smoke screen of rhetoric. The American people were being asked for their support, but were not being leveled with as to the extent of their commitment. In effect, the president said, "Trust me."

On Capitol Hill, response to the president's speech was supportive and bipartisan. Both the House and Senate had adjourned earlier that summer, and most members were at home organizing their campaigns for the November elections. House Speaker Tom Foley said that "Democrats and Republicans, House and Senate . . . are very strongly of the opinion that the president had to act."[9] Senate Majority Leader George Mitchell of Maine called the invasion of Kuwait "an outrageous act of aggression" and said all Americans would support the president's decision to deploy troops.[10] Robert Dole of Kansas, the Republican leader in the Senate, said Bush was "doing precisely the right thing. He's drawing more than a line in the sand, he's insisting the line go back" by demanding that Iraq withdraw from Kuwait.[11] All three leaders had been briefed by the White House prior to the delivery of the president's speech, and at that time, all shared Bush's desire to push Iraq out of Kuwait. To judge from their response, none ruled out the possibility of using military force to do so.

Several members of Congress who had not been briefed expressed concern about the open-ended nature of the president's move. Nevertheless, they were supportive. Sam Nunn of Georgia, running for reelection, told *The New York Times* that he thought a limited deployment would be backed by Congress if the Arab nations supported it. "My hope is that we'll continue to confine our role to protecting air bases and perhaps using American troops to mine highways from Kuwait on which Iraq might send tanks into Saudi Arabia," he said.[12] Nunn did not foresee any combat role for American forces. Senator Alan Cranston of California, the Democratic whip, was quoted as saying, "I hope we won't be the Lone Rangers the way we were in Vietnam."[13] Representative Lee Hamilton of Indiana, chairman of the House subcommittee on the Middle East, said he thought the president should have put more emphasis "on what diplomatic efforts he will make to get Iraq out of Kuwait."[14] Representative Pat Schroeder of Colorado sounded the strongest note of caution. "I hope that sanctions take hold and we get the U.N. flag up rather than the U.S. flag," said Schroeder. "If this thing breaks, this is going to be very costly in blood for anyone on the ground in Saudi Arabia."[15]

Throughout the country, support for the president was overwhelming. A *Washington Post*–ABC News poll indicated that 74 percent of Americans supported Bush's decision to send troops to Saudi Arabia. Sixty percent said they thought that ultimately the United States and Iraq would be at war. On the other hand, when asked whether the U.S. should invade Iraq to force it to withdraw from Kuwait, 68 percent of the respondents answered "No." Only 27 percent favored such a move.[16]

In Boston, former Democratic presidential candidate Michael Dukakis added his support for the president. "I think he's doing exactly the right thing," said the governor.[17] Jesse Jackson told the *Washington Post* that Saddam "must be driven back to the borders" of Iraq. Departing from his normal skepticism about military power, Jackson said that the United States must be prepared to "use military force, multilaterally or unilaterally."[18] But the Reverend Sloane Coffin, president of the citizens' group Sane/Freeze, while generally supportive of the president's diplomatic efforts, dissented from the possible use of force to push Iraq out of Kuwait. "It would be wrong to opt for a military solution," said Coffin. He added that U.S. intervention would be "very distressing and elicit a lot of sympathy for Iraq in the Arab world."[19]

Following the president's news conference, Secretary Cheney and General Powell briefed reporters at the Pentagon. They

designated the forces already under way: namely, the ready brigade of the 82nd Airborne, two squadrons of F-15s from the
First Tactical Fighter Wing at Langley Air Force Base, Virginia,
and the ships of the three carrier task forces steaming toward
the Gulf. Both Cheney and Powell declined to indicate the full
extent of the deployment.[20] Subsequently, Defense Department
officials said that the forces mentioned were merely "the tip of
the wedge," and that the numbers "would grow substantially
in the next few weeks." Cheney said, "The situation's uncertain. We don't know how long it will last. We don't know
when it will end."[21]

The New York Times, without identifying Cheney or Powell
as the source, said that the administration's aim was to deploy
"a force that would be sizable enough to deter an Iraqi attack
on Saudi Arabia but not large enough to wrest control of Kuwait from Iraq."[22] The *Washington Post* quoted a Powell aide as
saying that a direct confrontation on land had been ruled out,
since "it would take a 3 to 1 numerical advantage for U.S.
forces to go on the offense against the Iraqi army."[23]

On August 9, reflecting a White House briefing by John
Sununu, both the *Post* and the *Times* estimated that fifty thousand troops would be involved in the deployment, including
units from the 24th Division at Fort Stewart, Georgia, and the
101st Airborne at Fort Campbell, Kentucky.[24] It was a deliberate understatement. The administration was not putting its cards
on the table. By minimizing the deployment, the Bush team
believed that public opinion would not be aroused. The *Post*
also revealed that not everyone in the defense establishment
was pleased with the president's decision to intervene. According to veteran Pentagon correspondent Patrick E. Tyler, "Some
military officials and analysts express concern that U.S. leaders do not fully understand the risks of what may turn out to
be a military deployment that dwarfs both the Panama invasion
force and the Persian Gulf escort deployment of 1987–88."[25]

Only in the next several days was the enormous size of the
initial American deployment revealed—and then, only because

the Army insisted on it. General Carl Vuono, the Army chief of staff, was appalled when he saw Sununu's lowball figure of fifty thousand. The White House was concealing the facts—and the risks involved for American troops. If the public didn't have the true picture, there was no chance of maintaining their support. Vuono remembered Vietnam. On his own authority, the Army chief of staff leaked the real number of 250,000 to the Associated Press.[26] When AP ran the story, Sununu, described by The New York Times as "one of the handful of senior policy planners in the Administration," dismissed the true figure as "preposterous."[27] Vuono held his ground. The following day the Pentagon officially announced that the deployment would exceed 200,000 and could reach 250,000 by autumn, citing chapter and verse. In addition to the Army divisions previously designated, two Marine divisions as well as National Guard and reserve units from twelve states were being deployed. The Air Force was sending squadrons of F-16 fighters from Shaw Air Force Base, South Carolina; F-117 Stealth fighter-bombers from Nellis Air Force Base in Nevada; F-111 fighter-bombers from Europe; A-10 attack aircraft and giant C-5A transports from Pope Air Force Base in North Carolina, plus additional AWACS observation planes and aerial tankers. The Navy's sea-lift command activated its entire fleet of ships, while two mammoth hospital ships, the USNS Mercy and the USNS Comfort, were made ready to sail. "It's the full Central Command package," said one NATO official in Brussels. "Nobody ever thought they'd be free to commit all those forces because it was always assumed that they would be tied down in Europe by the Soviets. But what's happening is they're getting the full shot."[28]

The end of the Cold War provided the opportunity for the United States to assert its full power in the Middle East, and Bush took advantage of that. The fact that the huge size of the deployment was not initially announced by the White House was part of the administration's game plan. By asserting that principle was at stake, public support was mobilized behind the president. Only afterward, piece by piece, was the scope of the American commitment revealed. Objections, had they been raised at that point, would have looked quibbling. Or as one of the few critics of Bush's policy observed, bitter medicine is best administered in small doses.

Despite the lack of candor about his real objectives, Bush covered his constitutional tracks. To insure continuing congressional support, the president wrote to Speaker Foley and the Senate's president *pro tem*, Democrat Robert Byrd of West Virginia, to inform them of the deployment. The move, said White House spokesman Marlin Fitzwater, was "consistent with the War Powers Resolution,"[29] but was not a formal notification required by the statute.[30] The same procedure, he said, had been used at the time of the Grenada invasion in 1983 and the Panama invasion in 1989. Bush told the congressional leaders that he was not invoking the provisions of the War Powers Resolution because he did not believe that hostilities were imminent. "To the contrary," wrote the president, "it is my belief that this deployment will facilitate a peaceful resolution of the crisis." Bush said, "The Forces are equipped for combat, and their mission is defensive. They are prepared to take action in concert with Saudi forces, friendly regional forces, and others to deter Iraqi aggression and to preserve the integrity of Saudi Arabia." The president made no reference to possible offensive action.[31]

The War Powers Resolution, which had been passed over President Nixon's veto in 1973, reflected Congress's belated opposition to the war in Vietnam. The main thrust of the Resolution was that the president consult with Congress before sending American forces into combat. In case of hostilities, the troops had to be withdrawn after ninety days unless Congress specifically authorized the president's action. The Resolution also provided that Congress, by joint resolution, could instruct the president to remove the forces at any time.

But the War Powers Resolution had faced tough sledding from the day it was passed. The theory behind the ninety-day requirement of the Act was shaky, and the provision for recall by joint resolution, known as a "legislative veto," had been ruled unconstitutional.* All chief executives since Richard Nixon had asserted that the measure represented an unwarranted infringement on the president's authority as commander in chief, and, in varying degrees, all had ignored its provisions.

In twenty-three incidents involving the use of military force since the passage of the Resolution, only once—at the time of the evacuation of Saigon in 1975—did a president consult fully with Congress before deploying troops.[32] On that occasion, Gerald Ford vainly sought congressional approval beforehand. When Congress failed to act, Ford went ahead on his own authority. Major operations such as the liberation of the *Mayaguez* in 1975 by President Ford, and the attempted rescue of the hostages in Tehran by President Carter, were undertaken without reference to Congress. The Reagan administration ignored the Act altogether. In 1982, Reagan deployed the Marines in Lebanon; in 1983, he invaded Grenada; and in 1987, he dispatched U.S. naval forces to protect shipping in the Persian Gulf. In none of these cases was Congress consulted. In the case of Bush's invasion of Panama in 1989, the congressional leadership was informed of the action only after the troops were under way. Reports of the various actions, filed after the event, were provided to Congress on only nine occasions. In effect, every administration from Nixon to Bush had honored the Resolution through its breach, rather than its observance.

As a result, a consensus had developed both in Washington and within the legal community that the War Powers Resolution was a hortatory admonition to the president, but nothing more. In the view of Professor Lawrence Tribe of Harvard, one

---

*INS v. Chadha, 462 U.S. 92 (1983). The issue in *Chadha* dealt with the authority of Congress to overturn decisions of the Immigration and Naturalization Service by majority vote in one House. That gave final authority over the executive branch to Congress, hence the term "legislative veto." It was held by the Supreme Court to be unconstitutional. The War Powers Resolution, as such, was not ruled on, but the same rationale would apply.

of the country's leading liberal authorities on the Constitution, the law was unenforceable and "largely a dead letter."[33] As seen from the White House, the president was free to act as he wished. George Bush did not question whether his authority to deploy troops was conditional upon congressional support, and neither did any of his staff. Given the enormous size of the deployment and its purpose, that view may have misread the nature of the nation's war powers.

The Constitution divided the war powers between the president and the Congress. The president was made commander in chief of the armed forces, but the bulk of the war powers were left to Congress.* The framers intended that the powers be used in concert. Congress would decide on war or peace, and would provide the necessary forces, but the president would command them. As commander in chief, the president had the necessary authority to repel sudden attacks, but the power to initiate war rested with Congress. Those distinctions are clear in theory. In practice, they present a hopeless hodgepodge of conflicting authority and overlapping responsibility. In particular, the president's direct command of the armed forces has eroded many of Congress's constitutional war powers. Congress must still declare war and provide the funding for military operations, but numerous presidents have deployed U.S. forces abroad on their own authority, and that has sometimes resulted in hostilities. The War Powers Resolution had sought to remedy that by providing an explicit role for Congress before troops could be dispatched. But rather than clarify the issue, the Resolution merely proved to be a continuing

---

*Article I, section 8 of the Constitution provides that "Congress shall have the Power To . . . provide for the common Defense; . . . define and punish . . . Offenses against the Law of Nations; declare War; grant Letters of Marque and Reprisal, and make Rules concerning Captures on Land and Water; . . . raise and support Armies; . . . provide and maintain a Navy; . . . make Rules for the Government and Regulation of the land and naval forces; . . . provide for calling forth the Militia to execute the Laws of the Union, suppress Insurrections and repel Invasions; [and] provide for organizing, arming, and disciplining the Militia. . . ." In other words, everything except the power of military command resides in Congress.

source of friction. In 1987 Senator Sam Nunn acknowledged that the statute "has not worked";[34] and during the 1988 presidential campaign, George Bush had advocated its repeal.[35]

By writing to Congress immediately, as Bush did in August, he was tendering an olive branch. He was notifying Congress in writing of what he was doing, thus informally complying with the reporting provisions of the War Powers Resolution. But he carefully avoided triggering the ninety-day clock that would have required a congressional resolution of support. Senate aides told the *Washington Post* that Congress would probably regard Bush's letter as adequate.[36] Certainly, given the unanimity of support that greeted the president's dispatch of troops to Saudi Arabia, there was no reason to think otherwise. The only note of caution was sounded by Senator Claiborne Pell of Rhode Island, chairman of the Foreign Relations Committee, who warned that in the event of hostilities, Bush must obtain formal congressional approval. "That is the law," Pell said.[37]

Regardless of the constitutionality of the War Powers Resolution, the president's authority to dispatch a limited number of troops to Saudi Arabia (as opposed to the authority to initiate war) is well settled. The Constitution does not spell out, and the statutes are largely silent, but precedent, usage, and custom developed since the time of Thomas Jefferson generally support President Bush's decision. That does not mean the president can lead the country into war. It does mean that he can send troops abroad to meet an emergency. Whether he can send 250,000 or 500,000 begins to get murky.

There is no Supreme Court ruling directly on point. The authoritative Court holding pertaining to the president's authority as commander in chief was rendered almost 150 years ago by Chief Justice Roger Brooke Taney. Speaking for an all-but-unanimous Court in *Fleming v. Page*,[38] a case arising out of the Mexican War, Taney described the military power of the president in sweeping terms. "As commander in chief, he is authorized to direct the movements of the naval and military forces placed by law at his command, and to employ them in the

manner he may deem most effectual to harass and conquer and subdue the enemy."[39] Taney was talking about the authority of the president to command the armed forces in combat pursuant to a congressional declaration of war. He was not alluding to independent action by the president.

Two other nineteenth-century cases, neither of which dealt with military matters, recognized the president's broad discretion to act in the absence of specific congressional authorization. Those were *In re Neagle*[40] in 1890 and *In re Debs*[41] in 1895. In *Neagle*, the Court established the doctrine of the president's inherent power to defend "the peace of the United States." Justice Miller, who delivered the opinion of the Court, said the president's duty was not limited "to the enforcement of acts of Congress or of treaties of the United States according to their express terms," but also included "the rights, duties and obligations growing out of the Constitution itself, our international relations, and all of the protection implied by the nature of the government under the Constitution."[42] In *Debs*, a unanimous Supreme Court upheld presidential intervention in labor disputes, although there was no statutory basis for such action. Theodore Roosevelt, who dispatched American forces hither and yon while president, claimed that he not only had the right but the duty "to do anything that the needs of the Nation demanded unless such action was forbidden by the Constitution or by the laws."[43]

Shortly thereafter, William Howard Taft, the only person to serve both as president and chief justice of the United States, wrote that as commander in chief, the president "can order the army and navy anywhere he will, if the appropriations furnish the means of transportation."[44] Subsequently, in *Myers v. United States*,[45] Taft, as chief justice, upheld a broad, latitudinarian interpretation of presidential power.*

---

*Justices Holmes, McReynolds, and Brandeis dissented sharply from Taft's view in *Myers*. Holmes said, "The duty of the President to see that the laws be executed is a duty that does not go beyond the laws or require him to achieve more than Congress sees fit to leave to his power." *Myers v. United States*, 272 U.S. 52, 177 (1926). Justice

But neither *Neagle*, nor *Debs*, nor *Myers* dealt directly with foreign relations. Their application to President Bush's action, though strongly supportive, is by inference and analogy only. A strand of precedent that is directly related, and that supports the president's decision to deploy troops, pertains to the protection of citizens abroad. In his speech of August 8, George Bush listed his determination "to protect the lives of American citizens abroad" as the fourth principle underlying the dispatch of troops to Saudi Arabia. The tradition supporting such use of force stretches almost two hundred years, and virtually every president in modern times has cited the protection of American lives and property as one of the major reasons behind his decision to use troops. In 1965, President Johnson sent 25,000 Marines into the Dominican Republic to prevent a Communist takeover. But to justify the action (which was taken without consulting Congress), Johnson explained that "99 percent of our reason for going in there was to try to provide protection for these American lives and the lives of other nationals."[46]

In 1970, President Nixon cited the protection of "the lives of Americans who are in Vietnam" to justify his invasion of Cambodia.[47] President Ford's 1975 rescue of the crew of the *Mayaguez* (at the cost of forty-one dead Marines) and President Carter's ill-fated attempt to rescue the hostages in Tehran in 1980 were similarly justified. In 1983, President Reagan stretched the rationale to its limit when he ordered the invasion of Grenada, allegedly to protect the lives of American medical students enrolled at the unaccredited St. George's University of Medicine. All four actions were taken without congressional authorization.*

Brandeis, in an often cited remark, noted that the purpose of the separation of powers was "not to promote efficiency but to preclude the exercise of arbitrary power. The purpose was not to avoid friction, but, by means of the inevitable friction incident to the distribution of governmental powers among three departments, to save the people from autocracy." 272 U.S. at 293.

*Lesser actions involving the use of forces to protect American lives and property in recent years include the evacuation of U.S. citizens from Cyprus in 1974; the evacuation of Da Nang, Phnom Penh, and Saigon in 1975; the rescue of U.S. citizens in

The relevant judicial decisions are few, but they are supportive. In *Durand v. Hollins*,[48] decided ten years after Chief Justice Taney's definition of the commander in chief's military role, Justice Nelson upheld the president's use of force to protect American lives and property abroad. "Under our system of government," said Nelson, "the citizen abroad is as much entitled to protection as the citizen at home."*[49] Similarly in the famous *Slaughter-House Cases*[50] in 1873, Justice Miller, speaking for the Supreme Court, identified the "right to demand protection of the Federal Government on the high seas or abroad" as one of the privileges and immunities of citizenship guaranteed by the Fourteenth Amendment.

American statute law is equally supportive of presidential action to protect citizens abroad. An obscure but still valid piece of legislation known as the Hostage Act, passed by Congress in 1868, authorizes the president to take whatever action he deems necessary and proper, "not amounting to acts of war," to secure a hostage's release.[51] The deployment of 250,000 troops to the Persian Gulf might seem excessive, but no less a figure than Oliver North cited the Hostage Act as legal justification for the executive branch "to do whatever was necessary" during the Iran-contra affair.[52] President Carter regularly invoked the statute as providing legislative authorization for his actions during the Iranian hostage crisis.[53] And Chief Justice Rehnquist, speaking for the Court in *Dames & Moore v. Regan*,[54] the leading case to arise out of the drama in Tehran, said the statute was "highly relevant in the looser sense of indicating congressional acceptance of a broad scope of executive authority in circumstances such as those presented in this case."[55]

Lebanon in 1976; and the airlift of citizens from Zaire in 1978. Arguably, the interception of the *Achille Lauro* hijackers in 1985 was also so related.

*The idea that citizens are entitled to be protected by the government stems from historic common law concepts about the mutual obligation that exists between a British subject and the Crown. In return for the allegiance of the subject, the king is obliged to provide protection. And *vice versa*. The doctrine was formulated by the Lord Chief Justice of England, Sir Edward Coke, in *Calvin's Case* in 1608 (7 Coke's Reports 1, 5a) as *protectio trahit subjectionem, et subjectio protectionem*.

The pattern of presidential usage is even more compelling. Altogether, there have been over two hundred incidents in which presidents have deployed troops abroad on their own authority, and most of those occurrences have involved the protection of American citizens and property.* Almost all were defensive in nature. They were also relatively minor. Nearly all involved trivial naval engagements and other minor uses of force (fights with pirates or cattle rustlers, for instance) not directed at major adversaries or risking substantial casualties or large-scale hostilities over a prolonged period.

The general rule has been that the president is free to take the initiative, and if the matter is settled quickly and at little cost, congressional sanction is not required. If the matter drags on, or if it becomes serious, then the president must seek Congress's approval.

The distinction is not clear cut. For the most part, it depends on the president's judgment as well as the temper of Congress. In 1801, after the Bey of Tripoli declared war on the United States, President Jefferson dispatched a squadron of frigates to the Mediterranean to protect American commerce. When one of the frigates was attacked by a Tripolitanian cruiser, the frigate returned fire and in the ensuing battle defeated and captured the cruiser. After disarming the vessel, the American frigate released it because, as Jefferson told Congress, the president was unauthorized "to go beyond the line of defence" without congressional approval.[56]

---

*A list of such incidents is provided in *Congressional Record*, S-130, S-135, vol. 137, daily ed., January 10, 1991. Also see J. Terry Emerson, "War Powers Legislation," 74 W. Va. L. Rev. 53 (1972). For those incidents from 1798 to 1945, see James Grafton Rogers, *World Policing and the Constitution* (Boston: World Peace Foundation, 1945). Those from 1945 to the passage of the War Powers Resolution are treated in Barry M. Blechman and Stephan S. Kaplan, *Force Without War* (Washington, D.C.: The Brookings Institution, 1978). A recent listing of events after the War Powers Resolution is contained in Loch K. Johnson, *America as a World Power* (New York: McGraw-Hill, 1991), p. 278. Also see *Background Information on the Use of United States Armed Forces in Foreign Countries*, House Committee on Foreign Affairs, 91st Congress, 2d Session (Committee Print, 1970).

The rule was best illustrated by Andrew Jackson. When Argentine ships began to prey on American vessels in the vicinity of the Falkland Islands, Jackson reinforced the American naval squadron in the South Atlantic and sought diplomatic reassurances from Buenos Aires. But in his State of the Union message in 1834, Jackson said:

> I submit the case to the consideration of Congress, to the end that they may clothe the Executive with such authority and means as they may deem necessary for providing a force adequate to the complete protection of our fellow-citizens fishing and trading in these seas.[57]

In effect, having taken immediate action, Jackson was reluctant to go it alone. He asked Congress for support.

The most egregious example of a president's acting first and then submitting the issue to Congress involved President Polk's decision in 1846 to send a large force under General Zachary Taylor into disputed territory along the Rio Grande, triggering a Mexican attack. An unenthusiastic Congress passed the necessary resolution recognizing that a state of war with Mexico existed, but two years later the House of Representatives censured Polk for "unnecessarily and unconstitutionally" starting a war.[58]

Lincoln took unprecedented actions when the Southern states seceded from the Union in the spring of 1861. With Congress in recess, he issued proclamations calling out the remaining state militias, suspending the writ of habeas corpus, and placing a blockade on Southern ports. When Congress returned in July, Lincoln immediately sought their approval. "Whether strictly legal or not," Lincoln said, he had acted "under what appeared to be . . . a public necessity, trusting then, as now, that Congress would ratify those actions."[59] Unlike Polk, Lincoln had acted in an emergency to save the Union, and Congress generously responded, making valid "all the acts, proclamations, and orders of the President, as if they had been issued and done under the previous express authority and direction of the Congress of the United States."[60]

In 1869, President Grant thought it would be a good idea to annex Santo Domingo (now the Dominican Republic) and make it a state. After he had submitted a treaty to that effect to the Senate, war broke out between Haiti and Santo Domingo, and Grant, without congressional approval, ordered the Navy to defend Santo Domingo from Haitian attack. When the Senate rejected Grant's treaty, he canceled the order to the Navy.[61] Grant's action illustrates the point made many years later by Professor Alexander Bickel of Yale. While the president is free to exercise his initiative, said Bickel, "There are very few instances in our history when a President has taken the law in to his own hands against the will of Congress."[62]

In 1900, President McKinley dispatched five thousand American troops to China as part of an international force to relieve the besieged foreign legations in Peking and suppress the Boxer Rebellion. Again, the announced purpose was to protect American lives and property. Congress was not consulted.[63] Woodrow Wilson ordered American forces to Vera Cruz, Mexico, in 1914 in response to an attack on U.S. seamen from the USS *Dolphin* while on shore leave in Tampico. Unlike McKinley, Wilson asked Congress for approval.[64] But when the Senate chose to debate the measure, Wilson ordered the Marines landed on his own authority.[65] The U.S. occupation lasted seven months and eventually resulted in the downfall of the government of Mexican President Victoriano Huerta. Two years later, Wilson sent Major General John J. Pershing and another large force into northern Mexico on a "punitive expedition" against Pancho Villa. Congress approved Wilson's action, but not until Pershing's troops had crossed the border.[66] In 1914, Wilson intervened militarily in Haiti; American troops remained there until 1934. In 1918, he intervened in the Russian civil war. Five thousand troops were dispatched to Archangel, and seven thousand to Vladivostok. The casualties were heavy. In neither case was Congress consulted.[67]

Despite impressions to the contrary, Franklin Roosevelt, during his first two terms as president, punctiliously deferred to Congress when it came to the use of troops abroad. As late as June 14, 1940, with France on the ropes, he carefully hedged his message of sympathy to the French people. "These statements carry with them no implications of military commitments," said Roosevelt. "Only Congress can make such commitments."[68] But within three months, Roosevelt had decided that it was necessary for the president to take the lead. On his own authority, and in apparent violation both of the neutrality acts and Article IV of the Constitution,* FDR provided fifty refitted destroyers to beleaguered Britain in exchange for base rights in the Western hemisphere.[69] In the spring of 1941, again on his own authority, he dispatched U.S. troops to occupy Greenland and Iceland,[70] and on May 27 he ordered the Navy to "sink on sight" German U-boats in the North Atlantic.[71]

After World War II, presidents were more inclined to deploy troops without reference to Congress. On April 22, 1948, in a little-remembered episode, President Truman claimed the power, without the consent of Congress, to send troops to what was then Palestine as part of an international force under the United Nations. Both Senator Arthur Vandenberg of Michigan, the chairman of the Foreign Relations Committee, and former Senator Warren Austin of Vermont, the United States delegate to the U.N., supported the president.[72]

---

*Article IV, Section 3 of the Constitution provides that "Congress shall have the Power to dispose of and make all needful Rules and Regulations respecting the Territory or other Property belonging to the United States." For the opinion of Attorney General Jackson upholding the president's action, see 39 Op. Attorney General 484 (1940). ["No such dangerous Opinion was ever before penned by an Attorney General of the United States," said Professor Edward S. Corwin of Princeton, the late dean of constitutional law scholars. For competing views, see Quincy Wright, "The Transfer of Destroyers to Great Britain," 34 Am. J. Int. L. 680 (1940); Edwin Borchard, "The Attorney General's Opinion in the Exchange of Destroyers for Bases," 34 Am. J. Int. L. 690 (1940).]

In perhaps the greatest single display of executive initiative, President Truman dispatched American troops to repel the invasion of South Korea on June 25, 1950. Not until two days later did the president meet with congressional leaders. Explicit congressional approval was never sought. Truman was acting to repel aggression that threatened American security interests in the Pacific. Senator Paul Douglas of Illinois argued that Truman's action was consistent with the intent of the framers that permitted the president, as commander in chief, to respond to sudden attacks.[73] Senator Robert Taft and most Republicans disagreed. They thought Truman should have sought a declaration of war. But in addition to Douglas's argument, there were pragmatic reasons for not declaring war. Against whom would it be declared? How did one declare war against a power that one did not recognize? And did the United States really want to go to war with China?

The only strict constructionist among modern presidents was General Eisenhower. Ike undoubtedly would have acted on his own authority in an emergency, but when time allowed, as it usually did, he insisted on seeking authorization from Congress before sending troops abroad. In 1955, when China threatened military action against Chiang Kai-shek's forces in the Pescadores and Formosa, Eisenhower asked Congress for explicit authority to use American forces in their defense. The Formosa Resolution, passed immediately thereafter, "authorized" the president "to employ the Armed Forces of the United States as he deems necessary" to protect Formosa.[74] It was a blank check, but Congress had written it. Two years later when Lebanon threatened to erupt in civil war, Eisenhower again asked Congress for permission to intervene. The 1957 Joint Resolution to Promote Peace and Stability in the Middle East again explicitly "authorized" the president's use of military force.[75] As John Foster Dulles told the Senate Foreign Relations Committee, "President Eisenhower is very reluctant to use the Armed Forces of the United States in a war unless he has the authority of Congress."[76] Ike's caution was well served. Perhaps because he had the support of Congress, American forces were not challenged. Hostilities did not ensue.

Eisenhower has been the exception. Modern presidents have asserted their power to deploy troops abroad on their own authority without consulting Congress, and the courts have been supportive. When litigants sought to challenge FDR's destroyer deal in 1940, the courts invariably dismissed the suits because the plaintiffs lacked what the judiciary calls "standing." They could not demonstrate how they had been injured by the president's action.

An additional impediment to challenging a president's action in court involves what is known as the "doctrine of political questions." The concept goes back to Chief Justice John Marshall's 1803 landmark decision in *Marbury v. Madison*.[77] It was in *Marbury* that the great chief justice established the authority of the Supreme Court to declare acts of Congress unconstitutional. In so doing, Marshall noted that the Constitution was not only a legal document, but that it was also an important political document. In legal matters, said Marshall, the decision of the Supreme Court was final. But in political matters, it had no jurisdiction. In Marshall's words, "The Constitution invests the president with certain important political powers, in the exercise of which he is to use his own discretion, and is accountable only to his country in his political character, and to his own conscience." That is a powerful recognition by the Court of the president's discretionary authority. Marshall added:

> *Whatever opinion may be entertained of the manner in which executive discretion may be used, still there exists, and can exist, no power to control that discretion. The subjects are political. They respect the nation, not individual rights, and being entrusted to the executive, the decision of the executive is conclusive.*

The foreign relations of the United States are political re-lations. They involve the nation in its sovereign capacity, not individual rights. According to the Constitution, they are en-trusted to the president and Congress—not the courts.* Since the command of the armed forces is entrusted by the Consti-tution to the president, it is unlikely that the courts would entertain a challenge to his authority to deploy troops overseas. Indeed, there is no record of their ever having done so. To the contrary. In 1981 when several members of Congress sought to challenge President Reagan's sending of military advisers to El Salvador,[78] the suit was dismissed as a political question.† So too in 1983 when Representative John Conyers of Michigan and ten others brought suit to contest the president's invasion of Grenada.[79] President Reagan's dispatch of naval forces to the Persian Gulf in 1987 was challenged in court by 110 members of Congress.[80] That too was dismissed. The Court of Appeals held that the matter presented "a nonjusticiable political ques-tion." None of these congressional challenges ever reached the Supreme Court. The rule is so clear that no attempt was made by the congressmen to seek a review by the high court.

A final bar to litigation is the matter of "ripeness." Just as standing pertains to who may bring suit, ripeness concerns when it may be brought. In 1979, Senator Barry Goldwater and twenty other members of Congress sought to block President Carter's termination of a defense treaty between the United States and Taiwan.[81] They argued that since the treaty had been approved by two-thirds of the Senate, President Carter could not revoke it without the Senate's concurrence. The Su-preme Court rejected the suit, a plurality of justices asserting that it was a nonjusticiable political question. In a concurring

*This is sometimes referred to as "textual commitment": The foreign relations func-tions are textually committed to the president and Congress by the Constitution. *Baker v. Carr*, 369 U.S. 186, 210 (1962).
†In a concurring opinion, Judge Robert Bork expressed the belief that the congress-men lacked standing. *Crockett v. Reagan*, 720 F 2d. 1355, 1357 (1983).

opinion, Justice Powell maintained that the issue was not ripe for judicial intervention. In Powell's view, the Supreme Court could resolve disputes between the president and Congress, but only when the branches "reach a constitutional impasse." If Congress "chooses not to confront the President, it is not our task to do so," wrote Powell.[82] That meant that if a majority of both Houses of Congress officially raised an issue, it was Powell's view that the Court could act. But it had no power to adjudicate actions brought by small groups of congressmen. Since President Bush's decision to send troops to defend Saudi Arabia enjoyed virtually unanimous support in Congress, the question of ripeness would act as a final hurdle to any member who sought to bring suit.

Subsequently, in the autumn of 1990, Congressman Ron Dellums and fifty-three members of Congress brought suit in Federal District Court to restrain President Bush from initiating hostilities in the Gulf without congressional approval. The issue in *Dellums* related to the president's authority to make war, and not to his authority to send troops to Saudi Arabia. It will be discussed subsequently in the context of the president's war-making powers. Suffice it to say that the district court dismissed the suit on the basis of ripeness. If Congress as a whole had acted, the court suggested it would have entertained jurisdiction. But it could not act at the behest of individual congressmen.

The inescapable conclusion is that in initially sending troops to Saudi Arabia, President Bush acted within the bounds of his authority as commander in chief. The text of the Constitution, the uncontradicted pattern of judicial precedent, as well as custom and usage, support the president's action. Whether it was a wise move poses a different question. But that is not a question to be answered by the courts.

The vast authority lodged in the president as commander in chief has profound implications for American democracy. The executive branch's monopoly of the sources of intelligence, its constitutional authority to speak and listen for the nation, and its almost total control of the flow of information arm the president with unparalleled capacity to dictate the nation's course.

When the Constitution was written, the United States was a minor actor on the world scene, and military weapons seldom shot farther than the eye could see. Even as late as World War II, the conduct of military campaigns, except for air power, was not qualitatively different from the time of George Washington or Abraham Lincoln. But the advent of the nuclear age has wrought enormous changes both in the technology of war and its destructive consequences. Are the constitutional precepts that grew from an earlier age still appropriate? That question was asked by Justices Potter Stewart and William O. Douglas in 1968.[83] There are no easy answers. On the one hand, particularly when confronting a nuclear foe, the argument is stronger than ever that the president must enjoy full authority to respond instantly to a sudden attack. On the other, the vast arsenal that has accumulated to defend American interests permits the president unlimited opportunities to deploy it abroad, unchecked by any force other than his own good judgment. In August 1990, it would not have made any difference whether American decision-making was broadened to include more than just the president, because Congress was fully supportive of President Bush's action. But the fact that a president, acting on his own authority as commander in chief, can constitutionally deploy a vast military force halfway around the globe is an issue that deserves considerable scrutiny. While President Bush may have been within his constitutional authority to deploy troops for defensive purposes, did he have the same right for offensive objectives? And whether he did or did not, should he have been more forthcoming with Congress about the administration's ultimate aims?

It matters little whether one subscribes to theories about America's decline as a great power, or whether one sees events in the Persian Gulf as a testament to United States leadership. The danger is that with the forces available, the ready means of transporting them rapidly, and the elaborate array of weaponry with which they are equipped, the president enjoys virtual carte blanche to intervene in local and regional disputes anywhere in the world. The Founding Fathers would have checked that tendency by rejecting, as they did, a large standing army. With no forces available, there could be no foreign adventures. But that option has been foreclosed, and even the end of the Cold War has brought little reduction in American armed forces.

In 1788 the anti-Federalists recognized the potential for presidential aggrandizement. The opponents of the Constitution warned of the dangers of a *"military king."*[84] Writing under the pseudonym "Philadelphiensis," one critic charged that "the president is a King to all intents and purposes, and at the same time one of the most dangerous kind—an elective King, the commander in chief of a standing army."[85] But it was the redoubtable Patrick Henry who said it best when he asserted in the Virginia ratification convention that the Constitution "has an awful squinting, it squints toward monarchy" and absolutist power.[86]

In August 1990, President Bush intervened in the Persian Gulf to defeat aggression. During the ensuing seven months, the United States deployed the largest military force sent into action since World War II. In forty-three days, the international coalition assembled by the president pummeled Iraq into submission. Kuwait was liberated, and the aggressor was made to pay dearly. The president prevailed. But the tally sheet of costs has yet to be totaled.

4.

BUSH TAKES
THE HELM

In the family of nations, the
sovereignty of each government,
even the smallest, should be
scrupulously respected.

—Henry M. Stimson
(to the graduating class at Phillips
Academy, Andover, Massachusetts,
June 14, 1940)

Throughout the weekend of August 4–5, Bush worked fever-
ishly to bring America's allies into line. The European Community was first off the mark, freezing Kuwait's assets, placing
an embargo on arms sales to Baghdad, suspending Iraq's preferred trading status with the Community, and halting the pur-
chase of Iraqi oil. "As long as there is one Iraqi soldier in
Kuwait, as long as there is not a legitimate and sovereign gov-

ernment . . . we will not be satisfied," said Italian foreign minister Giovanni Castelleneta. In a surprising show of unanimity,
French foreign minister Roland Dumas added that France would
consider joining a naval blockade if diplomatic efforts failed to
dislodge Iraq from Kuwait.[1]

In Japan, Prime Minister Toshiki Kaifu announced that his
government had ordered a ban on the importation of Iraqi oil
and a halt to all other commercial transactions. Bush had leaned
heavily on Kaifu, telling him that the United States expected
Japan to go along with a "concerted effort" against Iraq. But
the cost for Kaifu would be high. Japan imported 12 percent of
its oil from Iraq, and already the Japanese stock market was in
free fall. The press reported that as soon as Kaifu reached his
decision, he called Bush (7 A.M. Washington time) to report
the move, reflecting the friendship that had developed between
the two.[2]

The Soviet Union and the Chinese came aboard as well.
Again, George Bush could take personal credit. For the past
two years, throughout the dissolution of the Soviet empire in
Eastern Europe and German unification, Bush and Secretary of
State Baker had painstakingly nourished their relations with
Mikhail Gorbachev and Eduard Shevardnadze. The remarkable
scene at Moscow's Vnukovo airport—with Baker and Shevardnadze standing shoulder to shoulder as they jointly called for
international action against Iraq—would have been inconceivable a year earlier. The Soviet press, recently freed from government censorship, heaped scorn on Saddam for his invasion
of Kuwait, and there was even talk, discouraged by Shevardnadze, that the Soviet Union might join in naval efforts to
interdict Iraqi shipping.[3]

In China, Bush's quiet efforts to restore relations after Tiananmen Square bore fruit as well. As former American ambassador to Beijing, the president understood the necessity of
working with China and not isolating it. In December, he had
dispatched National Security Adviser Scowcroft on a secret
mission to China's leadership. Now he dangled the prospect of

renewed international acceptance. On Saturday, August 4, the Chinese publicly dismissed the possibility of cooperating with Western sanctions against Iraq.[4] By Monday, they too were in tow. When the U.N. Security Council voted later that day, the result was a foregone conclusion. All five permanent members joined the move to impose the most complete economic sanctions on Iraq that had ever been voted. Only Castro's Cuba and Yemen abstained. There were no negative votes. "This is a new U.N.," said Britain's ambassador, Sir Crispin Tickell, and George Bush's behind-the-scenes efforts were largely responsible.

Saddam's response was predictable. Months later a senior Arab diplomat would lament that the Iraqi leader failed to understand the forces arrayed against him. "If he had acted like Bush in Panama, if he had gone in, taken what he wanted, and gotten out that weekend, he could have avoided what happened."[5] Instead of getting out, Saddam chose to sit tight. The more pressure that was brought, the more determined he became to hold on. Arabists in and out of government could have explained to Bush why Saddam would not back down if he was threatened, but Bush had little contact with such people, and neither did members of his inner circle. Indeed, he may not have cared. The president was determined that Saddam be humiliated. As a result, the confrontation accelerated.

On Sunday, August 5, the newly installed government in Kuwait (composed exclusively of Iraqi military officers) warned for the first time that foreign nationals could be in jeopardy. Since Kuwait's population was composed largely of foreign nationals, that threat was ominous. As announced by Baghdad radio, "Countries that resort to punitive measures against the provisional government of free Kuwait and fraternal Iraq . . . should remember that they have interests and nationals in Kuwait."[6]

Asked whether he believed Americans in Kuwait were in danger, President Bush replied he thought not. "But I think you know how I feel about the protection of American life and the willingness to do whatever is necessary to protect it."[7] At the same time, the State Department advised all Americans in Kuwait "to depart as soon as the situation permits."[8]

It was not until the following day, August 6—the day after the Security Council had voted to impose trade sanctions—that the first Westerners in Kuwait City, including twenty-nine Americans, were taken into custody. They were transported by bus to Baghdad, where they were installed in the Sheraton hotel. The United States and Iraq were now on a collision course. Any move by one required a response from the other. Saddam invaded Kuwait, Bush mobilized the U.N. The U.N. voted sanctions, Saddam took hostages. When Bush sent troops to Saudi Arabia, Saddam annexed Kuwait as Iraq's nineteenth province. An inexorable escalation had begun, compounded by a fearful set of mutual miscalculations. George Bush believed, incorrectly as it turned out, that Saddam would back down if confronted with overwhelming Western force. Saddam, equally incorrectly, believed that Bush was bluffing, that his shaky coalition would fall apart, and that in a showdown it would be the United States that backed down.

On Tuesday, August 7, a peace plan floated by Yasir Arafat was dismissed by the West. The PLO had proposed the complete withdrawal of Iraqi troops from Kuwait, a large cash payment to Baghdad, elections for a government to replace the emir, and the cession of Bubiyan and Warba islands to Iraq. That was essentially what Baghdad had sought in the first place.[9] The plan appeared to garner support in Arab capitals as nervous leaders sought to accommodate Saddam.[10] But Bush abruptly rejected the scheme, and shortly thereafter Mubarak did as well. Despite the lack of U.S. forces in the region, American aims were now fixed. The tactics might vary, the circumstances would change, but the goal of liberating Kuwait was not negotiable.

But if American aims were clear, the anti-Saddam alliance

had not yet jelled. Above all, Bush faced the urgent task of keeping the Gulf states on line. King Fahd had agreed to accept U.S. troops, but had not as yet given any indication whether Saudi Arabia would comply with U.N. sanctions and shut off the flow of Iraqi oil through the two massive pipelines that traversed the kingdom. Turkey, too, held back, the 810-mile pipeline from Mosul to the Turkish port of Yumurtalik still pumping oil. The Saudi and Turkish pipelines had a daily capacity of 2.3 million barrels, or about 85 percent of total Iraqi production. Only Egypt and Syria could be counted on. Mubarak had signed on for the duration, and for Syria's Assad, it was a case of the enemy of my enemy is my friend. In point of fact, Assad's record in virtually every category of terrorism and oppression was indistinguishable from Saddam's. But he was indispensable if the contest was to be more than the West versus the Arabs. To use a phrase Lyndon Johnson made famous, it was better to have Assad inside the tent pissing out than outside the tent pissing in.

The mood of the Gulf states was summed up in a journalist's report from Cairo: "In the first day [after] the invasion, Gulf diplomats were insisting that Iraq must withdraw its forces and that the Kuwaiti ruling family be restored to power. By the weekend, some of those same diplomats had conceded that the ruling family might not be allowed to return . . . But today [Monday], yet another version had surfaced in some Gulf capitals in which it would be conceded that Kuwait was effectively in Iraq's sphere of influence and that the new rulers would commit themselves to a settlement favorable to Baghdad."[11]

Turkey came through first. President Turgut Ozal had been called repeatedly by Bush over the past several days, and eventually those calls paid off. The Turks, who shared a two-hundred-mile border with Iraq, announced on Tuesday that they would comply with U.N. sanctions and halt the flow of Iraqi oil. The cost to Turkey in lost revenue was estimated at $5 million daily. President Ozal told ABC's Peter Jennings that Turkey had no guarantee it would be compensated for the loss. "I believe the most important thing is that we stop this aggression," said Ozal.[12]

There is no doubt that George Bush had brought Ozal around. The president's personal efforts had been flattering and effective. Since the time of Mustafa Kemal Attaturk, Turkey had sought an opening to the West. For its support against Saddam, Bush offered one. Whether he could deliver on Turkey's goal to become the thirteenth member of the European Common Market was problematic, but the strengthening of ties that an alliance with the United States provided made good sense to Ozal. "This is the first time in two hundred years that Turkey has allied itself with the winners," he said afterward.[13]

Saudi Arabia fell in line as well. The flow of Iraqi oil was closed down, and the Arab League states, meeting in Cairo, voted overwhelmingly to send troops to defend the Saudis from Iraqi attack. Only Libya and the PLO opposed the move. The vote was another victory for Bush's backstage efforts to add legitimacy to the deployment of American troops in Saudi Arabia. Virtually every Arab country had been lobbied intensively by Washington. And now, with strong League support, the president had undercut Saddam's pan-Arab appeal.

Nevertheless, *The New York Times*, like many observers at that point, was pessimistic about the prospects of an Arab force. The question of offensive action was beyond the pale. Even whether they could mount an effective defense was doubtful. "It would take a T. E. Lawrence to get these guys to act in concert," said one analyst, "and I haven't noticed any Lawrences in the corridors of the Pentagon."[14] That comment puts the magnitude of allied military accomplishments into perspective. In hindsight, Desert Storm looks like a cakewalk. But in early August, the prospects appeared dim.

In the midst of the crisis, before U.S. troops were deployed in strength in Saudi Arabia, and before the glue of self-interest had cemented the coalition, President Bush went ahead with a long-scheduled vacation at Kennebunkport. Ever since Jimmy

Carter came to be seen as a captive of the Iranian hostage crisis in 1980, presidents have been reluctant to let international events pin them down in the White House. As Thomas Griscom, who served as communications director for President Reagan, noted, "You don't let [a crisis] disrupt everything you were planning to do. It heightens everything. It really brings a different level of concern."[15]

In a curious way, by going ahead with his vacation, Bush enhanced his control of the situation. By leaving Washington, the president dissipated public pressure for an instant solution to the crisis. The buildup would continue, but the clamor for immediate results would be stilled. In addition, the Kennebunkport vacation reflected a minor point of principle for Bush: Saddam was not going to disrupt normal activities. Even more important, however, it would allow him time to reflect, to have long talks with aides and associates, and to plan strategy. Appearances to the contrary, it would allow him to focus exclusively on the problem in the Gulf, which a busy White House schedule would not. And so on Friday, August 10, the president left Washington, intent on not returning until after Labor Day. As aides fretted about television images of the president speaking to reporters while sitting on a golf cart,[16] Bush resolutely went through the motions of a seaside vacation: recharging his energy, sharpening his resolve, and demonstrating that he was at the helm. The seat of government might be in Washington, but the crisis command post was with the president.

The surface calm at Kennebunkport was deceptive. Bush continued his marathon telephone conversations with world leaders and watched nervously as the confrontation in the desert grew. What Saddam would do next was not clear. During those three critical weeks, Iraq could have marched through Saudi Arabia virtually unopposed. "We had nothing there to speak of," said General Powell months later. "We were scared to death he'd figure out that . . . there was no way we could have stopped him."[17] The fact that Saddam did not move against the meager allied force in Saudi Arabia suggests once again that his aims were limited: that he was determined to hold Kuwait, but had no intention, at least for the moment, of moving farther south.

Meanwhile, the buildup in the desert continued. On Saturday, August 11, the Pentagon announced that a fourth carrier task force, led by the *John F. Kennedy*, was being sent to the Gulf. The remainder of the 82nd Airborne Division, plus the 7th Division from Fort Ord, California, and the entire III Armored Corps based at Ford Hood, Texas, were ordered to move. The Air Force dispatched another 250 planes, including two dozen mammoth B-52s, sent to the Indian Ocean base at Diego Garcia.[18] The B-52s, workhorses of the war in Vietnam, were looked on by the Pentagon as the first line of defense should Saddam attack. With a wingspan the length of a football field, and a bomb load to match, the aging bombers could deflect any Iraqi thrust into Saudi Arabia—or hurl massive destruction against Iraq itself.

At sea, the United States had an enormous advantage. Except for an occasional torpedo boat, there was no Iraqi navy to speak of. The U.S. already had three carrier task forces in place with a fourth on the way. And it was now, during that first weekend at Kennebunkport, that Bush's impatience got the better of him. On Sunday, August 12, the president abruptly ordered American forces in the Gulf to intercept all Iraqi shipping. The Navy was told to enforce U.N. sanctions and to detain all vessels attempting to evade the embargo. The U.N. had not ordered the action, and it had not been cleared with America's principal allies. Bush, acting on his own authority, was ratcheting up the United States' response. As commander in chief, it was arguably within his authority to do so. But the legal justification for the U.S. blockade was weak. Secretary Baker claimed authority under Article 51 of the United Nations Charter, which gives countries the right of self-defense, as well as the right to request aid from others when they come under attack. Supposedly, the United States was responding to a request from Kuwait.[19] But since the emir's government was no longer in place, the rationale was thin. France, the Soviet Union, and China criticized the move, and for the next two weeks the administration worked frantically to retrieve their support.

Finally, after extensive presidential intervention, including more lengthy telephone conversations with Mitterrand and Gorbachev (these had become almost routine), the Security Council voted on August 25 to support the forceful interdiction of Iraqi shipping. It was the first time in the forty-five-year history of the United Nations that the organization had authorized the use of force to compel compliance with economic sanctions. To the consternation of many, all five permanent members voted in favor. There were no negative votes. Only Cuba and Yemen abstained.[20] Bush's direct involvement was duly noted. Whether his arguments had been convincing, or his leverage compelling, the major powers fell into line. As the once-reluctant Mitterrand said from Paris, "An embargo without sanctions would be a sham."

The naval blockade marked a decisive benchmark in American escalation. While Bush hoped it would bring Saddam to his senses, one White House aide, presumably Scowcroft, reported long afterward that it was the scariest moment of the crisis. "I would sit on my bed looking out the window down the Kennebunk River and I could almost see those destroyers on the horizon. Any moment I thought we were going to war."[21]

On August 18, it may have come close to that. U.S. ships fired warning shots across the bows of two Iraqi tankers that failed to heed repeated requests to halt for inspection. In the Gulf of Oman, the frigate USS *Reid* fired six warning shots across the bow of the tanker *Khanaqiin*; in the Persian Gulf, the USS *Bradley* fired three warning shots across the bow of the *Baba Gurgur*. The Navy did not press the issue, and both vessels continued on their courses under close American surveillance.

The fact is, despite Bush's impatience, allied forces in the Gulf were not ready to take on Saddam. They were too thin on the ground, the necessary logistical support was not in place, and the troops that were arriving were not yet prepared for combat in the desert. On August 14, the Defense Department announced the impending call-up of up to 200,000 military reservists, primarily in noncombat support branches to assist the deployment. This marked the first instance since the Tet offensive in 1968 that reserve units had been activated for tactical purposes.[22] General Powell and the Pentagon's military leadership insisted that the reserves be called early.[23] They wanted the public to be aware of the crisis, and there were few ways of doing that more effectively. By calling friends and neighbors to active duty, the military was telling the public that the situation was serious. In addition, it kept the White House honest. There would be no rosy scenarios.

At the same time, Saddam continued to dig in. There was still no indication that he planned to invade Saudi Arabia, but there was every indication that he planned to defend Kuwait. Speaking to reporters at Central Command headquarters, still located in Tampa, Florida, General Schwarzkopf said, "There's no question about the fact that they have dug in right now for a strong defense." Schwarzkopf warned that until the Allied buildup was complete, the Iraqis "have the capability to do just about anything they want to."[24]

As U.S. forces continued to flow into Saudi Arabia, the rhetoric escalated. Briefly interrupting his sojourn at Kennebunkport, the president returned to Washington on August 14 for an update on the situation. Speaking to reporters at the White House, Bush said he saw no hope of a diplomatic solution to the crisis unless Saddam backed down. The annexation of Kuwait, he said, was unacceptable, and he repeated his earlier vow that "it will not stand."[25]

The next day, Bush visited the Pentagon to deliver a blistering attack on Saddam. Speaking before an audience of ranking military officers and Defense Department employees, the president, in a rare flight of oratory, said that "our jobs, our way of life, our own freedom and the freedom of friendly countries around the world" were at stake in Kuwait. Bush warned that "no one should doubt our staying power or determination." Returning to a theme he would hit over and over, the president said it was a simple matter of punishing aggression. "A half century ago, our nation and the world paid dearly for appeasing an aggressor who should, and could, have been stopped. We are not going to make the same mistake again."[26]

The reference to Hitler was unmistakable. The Fuehrer was not mentioned by name, but the allusion to Nazi aggression was clear. The press picked up the comparison quickly. On August 24, William Safire devoted an entire column to "The Hitler Analogy."[27] The September 3 issue of *The New Republic* featured a cover photo of Saddam with his mustache clipped to resemble Hitler's. FUROR IN THE GULF, the headline said.

Hindsight suggests that Bush's Hitler analogy was a two-edged sword. It helped mobilize public opinion in support of administration policy, but by identifying Saddam with Hitler, negotiations were ruled out. Any discussion with Baghdad, assuming such had been possible, would have been immediately suspect as appeasement. It was Churchill, not Chamberlain, whom Bush sought to emulate, and so the reference to Hitler soon took on a significance of its own.

Saddam responded to Bush's attack in mid-August with his own vitriolic "open letter" to the president, accusing Bush of lying to the American people about the nature of the crisis, and threatening that the "thousands of Americans whom you have pushed into this dark tunnel will go home shrouded in sad coffins."[28] Saddam and Bush were taking each other's measure. Neither gave any indication of a willingness to compromise. Bush spoke the traditional language of Western politics; Saddam responded with the rhetorical overkill of the Middle East. Neither looked closely at what the other was saying. Whatever opportunities there might have been for settlement drifted away.

It was at that point that Saddam took one of many missteps that seriously undermined his cause. Baghdad announced that citizens of the U.N. coalition residing in Iraq and Kuwait, estimated by Washington at more than ten thousand people, would be detained "until the threat of war against our country ends." National Assembly Speaker Sadi Mahdi said the Iraqi people would "play host to the citizens of these aggressive nations," and that they would be housed at appropriate military and civil sites to serve as human shields.[29]

Why Iraq took that action is not clear. Just as the United States had been taken by surprise when Saddam invaded Kuwait, the Iraqis had been caught off guard by Bush's response. Saddam had not anticipated the strength of the president's resolve. Certainly, there was nothing in Washington's attitude prior to August 2 that would have alerted him. As a result, Saddam fumbled badly in trying to improvise a rejoinder.

Once the hostage issue emerged, whatever international support Saddam may have had quickly evaporated. The heartrending spectacle of innocent women and children herded into Iraqi holding areas prejudiced even the most sympathetic observer. Saddam, accustomed to bullying his way, had gone too far. France ordered its fleet in the Persian Gulf to cooperate with the U.S. Navy to ensure compliance with U.N. sanctions,[30] and within twenty-four hours the Security Council passed a unanimous resolution demanding that Iraq permit the immediate departure of all foreign nationals.[31] This time, both Cuba and Yemen joined the Council's action. In the words of U.S. Ambassador Thomas Pickering, Iraq had "crossed the Rubicon" by "planning to use innocent third-country nationals as human shields around military installations."[32] While the White House remained deliberately low-key to avoid endangering those Americans who might be detained, it was announced that the president was returning to Washington from Kennebunkport to review the crisis. Bush was reported by Marlin Fitzwater to be "deeply troubled" by the Iraqi action.[33]

Iraq responded to the Security Council action by offering to release the hostages in return for a lifting of U.N. sanctions and the withdrawal of American forces from Saudi Arabia. But Baghdad made no offer to evacuate Kuwait. The Iraqis continued to miscalculate the odds and, not surprisingly, Saddam's half-hearted gesture was summarily dismissed by the White House. "It contains no new relevant proposals and makes no reference to the United Nations and Arab League calls for them to leave Kuwait," said Fitzwater.[34] President Bush told reporters aboard Air Force One that Saddam's conditions were "totally unsatisfactory." "We must not delude ourselves," said Bush. "Iraq's invasion was more than a military attack on tiny Kuwait. It was a ruthless assault on the very essence of international order and civilized ideals. And now . . . Iraq has imposed restrictions on innocent civilians from many countries. This is unacceptable."[35]

The following day, August 21, Bush ordered the first fifty thousand reservists to active duty. In effect, the White House was agreeing with the military that the situation was serious; it was prepared to put its political capital on the line. The call-up included Army transport personnel, Navy doctors and medical technicians, and some Air Force pilots. At the same time the White House rejected another Iraqi request for negotiations, made this time by Foreign Minister Tariq Aziz. Until Iraq withdrew from Kuwait, there was nothing to negotiate, said administration spokesmen.[36] Washington's rapid dismissal of Iraq's overtures betrayed a concern that should negotiations begin, the Gulf states might feel under pressure to compromise with Saddam. Bush was determined to prevent that. To defeat aggression, it was essential that the aggressor be punished. Saddam must not only be defeated, he must also be seen to be defeated.

George Bush's concern to counter aggression was a personal feeling that he held strongly. It traced partially to his parental upbringing, and in ever larger measure to his schoolboy days at Andover. It reflected a romantic warrior ethic that runs deep in the values of the American establishment, a culture that prizes athletic accomplishment, martial virility, and moral certitude. As a child, Bush was taught to play fair. But he was also taught to punch a bully in the nose. "My family instilled some concepts in me at a very early age," he said. "They believed very strongly in Christian ethics and helping others, and I've embraced that."[37] Helping tiny Kuwait stand up to a bully like Saddam came naturally. Perhaps more important, it reflected what Bush's boyhood hero, the remarkable Henry M. Stimson, would have done.

Bush was a student at Andover when he heard Stimson speak. It was June 14, 1940. Hitler's armies had crashed through Belgium and Holland; Denmark and Norway had been overrun; and the fall of France was imminent. Andover's commencement speaker that year was the seventy-three-year-old Stimson. Himself a graduate of Andover, Yale, and the Harvard Law School, Colonel Stimson (as he preferred to be called) epitomized the virtues that Americans held dear: dedicated public service, ironclad integrity, unflinching patriotism, and a deep devotion to democracy.

As secretary of war under Taft, Stimson had organized the civilian administration of the Philippines. As secretary of state under Hoover, he had forged what became known as the "Stimson Doctrine": the refusal of the United States to recognize the fruits of aggression—specifically, the Japanese conquest of Manchuria.[38] When World War I had come, Stimson, at the age of fifty, left his prosperous New York law practice and enlisted in the Army. He served in France and was discharged as a colonel of artillery. In 1940, less than a week after his speech at Andover, the staunchly Republican Stimson would be tapped by FDR to return as secretary of war and guide the nation's rearmament.[39] Stimson hated Hitler as fervently as the most rabid New Dealer, and he provided Roosevelt with essential bipartisan support on the eve of the 1940 presidential election. "He was a giant," said one famous general who knew him well, and George Bush's admiration for the old gentleman was not misplaced.

Stimson spoke forthrightly to the schoolboys that spring. He took issue with the prevailing sentiment of isolationist America and warned of the titanic struggle that lay ahead. It was "a very dark hour for the civilized world," Stimson said. Hitler was bullying smaller countries. He was violating "Christian principles" of "respect for justice and fair play." Unaware of FDR's impending call, Stimson told his young listeners that he envied them because they had the opportunity to choose between "right and wrong," to stand up for good against evil. "I would to God that I were young enough to face it with you."[40]

The sixteen-year-old George Bush had been electrified by the colonel's speech. Stimson's words left an indelible impression. The president repeated them almost verbatim two weeks after the Iraqi invasion of Kuwait when he said he intended "to stand up for what's right and condemn what's wrong."[41] That black-and-white contrast between good and evil sketched out by Stimson more than fifty years earlier would dominate American policy for the next six months. Bush saw the struggle against Saddam as the moral equivalent of World War II. That justified the inordinate lengths to which he was prepared to go to reverse Iraq's aggression.

As Bush worked to strengthen American resolve, international support for the president's tough stand increased markedly. On Tuesday, August 21, Egypt announced the deployment of an additional twelve thousand troops, and for the first time, Assad's Syria said that it would be sending front-line armored forces to Saudi Arabia. The nine states of the Western European Union, meeting in Paris, also agreed to provide support. "We in Western Europe see the need to act so that the United States is not left to have to do the job alone," said WEU Secretary General Willem van Eckelen.[42] Belgium, Italy, the Netherlands, and Spain announced they were sending warships to the Gulf to augment British and French ships already deployed.

On Wednesday, the president met with the press at Kennebunkport. He ticked off the growing international support for America's position and said that Iraq was becoming increasingly isolated. Twenty-two nations, he said, had agreed to provide military forces. Ultimately, thirty-eight would do so. "This is not a matter between Iraq and the United States of America. It is between Iraq and the entire world community."[43]

It was apparent from the president's comments, and from those of Secretary Cheney and General Powell, who followed him, that the use of force to drive Saddam from Kuwait was an increasing possibility. Bush was reminded by reporters that when he made his initial announcement about sending troops to Saudi Arabia, he had said their mission was purely defensive. Did he still rule out the use of military force to drive Saddam from Kuwait? Bush replied, "I don't rule in or rule out the use of force."[44] That marked the first public acknowledgment by the president that offensive action by the United States was possible.

Q: Are you preparing Americans for the possibility of war and American deaths?

Bush: I think any time you move American forces and any time you are up against what most of the world now considers to be an outrageous violator of international law, the best thing is to be prepared.[45]

Bush's remarks sent Wall Street into a tailspin. Since the crisis began, the Dow had dropped 17 percent. On Thursday, August 23, it fell another 77 points (3 percent) to hit its lowest level in thirteen months. In Tokyo, the Nikkei index suffered its fourth worst loss in history, helping to cut its value by a quarter since August 1. The market plunge came as oil prices soared. The benchmark price of West Texas crude rose to $31.93 a barrel on the New York Mercantile Exchange, with no top in sight. "There's a lot of panic out there," one money manager noted.[46] Saudi Arabia and Venezuela agreed to step up production to compensate for the Iraqi shortfall, but the economic problems of a protracted standoff were fast becoming evident.

In some respects, the president had put himself in a no-win

situation. On the one hand, he had to prepare public opinion for a possible military move to oust Saddam from Kuwait. But on the other hand, whenever the administration turned up the heat, domestic doubts rekindled. Already, prominent voices on the conservative right had begun to question the president's policy. Former Reagan staffer and syndicated columnist Patrick Buchanan asserted that Bush had "gone too far in terms of his rhetoric and too far in terms of his commitment. There's no interest so vital that we should consider using American ground forces to disgorge Iraq from Kuwait." Even if Iraq withdrew, Buchanan observed, American forces would have to remain in the area to ensure that Saddam didn't try it again. "It looks like an open-ended commitment," he wrote.[47]

Conservative military writer Edward Luttwak told "Nightline's" Ted Koppel that he doubted whether the U.S. should be defending the oil interests of Europe and Japan, and expressed even greater skepticism about defending Saudi Arabia, "which, with the possible exception of Albania, is the most oppressive and reactionary and absolutist regime in the world."[48]

Ted Galen Carpenter, director of foreign policy studies at the libertarian Cato Institute, accused the president of a "knee-jerk cold-war reaction that the rest of us may soon regret." Writing on the Op-Ed page of *The New York Times*, Carpenter was one of the few to note early on that the size of the U.S. buildup in Saudi Arabia "portends offensive operations against Iraq." He noted that Washington's hyperactive policy might "gratify the egos" of policymakers obsessed with continuing America's "global leadership in a post-cold-war setting," but it makes the United States "the point man in the Middle East: a dangerous and thankless status that prudent statesmen would seek to avoid."[49]

Opposition was less vocal on the left, although *The Nation*, a bellwether of left-liberal thought, labeled the administration's approach "naked imperialist intervention." Democratic Senator Tom Harkin of Iowa, in a tough reelection fight, questioned why "we always have to do it by ourselves."[50] New York's

Daniel Patrick Moynihan, like many others, argued that U.N. sanctions be given a chance to prove themselves.[51]

Part of the problem stemmed from Bush's initial explanation that American troops were being dispatched to the Gulf solely to defend Saudi Arabia from Iraqi attack. Most took the administration's explanation at face value, and by mid-August they believed that the mission had been accomplished. But the defense of Saudi Arabia was merely window dressing to get American forces to the Gulf. From the beginning, the goal of the president's policy had been to force Saddam to relinquish Kuwait, and Bush now faced the difficult problem of explaining that.

The criticism came from across the political spectrum. Republican Senator John McCain of Arizona, a former Vietnam POW and normally a strong backer of the president, warned that "if you get involved in a major ground war in the Saudi desert, I think support will erode significantly. Nor should it be supported. We cannot even contemplate, in my view, trading American blood for Iraqi blood."[52] Former Secretary of Defense James Schlesinger told *The New York Times* in August that the American public would undoubtedly back the president's decision to defend Saudi Arabia. "But it is not clear that there is strong public support for a rollback in Kuwait, especially if it will require heavy American casualties."[53]

Senator Terry Sanford of North Carolina, a decorated World War II veteran, became the first member of Congress to flatly oppose the president's policy. Sanford warned against the initiation of hostilities by the United States and suggested that American troops be withdrawn as quickly as possible from Saudi Arabia. "We have accomplished our mission," said Sanford, meaning that the Iraqi threat to Saudi Arabia had been contained. "I would not risk a single life to restore the Kuwaiti royal family to the throne."[54]

As domestic skepticism accelerated, the problems of holding the international coalition together intensified. If oil prices continued to skyrocket, pressure in Europe and Japan to settle with Saddam might become irresistible. The Soviets were held in place temporarily by the need for Western aid, but at the same time Moscow was reluctant to jettison completely its major client in the Middle East. Some two hundred military advisers and over six thousand Soviet civilians were in Iraq, and Baghdad's bill for previous Russian military aid ran well into the billions—hard currency that the Kremlin could ill afford to write off.

China was even more of a riddle, although Bush seemed to enjoy greater credibility with the Chinese leadership than any American president since Richard Nixon. Among the Arabs, not only did Syria and Saudi Arabia make strange bedfellows, but Saddam's share-the-wealth appeal resonated loudly in the impoverished, oil-free lands of the Mediterranean littoral. Even the continued presence of large numbers of American troops in fundamentalist Saudi Arabia was fraught with peril should cultural differences prove insurmountable. In that context, Washington's impatience with sanctions was well placed. That helps explain why Bush orchestrated the pressure on Saddam, and why he was determined to force the issue to a speedy conclusion. If there were to be a confrontation, it had to be soon, before the fragile bonds of the coalition fell apart.

On August 27, in an effort to break the crisis, U.N. Secretary General Pérez de Cuéllar announced his intention to meet with Iraqi Foreign Minister Tariq Aziz in Amman to seek "full implementation" of Security Council resolutions calling for the withdrawal of Iraqi forces from Kuwait. The secretary general was acting on his own responsibility. "I've been a diplomat for fifty years," said the seventy-year-old de Cuéllar, and "I decided this was the time for diplomacy." He said he hoped to have "a good dialogue" with Aziz, because they had worked together for six years in the 1980s negotiating an end to the Iran-Iraq struggle.[55]

Washington reluctantly said it supported the secretary general's efforts, although President Bush, speaking to reporters in Kennebunkport, said once more that he saw no immediate hope for fruitful negotiations. With Prime Minister Brian Mulroney of Canada at his side, Bush said there was "no flexibility" in the United States' basic demand that Iraq withdraw unconditionally from Kuwait.[56]

Meanwhile, despite the continuous flow of inflammatory rhetoric from Radio Baghdad, Saddam began to move cautiously. The captains of Iraq's merchant marine were ordered to comply with American interdiction orders and allow their ships to be searched. In Washington, administration officials announced that there was "no evidence that Iraq had moved Scud missiles into Kuwait to threaten Saudi cities." A Pentagon spokesman added that the Iraqis "are being very careful with their air power so as not to violate the border with Saudi Arabia."[57]

Saddam's restraint may have reflected a renewed willingness on his part to compromise. On August 28, Iraq announced that it was releasing all women and children of foreign nationals as a "goodwill gesture." The Iraqi announcement, carried over Baghdad television, said that Saddam had been "deeply affected" after meeting some of the families and had decided to give them "the freedom of staying or leaving."[58] Coupling its goodwill gesture with a show of defiance, Iraq's government newspaper, Al Jumhuriya, printed a presidential decree officially incorporating Kuwait and giving the province the name of Kadhima, which Baghdad claimed it had been called under the Ottoman Empire. "The branch has been returned to the tree trunk," Saddam was quoted as saying.[59] Saddam's efforts to have it both ways—a common gambit in Middle East negotiations—served him poorly in dealing with Bush. The White House focused on the Iraqi leader's harsh words, and indeed, often cited them as reason for dismissing his more conciliatory statements.

In addition, Saddam simply had no feel for his audience. His grotesque appearance on Iraqi TV with a group of frightened British hostages only intensified international revulsion. The same could be said for his bizarre challenge to President Bush and Mrs. Thatcher to a global television debate. "I am prepared now—ready and prepared—for direct talks and dialogue with Mr. Bush and Mrs. Thatcher," he said.[60] In Washington, Margaret Tutwiler dismissed Saddam's offer to debate as "sick," and said that it didn't deserve a response.[61]

That same day, August 28, the president once again returned to the capital from Kennebunkport to brief members of Congress on administration policy. "Our intention, and indeed, the intention of almost every country in the world," he said, "is to persuade Iraq to withdraw; that it cannot benefit from this illegal occupation; that it will pay a stiff price by trying to hold on, and an even stiffer price by widening the conflict. And, of course, we seek to achieve these goals without further violence."[62] The president emphasized that his basic demand, that Iraq withdraw from Kuwait, was not negotiable. From his remarks, it was clear that Bush assumed that once overwhelming allied force was deployed in Saudi Arabia, Saddam would recognize that he was in an untenable position and back down; that he would, in the president's words, "do a 180 and reverse course."[63] And it was that calculation that drove American policy in the closing weeks of August.

House Speaker Tom Foley said after the meeting that "there's very strong support for the president's actions. He was commended by speaker after speaker. There were really no overall reservations expressed." House Democratic whip William Gray of Pennsylvania balanced his support for Bush with a note of caution. The nation would back the president, he said, "provided we do not get into a protracted struggle with loss of life and no prospect for victory."[64]

Whatever congressional reservations there were at that point focused on the cost of the operation and who would pay for it. Bush did his best to reassure his listeners that Germany and Japan would be offering significant financial assistance, and that the other nations, particularly the Gulf states, would make large contributions in the near future.[65] None of the 170 members of Congress present raised the question of the War Powers Resolution. The lawmakers said that Bush had gone far enough in consulting them with his letter of August 9, and they appeared satisfied.[66] There was no urge to intrude on the president's response to the crisis—a traditional strength of the American system or a perennial failing of legislative oversight, depending on how one looked at it.

On Thursday, August 30, Bush moved to meet congressional concerns over costs by announcing a multibillion-dollar plan of allied assistance in the Gulf. At a news conference in Washington, the president said that the United States expected others "to bear their fair share." He said that an American delegation led by Baker and Treasury Secretary Nicholas Brady would visit Germany, Japan, Saudi Arabia, the Gulf states, and South Korea to "twist their arms a bit," seeking as much as $25 billion to defray the costs of the deployment.[67] For the first time since his television address to the nation on August 8, the president restated his personal view of what was at stake. It was, he said, "the dependability of America's commitments to its friends and allies, the shape of the post-postwar world, opposition to aggression, the potential domination of the energy resources that are critical to the entire world. . . ."[68]

The president's remarks were more than standard boilerplate turned out by a bevy of West Wing speechwriters. They went to the heart of his belief about America's role in the world—a belief that had not changed since that June day at Andover fifty years earlier. There was no room to compromise with aggression: The aggressor must be punished, and that punishment must be humiliating. The long-term problem was that the beneficial effects of that punishment were taken for granted. Little consideration was given to what shape the region would take in its aftermath.

Asked by reporters whether there were any negotiations in progress, or whether there had been any back-channel contacts with Iraq, Bush replied, "None that I'm aware of." As for Saddam's challenge to a debate, "You can put an empty chair there as far as I'm concerned," the president said.[69]

When Pérez de Cuéllar met that day with Tariq Aziz in Jordan, a brief glimmer of hope appeared, shrouded in the haggling of a Middle East bazaar. Aziz, the most worldly and sophisticated member of the Iraqi leadership, made no effort to defend the annexation of Kuwait, and brushed aside reporters' questions with a crisp "No comment." He indicated to the secretary general that Baghdad would be prepared to release all of the hostages in return for an allied pledge not to attack Iraq. Speaking of the growing confrontation, Aziz said, "You cannot solve such a situation by a magical solution. We need patience, we need some degree of quiet diplomacy."[70] Pérez de Cuéllar said the Iraqi hostage offer was "an important step forward, but it is not enough."[71] Later he said he had been disappointed because he had "hoped for more" in his discussions with Aziz.[72]

In Washington, the Iraqi proposal once again was rejected. The United States repeated its demand for the unconditional release of all hostages without preconditions or guarantees.[73] The swift American rejection of Aziz's offer reflected Bush's determination not to let the hostage issue dominate United States policy. For the initial two weeks after the first Americans were seized in Kuwait, the administration declined even to use the word *hostage* in describing them. Afterward, the president was careful not to stress their importance. To have done so would have increased their value to Saddam and in the end undoubtedly would have delayed their release. "We cannot permit hostage-taking to shape the foreign policy of this country," Bush told his press conference on August 30.

Q: Sir, does that mean that their lives would be expendable if you judge in the national interest . . .

Bush: That's too hypothetical a question. It
                         means I will not change the policy of the
                         United States, and I don't think other
                         leaders whose foreign nationals are in the
                         same predicament will change their policy
                         to pay homage or give credibility to this
                         brutal move . . . of holding citizens against
                         their will.[74]

Aside from the intrinsic merits of that position, Bush's views
had been shaped by his chairmanship of the Vice President's
Task Force on Combatting Terrorism four years earlier.[75] The
task force, composed of nine Cabinet officers, ultimately made
forty-four recommendations and, in effect, codified the U.S.
response to future terrorist acts. Bush was the moving force
behind the report and had spent more than a year in the mid-
1980s pulling the various contributions together. The report's
principal finding was that:

> The U.S. Government will make no concessions to terror-
> ists. It will not pay ransoms, release prisoners, change its
> policies or agree to other acts that might encourage additional
> terrorism.[76]

That policy was based upon the view that "to give in to terrorists' demands places even more Americans at risk." Accordingly, "this no-concessions policy is the best way of ensuring
the safety of the greatest number of people."[77]

That perspective, written when Bush was vice president, set
the tone of American policy. The president was determined to
downplay the hostage issue and to concentrate instead on
bringing maximum pressure on Saddam to withdraw from Kuwait. In his view, the mistakes of Carter and Reagan would be
avoided, and administration policy would remain sharply focused. That meant keeping the allied coalition intact. If the
subsequent military struggle was George Bush's war, the allied

coalition was George Bush's coalition. The president worked overtime to cement his ties with world leaders.

For Mubarak, Washington now provided one of the many quid pro quos that ensured Egyptian support. The White House announced that it was forgiving Egypt's $7.1 billion military debt to the United States. Despite opposition from the Treasury and the Office of Management and Budget, the president said his "gut instinct" was that Egypt's pivotal role in the current crisis justified the decision. It was government by the seat of the pants, another example of Bush's willingness to pull all the levers at his disposal to hold the alliance together. As former NSC staffer William Quandt observed, "We need to demonstrate to the key Arab party that has stood with us in this crisis that there are benefits to them for staying with us because we are going to be in this for a while."[78]

At the same time, the massive American deployment in Saudi Arabia moved ahead. Displaying the robust confidence that would soon make his name a household word, General Schwarzkopf told reporters in Riyadh that Iraq would pay a "terrible price" should it attack. It was pure bluff. Allied forces were still exceedingly vulnerable to an Iraqi assault, since the bulk of the Army's armor and artillery had yet to arrive. But Schwarzkopf's beefy presence was reassuring, and his candor and plain speaking provided a welcome change from the jargon commonly associated with the military. "Murphy's Law is alive and well out there," he confessed, while assuring reporters that the buildup was on schedule. What other general officer in recent memory would have parried a reporter's question about how the troops were adjusting to the brutal Saudi sun by observing, "These are not potted plants. They're not greenhouse shrubs. They're trained for this environment and they're very very tough folks."[79] Schwarzkopf was proving what the Army seemed to have forgotten: A sense of humor goes a long way in dealing with the media.

Bush's payoff to Mubarak marked a willingness by the White House to make whatever concessions were necessary to hold the alliance against Iraq together. But it was small potatoes when compared to the president's efforts to keep the Soviet Union in line. On Sunday, September 2, Bush announced from Kennebunkport that he and Mikhail Gorbachev would meet the following weekend in Helsinki. The meeting was scheduled at Bush's initiative. It was another powerful signal that the United States and the Soviet Union were working hand-in-hand to reverse the Iraqi takeover. Bush told reporters somewhat disingenuously that there was no special Middle East agenda. But White House aides made clear that the image of the two world leaders standing together would be beneficial. "I don't think that's the expressed purpose of them going, but if that's a product that comes out of it, that's fine with us," said Marlin Fitzwater.[80]

The meeting with Gorbachev was part of Bush's strategy to keep the pressure on Saddam. The president restated his view that he saw "no reason for optimism" about a diplomatic breakthrough. At the same time, Robert Gates, then the deputy national security adviser and one of the most hawkish of the president's staff, was dispatched to Amman to deliver a hardball message to King Hussein. If Jordan didn't join in condemning Iraq, there would be a significant slowdown in economic assistance.[81]

On Labor Day, after a late round of golf, President Bush ended his twenty-five-day vacation in Kennebunkport and returned to Washington. In addition to the Gulf crisis, the administration faced an increasingly intractable stalemate with congressional Democrats over the budget, sweeping civil rights legislation that the president had threatened to veto, and a potential controversy over the nomination of Judge David Souter of New Hampshire to the Supreme Court—not to mention the upcoming November elections. But it was the crisis with Saddam that held center stage. Bush was proving to be a consummate crisis manager, and in a remarkable display of political coordination, all of the administration's guns seemed to be pointing in the same direction. Secretary of State Baker told the House Foreign Affairs Committee that the United States rejected suggestions that Saddam be offered a face-saving exit from Kuwait. "We don't buy this idea . . . that you've got to find a way to give Saddam a face-saving way out for his aggression," he said. "We think that's totally unprincipled."[82] Whether Baker believed that was the best strategy is unclear. He, too, like Powell, deferred to the White House steamroller.

The day after his congressional testimony, Baker was in Jidda, where he obtained a commitment from King Fahd to use Saudi Arabia's windfall oil profits to help defray the costs of Desert Shield. No dollar amount was set, but American sources placed the figure in the billions. The Saudis could afford that. The price of oil, which was as low as thirteen dollars a barrel before the crisis began, had jumped above thirty-two dollars and was still rising. In addition, Saudi production was up 20 percent. Baker indicated that he thought Fahd's commitment, combined with similar contributions from the smaller Gulf states, Germany, and Japan, would cover most of the estimated $11 billion in additional expenses the United States would incur. Eleven billion dollars was a shockingly low estimate in early September, but the fact is, Bush, Baker, and Brady were on the ground running to raise money virtually from the beginning of the crisis. And the Saudis, who were becoming increasingly sophisticated about U.S. public opinion, recognized that it was essential to be forthcoming to maintain American support.

The following day, Baker met with the exiled emir, Sheik Jabir al-Ahmed al-Sabah, in the presidential suite of the Sheraton hotel in Taif, Saudi Arabia—home away from home for the emir. Sheik Jabir agreed to provide $5 billion immediately and "whatever is necessary" to bankroll the American effort. Receiving reporters with Baker at his side, the emir said, "As a person whose country has been aggressed against, I hope that the issue will end as soon as possible, no matter what it means."[83] Already, the Kuwaitis had retained the top-drawer public relations firm of Hill & Knowlton to polish their image in the United States. Henceforth, whenever a Kuwaiti went before the media, a Hill & Knowlton executive was at his side. That was an inordinate help to the country's leadership, which was, at best, languid and lethargic in dealing with the public.

Emboldened by the fast-growing American presence in the desert, both the Saudis and the Kuwaitis became increasingly bellicose about Saddam. Fahd had become convinced that if sanctions did not force Iraq to relinquish Kuwait, "force, of course, will have to be used."[84] In fact, as early as the beginning of September, Saudi Arabia's intelligence service was remarkably prescient as to the shape of things to come. They said Iraq's army was not what it appeared, that its effective strength was more like 300,000, not one million. They also claimed that its air force had only 120 top-of-the-line MiG-29s and Mirage fighters, and that the remainder were not worth much. The Saudis said that Saddam's command centers, communications, air bases, and antiaircraft emplacements could be knocked out quickly by allied bombing and sea-launched cruise missiles. Once the skies over the desert had been cleared, Saudi military specialists said, the Iraqi tanks could be systematically destroyed by U.S. aircraft. That would open the way for allied tanks and infantry to clear out Kuwait, driving Saddam's forces back into Iraq or isolating them.

"They will panic," one Saudi official said. "Without communications, how will they know what to do?"[85]

That early Saudi estimate proved to be remarkably accurate. Was it widely shared? Was the American intelligence community privy to the same data? Did Central Command, the Pentagon, and the White House know in September of the weakness of the Iraqi position? Or was it merely wishful thinking on the part of the Saudis?

Regardless of the answers to these questions, the fact is that in early September, the administration was not buying the need for offensive operations, and still believed that the combination of sanctions plus a well-orchestrated buildup of allied forces would convince Saddam to back down. France and Britain were equally leery of attacking Iraq. On September 6, President Mitterrand said that French troops would be sent into battle only in the event of further Iraqi aggression. He ruled out their participation in any offensive strike, saying that French involvement would be guided strictly by Security Council resolutions.[86] In effect, a curious juxtaposition had taken place. The Arab states, initially trembling before Saddam, now called for his destruction while the Western powers, bent on halting Iraq's aggression, stressed the need to do so without further bloodshed.

It was in that context that Bush and Gorbachev arrived in Helsinki on September 8 for their meeting the following day. Bush was upbeat. He told reporters that he hoped the talks would "strengthen our common approach" against Saddam. "If the nations of the world act together . . . to deny Saddam the fruits of aggression, we will set in place the cornerstone of an international order more peaceful, stable, and secure than any we have known."[87]

Gorbachev, more subdued, said the talks were occurring at a "crucial moment in history when it is very important to compare our political approaches and to cooperate in order to protect the positive trends evolving in the world today."[88]

If Bush was determined to cement the alliance by meeting with Gorbachev, the Soviet leader's attendance in Helsinki was even more remarkable. Since shortly after World War II, the United States and the Soviet Union had found themselves on opposite sides of most major conflicts in the Middle East, from the Arab-Israeli war of 1967 to Israel's invasion of Lebanon in 1981. And Baghdad had been the Russians' most loyal ally. The Soviets had first gained a foothold in Iraq in 1958 after the overthrow of the pro-Western monarchy by Arab nationalists. That tie intensified when the Baath took over in 1968, and became especially tight when Saddam gained full power in 1979. If the traditional Soviet view of Third World conflict had prevailed, the Iraqi takeover of Kuwait might even had been interpreted as a victory for socialism against the "corrupt oil sheiks" and their American masters.

Instead of siding with Iraq, Gorbachev and Shevardnadze backed Bush from the beginning, sometimes against a rising tide of hard-line opposition in Moscow. Beset with a full range of domestic problems, Gorbachev sought to cement his ties to the West while at the same time nudging American policy toward moderation. When Soviet generals questioned the massive U.S. buildup in Saudi Arabia, they were quickly slapped down by Kremlin foreign-policy spokesman Gennadi Gerasimov, who said there was no connection between the military balance in Europe and American actions in the Gulf. By cutting off arms sales to Iraq, supporting U.N. trade sanctions, and approving the interdiction of Iraqi shipping by the U.S. Navy, Gorbachev was dismantling years of Soviet policy. It was a classic example of the flexibility of Great Power diplomacy as it had been practiced in the nineteenth century. Bush needed Gorbachev's support if Saddam was going to be faced down. But in many ways, with the Soviet Union unraveling, Gorbachev needed Bush even more. That made the meeting in Helsinki a timely necessity.

After seven hours together on Sunday, the two leaders issued an unprecedented joint declaration condemning Iraq. "Nothing short of a return to the pre–August 2 status of Kuwait can end Iraq's isolation," they said. "Nothing short of the complete implementation of the United Nations Security Council resolutions is acceptable." Bush and Gorbachev called for Iraq to pull out of Kuwait, restore its legitimate government, and free all hostages.[89] Bush did not bring Gorbachev around to support the possible use of force, but the communiqué made it clear that military means had not been ruled out.

Our preference is to resolve the crisis peacefully. . . . However, we are determined to see this aggression end, and if the current steps fail to end it, we are prepared to consider ad-

*ditional ones consistent with the UN Charter. We must
demonstrate beyond any doubt that aggression cannot and
will not pay.*[90]

If symbols are important, the meeting had been an overwhelming success. While Gorbachev continued to stress his
preference to find a peaceful solution to the crisis, the friendly
banter of the two leaders at a joint press conference in Helsinki's Finlandia Hall captured an unparalleled mood of superpower cooperation. In their private meetings, Gorbachev had
raised no objection to the American buildup in the Gulf except
to ask how long it would last. Bush, on his part, acknowledged
that the Soviet Union had an important role to play in the
Middle East. That was a major concession. It reversed four decades of United States policy in the region and came as an un-
welcome surprise to many in the American foreign-policy
establishment. But for the White House, it was a small price to
pay for Russian support.[91]

Meanwhile, Washington announced that Secretary Baker
would visit Damascus to discuss the Iraqi situation with Saddam's longtime antagonist, Hafez Assad. It was yet another
move by Bush to increase the pressure in Iraq, another stark
display of American realpolitik. No high-level American official
had been to Syria in more than two years, and Assad's government remained on the State Department's list of countries that
sponsored international terrorism. Bush said simply that the
time had come for "face-to-face discussions." Once again,
Washington was jettisoning some long-held principles to cement the alliance against Saddam—another reflection of the
extent to which a forceful chief executive can dictate American
policy. "It is very important," Bush said, "that we cooperate
with a major Arab country who happens to share the same goals
that we do. That does not mean that . . . we won't continue
to have some differences. But on this very, very important issue
of what happens to reverse Iraq's unprovoked aggression, we
share the same goals."[92] In fact, President Bush had already

spoken with Assad three times over the telephone since the crisis began, and the two had exchanged a number of written messages. Not by accident, the Saudis announced at the same time that they were providing an unspecified amount of financial assistance to Damascus to compensate the Syrians for the cutoff of their trade with Iraq.[93] They would shortly do the same for the Soviet Union.

Bush's overture to Assad was understandable only in the context of the confrontation with Saddam. In many respects, Assad and Saddam were interchangeable parts: This year's Hitler was last year's ally, and vice versa. Assad, certainly, had not been Washington's friend in the past. From 1982 to 1984, the United States had sought unsuccessfully to prevent Assad from exploiting the bitter civil war in Lebanon to assert Syrian hegemony over that country. Ironically, part of Secretary of State George Shultz's strategy at that time had been to draw a contrast between the extremism of Assad's Syria and the reasonableness of Saddam's Iraq—which the United States said was abandoning terrorism and embracing moderation. In fact, one of Shultz's first acts after working out a peace agreement between Israel and Lebanon in 1983 was to meet in Paris with Tariq Aziz and urge him to praise the Lebanon accord publicly as an important step toward peace in the region.[94]

From Syria, Baker went to Bonn, where he spent the day closeted with Chancellor Kohl and Foreign Minister Hans-Dietrich Genscher. Germany, like Japan, was heavily dependent upon oil from the Gulf, and so far had been laggard in providing support for the U.S. effort. After the invasion on August 2, Kohl had moved swiftly to freeze Kuwaiti assets and had blocked German trade with Iraq. But his offers of financial support appeared small and grudging (the enormous costs of unification—which Kohl had grossly underestimated—claimed priority), and the German constitution, written during the Occupation period, barred troop service outside the NATO area. There was also a feeling that if the United States wanted Germany to pay, Bonn should have been consulted beforehand.

Moreover, Kohl's coalition partner, the Free Democrats (FDP), were exceedingly nervous about too close an alignment with the United States. Of all German political parties, the FDP had long sought to serve as a bridge between East and West. Their increasingly neutralist position served as an additional restraint on Kohl. The opposition Social Democrats and the Greens, who were congenitally anti-American, were outright critical of Bush's efforts in the Gulf.

But Kohl did his best. After meeting with Baker, he announced that Germany would provide $4 billion in Gulf aid, half to defray American troop costs and half to aid Egypt, Syria, and Turkey, all three of which had suffered economically because of the sanctions. Kohl, who was firmly behind Bush, lamented that "we are not fully assuming our responsibility in the Persian Gulf. Let me say very frankly that I am dismayed we are not completely free to act in the community of nations in a way we would like to act."[95] Kohl announced that he would seek to amend Germany's constitution to permit military support for U.N.-sponsored actions, but his offer stood little hope of early success. Given Germany's past experience, whether such an amendment was desirable is not self-evident.

Of all the members of the coalition, the German connection was the most difficult for Bush. As a result of America's staunch support of the chancellor during unification discussions with Moscow the year before, Bush and Baker enjoyed enormous credibility in Bonn. In addition, the German government was compromised for having closed its eyes to the support rendered by German companies to Saddam's chemical and nuclear weapons industry. Despite that, the German public was deeply troubled by the use of military force, and it was not solely because of the lingering memory of World War II. American involvement in Vietnam had been deeply divisive in Germany. Pacifism ran high in many circles, and the end of the Cold War had convinced most Germans that the military should be scaled back drastically.

Polls showed that the public supported the U.N. action in

the Gulf but wanted Germany to stay out. When asked about a model for a united Germany, respondents overwhelmingly chose Switzerland. The fact that Kohl's political opponents sought to capitalize on those sentiments restricted the chancellor's freedom of action. Above all, it was the enormous problem of unification that confronted Bonn. The Persian Gulf seemed to be an unnecessary diversion. Kohl did his utmost to support Bush, but unlike Thatcher and Mitterrand, he could not devote his primary attention nor invest all of his political capital on the situation in Kuwait. Ultimately, Germany would contribute $11 billion to the allied effort. But the political costs to Kohl would be high. From an approval rating of 74 percent in the summer of 1990 when the crisis began, the chancellor would drop to 37 percent by the time hostilities in the Gulf ended in 1991.[96]

Japan was an equally hard nut for Bush to crack. Again, despite the close personal relationship between the president and Premier Kaifu, the Japanese, like the Germans, hung back from the use of military force. The fact is, these two great economic powers still were traumatized by World War II, and both sought to tread softly. Germany and Japan desperately wanted acceptance by the international community, and the governments of both countries attempted to do their share. But they were firmly constrained, not only by their constitutions, but by overwhelming public sentiment against foreign military undertakings. The Japanese government initially pledged $1 billion to support allied efforts, raised that to $4 billion in September, and ultimately would contribute $14 billion to the cause. Like Germany, no Japanese forces joined the undertaking, and even Kaifu's efforts to provide medical and transportation personnel ran aground on the shoals of domestic protest.

Bush's efforts to deal with Germany and Japan reveal the limitations of the president's personal diplomacy. Both countries are parliamentary democracies, with strong cabinets and active opposition parties. Bush dealt with Kohl and Kaifu. But unlike Thatcher and Canada's Mulroney, neither Kohl nor Kaifu could guarantee where their cabinets stood, much less the outcome in parliament. Bush built his coalition with heads of government, but few leaders of parliamentary democracies enjoyed the same constitutional freeplay as did those who headed presidential systems, such as Mitterrand, or the outright authoritarian regimes of the Middle East.

Admittedly, Germany and Japan were the exceptions. For the most part, Bush's coalition became stronger as the crisis evolved. And as is often the case, it was Saddam who proved to be his own worst enemy. On September 14, in clear violation of the standards of diplomatic comity, Iraqi troops in Kuwait City entered the French diplomatic compound, as well as those of three other Western nations. The French military attaché was briefly detained. For France, which of all the Western powers had sought to remain on speaking terms with Iraq, Saddam's move was the last straw. Mitterrand responded by sending four thousand additional ground troops to Desert Shield and warned Baghdad that conflict might be inevitable. With the five permanent members in complete agreement that Iraq had gone too far, the Security Council voted 15–0, with no abstentions, to tighten the trade embargo and to threaten unspecified "additional measures" if Saddam did not withdraw from Kuwait. In particular, France urged that all air traffic into Iraq be blocked, even if it meant forcing planes to land or be shot down. Mitterrand's vigorous response was in keeping with the long tradition of French involvement in the Third World. Bush offered immediate support. "I don't know what France is going to do," he told reporters aboard Air Force One, "but I told [President Mitterrand] I would do anything I could to support whatever he decides to do."

Q: Mr. President . . . is there an escalation
                now required from you and your allies?

Bush: When an escalation is required from us,
                Saddam Hussein will know it.[97]

With the international coalition against Iraq coming together, thanks to Saddam, Bush turned his attention to Congress and American public opinion. Addressing a nationally televised joint session of the House and Senate on September 11, the president reiterated the goals he had announced on August 8: the unconditional withdrawal of Iraqi forces from Kuwait; the restoration of the Kuwaiti government; the stability of the Persian Gulf region; and the protection of U.S. citizens in the area. Bush did not mention military action to liberate Kuwait, but he warned once again that "we will not let this aggression stand." The president said he was reviewing all options. "Iraq will not be permitted to annex Kuwait. And that's not a threat. It's not a boast. That's just the way it's going to be."[98]

The president's September speech marked a decisive transition in American policy. For the first time, Bush made no reference to the defense of Saudi Arabia. Instead, he focused exclusively on what he referred to as Saddam's illegal occupation of Kuwait. A new phase of the crisis had begun. When asked by the press whether he would commit the United States not to strike the first blow in a shooting war, Bush said, "I'm not making any commitments."[99] According to the president, "If we do not continue to demonstrate our determination . . . to stand up to aggression . . . it would be a signal to actual or potential despots around the world."[100]

Bush held tenaciously to that view. He repeated the message one week later to the people of Iraq when invited by Saddam to appear on Iraqi TV. Saddam's invitation was another curious episode that defied explanation. Nevertheless, Bush's eight-minute address, which aired on September 16, firmly restated his determination that Iraq must withdraw from Kuwait or face the prospect of military defeat.

No one—not the American people, not this President—wants war. But there are times when a country, when all countries

who value the principles of sovereignty and independence
must stand against aggression. As Americans, we're slow to
raise our hand in anger and eager to explore every peaceful
means of settling our disputes. But when we have exhausted
every alternative, when conflict is thrust upon us, there is
no nation on Earth with greater resolve or stronger steadiness
of purpose.[101]

Henry M. Stimson could not have said it better. Bush's
remarks went to the core of what it meant to be an American—
or at least, what it had meant to generations of Americans
before the sad experience in Vietnam. In that sense, Bush's
one-dimensional policy was less of an outgrowth of the Cold
War than a throwback to the days of Manifest Destiny, the
frontier ethic, and the leadership of Theodore Roosevelt and
Woodrow Wilson.

And by mid-September, Bush's patience was wearing thin.
On Friday, September 21, the president met with key members
of Congress for a long and sober discussion about the situation.
Administration analysts were beginning to warn that trade
sanctions would have little impact on Iraq for at least six
months. In addition, the intelligence reports flowing into
Washington indicated that Saddam's resolve to stay in Kuwait
showed no sign of flagging.[102] Outside experts such as Henry
Kissinger were warning publicly that the stalemate could not
be continued for long. Writing in the *Washington Post*, Kissinger suggested that the economic and political pressures on the
allies were simply too great. He urged that military action be
taken quickly, otherwise "the entire enterprise might begin to
unravel."[103] Since both Scowcroft and Under Secretary of State
Lawrence Eagleburger had worked for Kissinger's consulting firm
before joining the Bush administration, and since both may
have wished to return there, the former secretary of state was
scarcely a voice crying in the wilderness. His opinions were
listened to, and they had a marked effect on administration

policy, as did such hawkish opinion makers as *New York Times* columnist William Safire and the *Washington Post's* former Baghdad correspondent, Jim Hoagland.[104]

According to members of Congress present at the meeting with Bush, the president laid out any number of events that could trigger a war—aside from the unlikely prospect of an Iraqi invasion of Saudi Arabia. House Armed Services Committee Chairman Les Aspin said Bush gave them the clear sense that the administration was "looking more favorably on an early war option." Among other things, Aspin mentioned the annual pilgrimage of millions of Moslems to Mecca in June, and the growing concerns about how long American forces could remain in the desert without "losing their edge." By deploying so large a force so quickly, the administration made its use almost inevitable unless Saddam backed down, said Aspin.[105]

Senator William Cohen of Maine, vice chairman of the Senate Select Committee on Intelligence, another of the participants, pointed to the possible erosion of domestic support as an additional factor driving policy. "There is a kind of loose consensus now," said Cohen. "But you can start to see it fray at the edges. The longer this goes on, the more doubts that are going to be expressed: Is this really blood for oil? You mean we don't have a democracy in Kuwait? How about free elections? And what about Saudi Arabia?"[106]

On their way out of the White House, one senator turned to several colleagues and asked, "Is this the briefing that's pointed to later as the one where they said 'We told the congressional leaders there's going to be shooting'?" His colleagues agreed that it was.[107]

Shortly after the congressional briefing, Bush hosted the exiled emir, Sheik Jabir al-Sabah, at the White House. The PR firm of Hill & Knowlton was leaving no stone unturned in its effort to win support for the Kuwaitis. Media coverage of the emir's visit was exhaustive. The president, who needed no convincing, used the occasion to highlight Iraq's pillage of Kuwait. Saddam's efforts "will fail," Bush said. "Kuwait, free Kuwait, will endure. . . . America's resolve to end this aggression remains firm and undiminished."[108]

Scowcroft told the press afterward that "there is no question that what happens in Kuwait affects the timetable" of the administration. The emir had not asked Bush to strike militarily to regain Kuwait, he said, but "you can subliminally read between the lines if you wish."[109] Scowcroft's remarks, added to those of the congressmen, were part of the White House campaign to convince public opinion that military action might be inevitable. "The plundering of Kuwait" was yet another factor that reduced "the time we have to allow sanctions to work," said one congressional leader after the emir's visit.[110]

To present a united front to Saddam, both the House and the Senate quickly passed resolutions in late September supporting the president's actions thus far. The measures did not endorse the use of force, but expressed support for "continued action by the president . . . to deter Iraqi aggression and to protect American lives and vital interests."[111]

Throughout the autumn of 1990, conventional wisdom suggested that George Bush was at his weakest when attempting to explain his policy domestically. But that judgment was rendered too hastily. Beginning from a standing start, with American public attention focused anywhere but on the Persian Gulf, Bush and his spokesmen adroitly brought it along, step-by-step, to support not only military intervention to defend Saudi Arabia but, when all else failed, the launching of the most massive assault since World War II to drive Iraqi forces from Kuwait. By any standard, it was a superlative performance.

Initially, the president explained his policy solely in terms of defending Saudi Arabia. That was a ruse. It won overwhelming support, but at bottom it was not true. From the beginning, Bush's policy was to punish Saddam's aggression and to liberate Kuwait. Would the American public have accepted that in the beginning of August? Given their almost total lack of knowledge concerning Saddam and Kuwait, it is unlikely. It must also be noted that throughout the crisis the administration was improvising. American tactics reflected less of a preconceived game plan than the grappling with changing events on a day-to-day basis. The White House exhibited enormous flexibility. That was one of Bush's hallmarks. And after the first wobbly twenty-four hours, the various zigs and zags that sometimes left observers gasping were motivated by a single purpose that was fiercely held by the president: Iraq must withdraw from Kuwait.

That was a hard case to make in August and September. The public wasn't ready for it and neither was Congress. And Bush didn't push. The president had articulated the four-fold purpose of American policy in his address to the nation on August 8. But there was no indication that the use of military force would be necessary to achieve those objectives, and it is doubtful that the White House assumed that it would.

Bush's success is reflected in the public-opinion polls taken throughout the crisis. If he did a poor job of convincing the public, the polls don't show it. Before the invasion of Kuwait, Bush's popularity hovered in the 55 percent range. By mid-August, it had soared to 76 percent. Not since John Kennedy's showdown with the Soviets during the 1962 Cuban Missile Crisis had a president scored higher.[112] More to the point, the percentage of those surveyed who favored invading Iraq rose even more precipitously as Bush gradually, almost by sleight of hand, made his case. On August 8, only 38 percent of those interviewed in a *Washington Post*–ABC News poll said they were in favor of such a move. By September 9, the figure had risen to 48 percent, and by January, more than two-thirds of the respondents voted yes.[113]

Throughout the crisis, Bush's diplomacy was superb. Despite abundant evidence in early August that Saddam was poised to attack, the Iraqi invasion of Kuwait had caught the world by surprise. After meeting with Thatcher in Aspen, the president had reversed American policy, made ready to intervene militarily, and begun a marathon effort to enlist international support. Not since World War II has such a disparate allied coalition been stitched together, and never in history had it been done so quickly. On all counts, Bush could take personal credit.

Unlike Jimmy Carter, who dwelt on detail, or Ronald Reagan, whose loose management style allowed others to act in his name, George Bush stayed on top of the crisis, dealing with the major issues and delegating broadly to his subordinates. American policy was his policy, and it was he who provided the overall direction. In the president's words, "When you get a problem with the complexities that the Middle East has now, and the Gulf has now, I enjoy trying to put the coalition together and keep it together. I can't say that I just rejoice every time I go up [to Capitol Hill] and talk to my good friend [House Ways and Means Committee Chairman Dan] Rostenkowski about what he's going to do on taxes."[114]

It is difficult to overstate Bush's involvement in the crisis or his effectiveness in working with other heads of government. It was not simply that the cause was just. There are many just causes that fail for lack of interest, insufficient commitment, or inadequate resources. Bush reached out to world leaders. His easy informality forged a bond among those at the heights of power—where friendships are difficult and suspicion runs rampant. Thatcher, Mitterrand, and Gorbachev became active coworkers in a striking realignment of world power. Fahd, Mubarak, and Ozal willingly acquiesced to Washington's hegemony in a region hitherto off-limits to American power. Later, when the stakes became clear, Syria's Assad joined the team as a witting accomplice. Only King Hussein of Jordan remained odd-man-out. If Bush's hyperbolic comparison of Saddam with Hitler had any legitimacy, it was in the breadth of the alliance that had been forged against him.

The president's adroit direction of American policy was equally compelling. His foreign-policy team can be faulted for inadequately considering the impact of American intervention on the region, and for underestimating the destructive consequences of Desert Storm, but certainly not for the efficiency with which the president's policy was executed. That policy may prove to be flawed. But it was carried out with a vigor and a singleness of purpose not seen in Washington since the wartime days of FDR and Mr. Stimson.

Like Stimson and Roosevelt, Bush accepted the necessity of war as a means to punish aggression.[115] And like both, he regarded the president as primarily responsible for directing American policy. George Bush's view of the president's preeminent role in foreign affairs traced not only to Stimson and Roosevelt, but to his own experience in government. That view reverberated through Iran-contra.[116] In January 1987, addressing the conservative Federalist Society in Washington, Bush, as vice president, urged Congress and the judiciary not to interfere with the president's conduct of foreign policy. Bush claimed that the framers of the Constitution intended that the president play the paramount role.[117] "John Marshall spoke of the President as 'the sole organ of the nation in its external relations, and its sole representative with foreign nations,' " said Bush.[118] Although Marshall was alluding merely to President Adams's authority to *speak* for the nation,[119] Bush interpreted Marshall's words to mean that the president was primarily responsible for formulating foreign policy as well.

That view of presidential power has enjoyed wide acceptance. The Supreme Court decision that is often cited in support is the celebrated case of *United States v. Curtiss-Wright* in 1936.[120] The *Curtiss-Wright* case, as Saddam might have said, is the mother of all foreign-policy litigation. Speaking for a virtually unanimous Court, Justice George Sutherland, the great conservative jurist, restated John Marshall's dictum in sweeping fashion when he spoke of *"the very delicate, plenary and exclusive power of the President* as the sole organ of the federal government in the field of international relations."[121] Sutherland apparently meant to endow the president with more than simply the power to speak for the nation,[122] and most presidents since the *Curtiss-Wright* decision have so interpreted it.

The issue in *Curtiss-Wright* would seem to provide an unlikely vehicle for presidential aggrandizement. In the early

1930s, a minor war broke out between Bolivia and Paraguay contesting ownership of the headlands of the Chaco River. To contain the fighting, Congress passed a joint resolution authorizing President Roosevelt to impose an embargo on arms shipments to both countries if, in his judgment, it would help restore peace. The day after the joint resolution was passed, FDR imposed a sweeping ban on all arms sales to the belligerents. The Curtiss-Wright company violated that embargo by conspiring to ship fifteen machine guns to Bolivia. When they were indicted in Federal court, Curtiss-Wright argued that Congress had delegated excessive power to the president: that it had set no standards to guide his action, in effect, allowing him to act as he chose. The trial court agreed and dismissed the indictment. The government appealed that decision to the Supreme Court.

The *Curtiss-Wright* case has to be seen in the context of the 1930s. The Supreme Court, with Sutherland often in the lead, was in the process of striking down much of the New Deal's economic program based on an old common-law theory that governmental powers, once delegated, could not be delegated further (*delegata potestas non potest delegari*). The Constitution had delegated legislative powers to Congress; the Congress, therefore, could not redelegate those powers to the president. Much of the New Deal's economic legislation delegated broad discretion to the president to act as he deemed necessary, and it failed the Court's test. Sutherland himself had just written a powerful decision for the Court striking down the Guffey Coal Act on precisely those grounds.[123]

The issue in *Curtiss-Wright* was whether Congress could delegate broad discretionary authority to the president in the field of foreign affairs. There was no conflict between the president and Congress, and Roosevelt was not undertaking any independent initiatives. He was acting pursuant to the powers Congress had delegated to him.

The trial judge, in dismissing the indictment, believed that the delegation of powers in *Curtiss-Wright* was similar to that in the other cases that the Court had struck down. If the president's embargo was to be sustained, Sutherland had to explain why foreign affairs were different, and why it was permissible for Congress to delegate broad authority to the president in that area if it could not do so in domestic matters.

The distinction between the domestic power of the national government and its authority in foreign affairs had long been recognized.[124] According to the Supreme Court, the domestic powers were carved from those that the States had previously enjoyed, and were strictly enumerated by the framers of the Constitution. But the foreign-relations powers were inherent. To some extent they existed outside the constitutional framework. The argument ran as follows:

- The United States came into existence when it declared independence from Great Britain on July 4, 1776.
- Accordingly, the United States existed *before* the Constitution, which was adopted in 1789.
- As an independent nation, during the period from 1776 to 1789, the United States enjoyed full sovereignty. It could wage war, make treaties, and conduct foreign relations.
- Consequently, the power of the United States to act in foreign affairs existed prior to the Constitution. It did not depend on any affirmative grant contained in that document.

In *Curtiss-Wright*, Sutherland drew on that traditional distinction to hold that while the domestic powers of the national government are enumerated in the Constitution and therefore limited by it, the foreign-relations powers, being outside that document, are not limited by it. Breathtaking as it may appear, that aspect of the holding was not exceptional. It simply restated the traditional view of the nation's international sovereignty. The difficulty is that Sutherland went far beyond that to expand the power of the president as the "sole organ" of the national government in foreign affairs. As expressed by Sutherland:

> Not only . . . is the Federal power over external affairs in origin and essential character different from that over internal affairs, but participation in the exercise of the power is significantly limited. In this vast external realm, with its important, complicated, delicate and manifold problems, the President alone has the power to speak or listen as a representative of the nation. He makes treaties with the advice and consent of the Senate, but he alone negotiates. [Sutherland's emphasis.] Into the field of negotiation the Senate cannot intrude, and Congress itself is powerless to invade it. . . .

When lifted from its context, Sutherland's disquisition on presidential authority appears to give the White House a blank check in foreign affairs. But Sutherland's broad language was merely dictum. It was gratuitous and unnecessary because in *Curtiss-Wright* President Roosevelt was acting pursuant to explicit congressional authorization. Over the years, the issue in *Curtiss-Wright* has faded, and Sutherland's dicta has been remembered.

Many legal scholars have questioned Sutherland's reasoning.[125] Almost all have rejected its application to circumstances dissimilar to those in *Curtiss-Wright*.[126] Congress itself is on record that the holding pertains exclusively to situations in which the president acts under congressional authorization. The final report of the Iran-contra committees in 1987 specifically rejected claims by the Reagan administration that *Curtiss-Wright* gave the president the authority to act unilaterally.[127]

Subsequent Supreme Court decisions have been equally chary of applying Sutherland's language to dissimilar situations. In the famous steel seizure case during the Korean war, Justice Jackson argued that *Curtiss-Wright* should not be interpreted too broadly.[128] In *Dames & Moore v. Regan*, the Iranian assets case, Justice Rehnquist (who had been Jackson's law clerk) cautioned against taking Sutherland's words out of context.[129] The United States Court of Appeals for the District of Columbia circuit, often regarded as the nation's second most influential court, has been much more explicit in limiting the scope of *Curtiss-Wright*. "To the extent that denominating the President as the 'sole organ' of the United States in international affairs constitutes a blanket endorsement of plenary Presidential power over any matter extending beyond the borders of this country, we reject that characterization."[130]

The *Curtiss-Wright* case remains a crucial decision in foreign affairs. It holds that the national government is endowed with sovereign powers in its dealings with foreign countries. The government cannot do what the laws or the Constitution forbid, but short of that it is free to proceed as it deems necessary. The decision holds explicitly that Congress may grant extensive discretionary powers to the president to meet contingencies abroad. But it does not hold, despite Sutherland's broad language, that the president is free to set the nation's course as he chooses.

5.

DESERT SHIELD

I can tell you this: If I'm ever in a position
to call the shots, I'm not going to rush to
send somebody else's kids into a war.
George Bush
Man of Integrity (1988)

Throughout the autumn the Bush administration followed a
policy of minimum candor. When the allies became restive,
Baker hinted of compromise. When public opinion seemed to
waver, administration spokesmen embellished tales of Iraqi
atrocities. When it appeared that Washington was moving too
fast toward a military showdown, Bush adroitly deflected the
criticism by suggesting alternative ways out of the crisis. But
the president's rhetoric was a tactical smoke screen. At bottom,
administration policy had not changed. If anything, the White
House was more resolute. Iraq must not only withdraw from
Kuwait, but its military threat to the region must be lessened.
That represented another unilateral escalation of American
goals in the Gulf. Congress had not been consulted. The State

Department, as usual, had been ignored. The military had not been asked for its opinion. Given Saddam's grim determination, the president's decision made war virtually inevitable.

On October 1, in response to growing international concern, President Bush momentarily stepped aside from the tough tone the White House had adopted and appeared to offer Saddam a face-saving way out. Speaking to the U.N. General Assembly, Bush said he was hopeful that a diplomatic solution to the crisis could be found. Repeating his vow that Iraq's annexation of Kuwait "will not stand," the president went on to say that after an unconditional Iraqi withdrawal, "I truly believe there may be opportunities for Iraq and Kuwait to settle their differences permanently; for the states of the Gulf themselves to build new arrangements for stability; and for all the states and peoples of the region to settle the conflicts that divide the Arabs from Israel."[1]

It was one more of George Bush's tactical masterstrokes. By offering Saddam a seeming opportunity to negotiate, Bush placed the onus for war on Iraq. The president's move was intended to calm fears that Washington was pressing for a military solution. By referring to the conflict with Israel, it also provided assistance to those Arab states aligned with the United States in their battle with Saddam for popular support. President Mitterrand had made much the same offer at the U.N. the week before,[2] but for George Bush and the United States, the suggestion marked a new departure.

Administration spokesmen moved quickly to stiffen the president's remarks. A public relations overture to compromise had been made, but in reality Washington was uninterested. Despite the president's statement, spokesmen were quick to point out that there was no "linkage" between Iraq's withdrawal from Kuwait and the settlement of the Arab-Israeli dispute. Bush "was speaking to the United Nations," said a senior State Department official. "So he emphasized a peaceful solution. But he in no way backtracked from U.S. demands that Iraq must withdraw unconditionally from Kuwait, restore the legitimate government there, and release all the foreign nationals it is holding hostage."[3] Seasoned observers saw through Bush's gambit. The press reported that despite the president's speech, the mood at the United Nations was haunted by "an inexorable movement toward war in the Persian Gulf."[4]

Two days later Saddam responded with typical heavy-handedness. Whether Bush's offer was genuine or not, a more adroit politician in Baghdad might have taken him up. That would have caused difficulties for Washington. Instead, Saddam scorned the overture. While visiting Iraqi troops in Kuwait, Saddam, whose remarks were rebroadcast nationwide over Iraqi TV, said, "There will be no compromise. Iraq will never give up one inch of this land now called Province Number 19."[5]

Bush did not follow up his U.N. offer. Instead, he directed his attention to shoring up the alliance against Saddam, and ironically, the Soviets appeared to be among the president's staunchest supporters. On October 3, Yevgeny Primakov, Gorbachev's diplomatic troubleshooter, stated in Moscow that "very much depends on Soviet-American solidarity, on parallel activity, on mutual support." Using words closely akin to those Brent Scowcroft might have chosen, Primakov said that the situation in the Gulf provided "a unique laboratory where we are testing our efforts to create a new world order after the end of the Cold War."[6]

Even Syria's Hafez Assad emerged as a key player on Bush's team. A dubious ally at best, Assad journeyed to Tehran to neutralize anti-American rhetoric emanating from the Ayatollah Khomeini's successors. Before Assad's visit, Tehran had declared a "holy war" against American forces in the Gulf. Assad convinced the Iranians to recast the call to holy war as something to be undertaken only if the United States stayed on in the region. As a result, Iran moved nearer to the allied position. In fact, Assad was reported to see no alternative but war, and thought it should come sooner rather than later.[7]

If the Russians and the Syrians were cooperating, the French, true to form, were going their own way. Mitterrand's spokesmen confirmed that while France was "prepared to fight for the restored sovereignty of an occupied country," it was not ready to go to war on behalf of the al-Sabah dynasty.[8]

At the same time, Iraq's deputy prime minister, Taha Yassin Ramadan, attempted to put the responsibility for war back on Bush's shoulders. "We have decided," said Ramadan, "not to fire the first shot. If others do, they will not be able to estimate the end nor the scope of the battle and they will lose, God willing."[9] In typical Middle East fashion, Saddam was still working both sides of the street. Nevertheless, when asked by reporters, White House spokesmen pointedly declined to make a similar commitment not to fire the first shot. War was not ruled out. If Baghdad was floating a trial balloon, Washington rejected it.

Given the drift of administration policy, Bush now came under increasing pressure from members of Congress for greater consultation. The fear of conflict had become real. In keeping with past practice, congressional concern was effectively ignored by the White House. Foreign policy, in the view of Bush's men, was the president's prerogative. A meddlesome Congress was a pernicious influence. Dick Cheney flippantly dismissed the concerns of his former colleagues. "Some members want consultation more than others," he said. "As a former member, I have to say it was an advantage that Congress was out of town" when the initial deployment to the Gulf took place.[10]

As the buildup continued, the Senate, in particular, became increasingly restive. With the 1990 session coming to a close and the members returning home to face reelection, Sam Nunn suggested establishing a bipartisan leadership group to consult "on a regular basis" with Bush. That would provide for legislative input while Congress was adjourned. Senator Mark Hatfield of Oregon, one of three senators who had voted against the resolution of support for U.S. policy in the Gulf,* intro-

---

*Senators Kerrey of Nebraska and Kennedy of Massachusetts also voted against the resolution.

duced legislation that would require the president to invoke the War Powers Resolution or seek specific congressional approval before sending U.S. troops into combat.[11] No action was taken on Hatfield's proposal, but the debate was sharp and unpleasant from the president's point of view. The bipartisan coalition that traditionally supports presidential initiatives in foreign policy seemed to be collapsing. Even worse, Saddam drew encouragement from the Senate debate, or so the White House suggested.

To complicate matters further, just as the Senate became restive, seven mainline Protestant church leaders, including the presiding bishop of President Bush's Episcopal faith, urged the White House to rule out the use of force in the Gulf. "I beg that we do not fall into the trap of war as a means of solving the problem," said Bishop Edmund Browning.[12] The *Washington Post* reported that the timing of the statement from the church leaders "partly reflected reports that Bush is frustrated by the apparent Gulf stalemate and is giving greater consideration to unilateral U.S. military action."[13]

Those reports were well founded. By mid-October, it was clear that the United States and Iraq had reached an impasse. Bush continued to discuss the occupation of Kuwait as a case of "Hitler revisited" and pledged no compromise.[14] Saddam, clumsy as always, tried to have it both ways. Occasionally signaling moderation, the public line from Baghdad remained inflexible. Iraqi information minister Latif Nassif Jassim, speaking on Saddam's behalf, insisted that "there is no room for any compromise on Kuwait."[15] Renewed mediation efforts quickly fell apart as the rhetoric escalated. King Hussein of Jordan, King Hassan of Morocco, and President Chadli Bendjedid of Algeria undertook to find a solution that would restore an independent Kuwait but would also satisfy Saddam.[16] Yasir Arafat met with Saddam on Sunday, October 14, and then flew to Tunis to meet with French Foreign Minister Roland Dumas. They too were looking for a compromise. Soviet envoy Yevgeny Primakov met with Saddam for several days of talks, but also without success. Despite the multiple contacts, no solution appeared in sight. Saddam refused to budge from Kuwait until assured that Iraq would benefit from subsequent discussions, while Washington insisted on an unconditional Iraqi pullout before discussions could begin.

"We don't have a decision point," a senior White House official said on October 13. "The passage of time helps us in terms of sanctions. But it hurts us with the rape of Kuwait and other diversions. No one wants to rush to war. But we're not coming closer to our objectives, either."[17] Administration officials dismissed the renewed peace feelers from Baghdad as an attempt to sow discord among the allies and restrict Washington's room to maneuver. "By hinting he is ready to consider other options," said one official, Saddam "hopes to reduce the prospect that the United States . . . will use military force anytime soon."[18]

In analyzing the administration's attitude, *The New York Times* reverted to traditional Cold War categories of hawks and doves.[19] According to the *Times*, the head hawk was the president himself. The fact was, Bush had painted himself into a corner. The alliance was shaky. Domestic support, to judge from the criticism in Congress and the opposition of church leaders, was eroding rapidly. And the military situation in the desert was grim. The troops could not be kept there indefinitely. Already the Pentagon was talking about rotation. Worst of all, Saddam showed no sign of yielding. With presidential elections two years away, time was running out for George Bush.

Other hawks included National Security Adviser Scowcroft, Chief of Staff John Sununu, Vice President Quayle, and Defense Secretary Cheney. Scowcroft saw the crisis through the eyes of his longtime mentor, Henry Kissinger. A late-in-life doctoral candidate in political science,* Scowcroft had adopted the jargon of academia and an attachment to realpolitik as practiced by Metternich and Castlereagh. His view of the world

---

*Scowcroft was awarded a Ph.D. by Columbia in 1979 for a dissertation on Congress and foreign policy.

was laced with abstractions, most of which were coin of the realm for Washington's "defense intellectuals." Scowcroft's thinking rarely transcended the slogans that had become fashionable.[20] Like Bush, he looked on the use of force as an option that was always available to policymakers, and he deplored the tendency of the American military to shy away from potential hostilities. "Can the United States use force—even go to war—for carefully defined national interests, or do we have to have a moral crusade or a galvanizing event like Pearl Harbor?" he asked.[21] Scowcroft had been Bush's constant companion since the first day of the Iraqi invasion and was temperamentally reluctant to present the president with policy alternatives. The National Security Council, Scowcroft's bailiwick, seldom met in structured fashion, and outside advice—especially from regional experts—was rarely canvassed.[22]

John Sununu, the president's less-than-lovable chief of staff, reduced the issue to domestic politics. Little versed in foreign policy, Sununu uncharacteristically deferred to Scowcroft's judgment, content to stress the electoral advantages of a quick military campaign against Saddam. A victorious war, he told the press throughout the autumn, would make Bush unbeatable in 1992.[23] His was not a voice urging restraint.

Similarly with the chickenhawks, Quayle and Cheney. Both shared Sununu's political calculus, and Quayle, according to Elizabeth Drew, the experienced Washington correspondent for *The New Yorker*, was busily cultivating the Israeli lobby, hoping to remain on the GOP ticket in 1992.[24] Cheney, for his own political future, and perhaps also aiming at a slot on the 1992 ticket, saw no reason to oppose the president, and continually prodded the Pentagon to provide viable military options.[25]

In effect, the men closest to the president shared his assessment and resonated with his determination. The White House staff, the vice president and his staff, and the secretary of defense jumped on the war wagon early and were determined not to give Saddam a graceful way out. For the hawks, a surprise Iraqi withdrawal from Kuwait was the "nightmare scenario" they wrestled with that autumn, since it would leave Saddam's military might intact.[26] If Saddam pulled out voluntarily, Iraq would remain the dominant force in the region, and the threat to the Gulf states, and to Israel in particular, would be undiminished.

Not surprisingly, the Arab leaders who had joined Bush's coalition were equally insistent in clamoring for Saddam's scalp. Assad, Fahd, and Mubarak had gambled their futures on Iraq's defeat and scarcely contemplated a world in which Saddam might menace them. The belligerence of the Kuwaitis was taken for granted. So too was that of Thatcher's Britain, a relic of a bygone era, like the prime minister herself.[27]

Opposition to military action was centered among the professionals responsible for executing American foreign policy: the diplomats and the armed forces. Unlike the White House staff, which comes and goes with a president, the State Department and the Pentagon took a long view of the crisis. Presidential staffs are transitory. Their obligations are personal. By design as well as instinct they see issues through the president's eyes. Their very existence is defined in terms of effecting the president's will. Scarcely a brake on policy, they exert the thrust that drives a presidential decision forward.

By contrast, the State Department, cranky and cumbersome as it often is, provides indispensable expertise and continuity for American policy. Presidential concern lurches from crisis to crisis. The diplomatic machinery, staffed by career professionals, is ongoing. The problems of Latin America, Europe, and the Middle East transcend the four-year term of a president and form a permanent part of the international landscape with which the United States must deal. Individual presidents—Bush, Reagan, Carter—have their own ideas how those problems should be addressed. But presidents come and go. The problems usually remain.

Viewed cynically from Foggy Bottom, Iraq's invasion of Kuwait was but another in the long series of crises that had plagued the Middle East. Saddam's method of settling his border dispute

with the emir was high-handed, the subsequent looting of Kuwait regrettable, and his treatment of diplomats and foreign
nationals totally unacceptable. Nevertheless, a military struggle, even a brief one, would probably create more problems
than it would solve. Iraq's multinational population could easily
come unglued, and the resulting instability could pin American
forces down in the Middle East for a generation. Add to that
the ongoing problem of Moslem fundamentalism emanating
from Iran, the dubious nature of Assad's Baathist regime in
Syria, as well as the continuing obduracy of Kuwait's be-
nighted leadership, and the future, even with Saddam's defeat,
looked less than rosy. In fact, a negotiated settlement that would
secure Iraq's withdrawal, admittedly at Kuwait's expense, had
much to recommend it. Baghdad's secular, modernizing example would continue to provide an alternative to the feudal regimes of the Gulf; the Iraqi army would block any Iranian move
into the oil fields; an accord on arms levels was perhaps not
beyond reach, and it was just possible that the intractable Arab-
Israeli dispute might be tempered. Those had, after all, been
key ingredients in Bush's U.N. address, and to achieve them
without bloodshed seemed to be a desirable objective. Whether
economic sanctions would do the trick was open to doubt. Over
time, they might make Saddam more reasonable. Ultimately,
negotiations would have to be held, and Iraq's position would
have to be accommodated.

To the White House such talk smacked of appeasement.
But Secretary Baker was not unsympathetic. Baker did not share
Bush's avuncular determination to humiliate Saddam. Perhaps
because of the diplomatic brief he carried, he was prone to seek
a negotiated solution to the crisis. In fact, Baker was instinctively inclined to seek common ground with his opponents, and
he despaired of Bush's unwillingness to cut a deal.[28]

If Baker and the diplomats fretted, the military leadership
was genuinely appalled by the rapid escalation. Except for Colin
Powell, the joint chiefs of staff had been shut out from White
House decisions. They had not met with Bush since the crisis

began, and they worried that the United States was moving too quickly toward war. Army Chief of Staff Carl Vuono and Marine Commandant Alfred Gray, in particular, were concerned that American ground forces would be committed to combat before they were adequately prepared, or before they were deployed in sufficient strength to ensure success. Vuono and Gray were hard-bitten foot soldiers. They remembered the piecemeal escalation in Vietnam, and unlike Cheney and Quayle, both knew the meaning of war for those who had to fight it. They thought in terms of dead and wounded, not beltway clichés. Both urged caution in the councils of the Pentagon.[29]

As it turned out, it fell to the military, particularly generals Powell and Schwarzkopf, to brake the president's impetuosity. By law, Powell was the president's senior military adviser. The chain of command in the Gulf ran from Bush to Cheney to Powell to Schwarzkopf. Unlike the service chiefs, Powell saw Bush frequently. He was close to the president's inner circle. From the beginning of the crisis, Powell had urged that if American forces were to be deployed in Saudi Arabia, the deployment should be massive. If war came, said Powell, the United States should fight all-out. In his view, any Iraqi assault on Saudi Arabia should be met with devastating force. A protracted campaign should be avoided at all costs. Powell's thinking was defensive. He had not contemplated offensive action to oust Saddam from Kuwait, and he was wary of undertaking it.

Schwarzkopf shared Powell's sentiments. In his daily telephone conversations with Washington, he urged the chairman to speed up the deployment and warned against a premature order to attack. No one knew better than Schwarzkopf that his troops were unprepared to take on Saddam. He queried Powell as to whether the White House knew that, too.[30]

In effect, Schwarzkopf and Powell reinforced each other. Though Schwarzkopf was several years senior in the Regular Army, he had accepted Powell's promotion to chairman gracefully. He recognized that Powell had the political savvy that few military officers possess, and he welcomed having a fellow combat infantryman in charge at the Pentagon. Powell had been wounded in Vietnam, just as Schwarzkopf had been, and both shared the infantryman's skepticism of high command. It was their strong advice to the president that force not be used capriciously or incrementally that so far had prevailed. How long that would continue to be the case was problematic.

One of the noteworthy aspects of the Gulf crisis was that the United States was able to call routinely on the talents of a Powell and a Schwarzkopf. At the outbreak of World War II, Harry Hopkins mused frequently at the ability of the Army and Navy to endure the deprivation of the interwar years and yet produce such gifted commanders as Marshall, Eisenhower, and Nimitz. "Where were they all those years when the Army had been kicked around like a mangy old dog and the Navy had been used only for target practice?" asked Hopkins. The Vietnam war had a similar effect on the Army. Like the interwar deprivation, the tragedy of Vietnam forced the military to reexamine its values: to stress professional competence, discipline, and esprit. Turned against by much of American society, the Army found an inner strength and a sense of mission. There was a firm determination to avoid the mistakes of Vietnam, just as the Army of the 1920s and 30s determined not to repeat the trench warfare blunders of World War I. The Command and General Staff School at Leavenworth, the War College, the various service academies and branch schools all stressed the lessons of Vietnam: Force should not be applied incrementally. Combat is not a football scrimmage or a board game. "This is not Nintendo." If war was necessary, it should be fought all out and brought to a swift conclusion.

It takes nothing away from the deserved accolades that Powell and Schwarzkopf have received to note that both were typical of the post-Vietnam American officer corps. Powell earned his elevation to chairman through demonstrated competence and a long track record of political sensitivity. Schwarzkopf, more surprisingly perhaps, was simply the commander on the spot when the crisis erupted: a final posting before heading into retirement. Central Command, based in Tampa, was not the Army's prime billet for a four-star general. Unlike the NATO assignment in Europe, or the Far East, there were no troops to command. Staff work was largely a shadow exercise. Critics charged that Central Command was a phantom head-quarters and many had urged its abolition.

Yet when Saddam invaded, Schwarzkopf was not only ready, he had just prepared a battle plan for exactly such a contin-gency—a remarkable demonstration of professional initiative and the attention to detail so essential for military success. The Pentagon and the White House had the good sense to stick with Schwarzkopf. There was no effort to insert a hotshot com-mander from Europe or Washington—someone younger per-haps, and leaner. Instead, the Army went with the commander on the spot. Schwarzkopf, in turn, stuck with his own subor-dinates. Lieutenant General Charles Horner, who was Schwarz-kopf's air chief, and Gus Pagonis, his supply man, provided outstanding direction for a military campaign that has had few equals in American history.

Success did not come easily in the Gulf. Both Powell and Schwarzkopf wanted to stick with sanctions: to contain Saddam and gradually pressure him into signaling a withdrawal. In the beginning of October, Powell took his case to Cheney. To launch an attack while there was still a chance that sanctions might work seemed to be a mistake, said Powell.

Cheney wasn't convinced. "I don't think the president will buy it," he told Powell.[31] Bush, said Cheney, needed to win, and there was no guarantee that sanctions would force Saddam to pull out. "That would constitute policy failure; it would be unacceptable to the president."[32]

Bob Woodward, whose account has been uncontradicted, reports that Powell took his case to Baker. Woodward said:

The Secretary of State was Powell's chief ally in the upper ranks of the administration. They thought alike on many issues. Both men preferred dealmaking to confrontation or conflict. . . . Baker was very unhappy about the talk [emanating from the White House] of developing an offensive military option. He wanted diplomacy—meaning the State Department—to achieve the policy success.[33]

Baker told Powell that the State Department was preparing a report on the advantages of waiting for sanctions to work. When it was ready, that should force a discussion of alternatives by the National Security Council, he said.

For whatever reason, the State Department report never came forward, and a formal discussion of alternative strategies was never held. The National Security Council failed to function as it should have. Designed immediately after World War II, the NSC had been patterned on the British war cabinet. By bringing together, under the president's leadership, the secretary of state, the secretary of defense, the head of Central Intelligence, and the chairman of the joint chiefs of staff, the NSC was intended as the body to formulate American strategy. To some extent, the creation of the NSC was a reaction to the disaster at Pearl Harbor and the failure of the wartime Roosevelt administration to coordinate military and diplomatic strategy effectively. But even more, it was a reflection of the complexity of America's new role in world affairs. The military services, the State Department, and the intelligence community could no longer go their separate ways. Policy coordination was essential. The National Security Act of 1947 sought to accomplish that by providing a formal statutory setting where those responsible would meet regularly.

Various presidents have used the National Security Council differently. Truman and Eisenhower scrupulously adhered to the intent of the 1947 Act, utilizing the NSC as the forum where national policy was thrashed out. Both Acheson and Marshall under Truman, as well as Dulles and a succession of defense secretaries under Ike, met in the NSC and resolved their differences. Whatever staff the NSC acquired was designed exclusively to keep track of what the principals had decided. There was no operational capacity and no independent analysis. Responsibility for implementing NSC decisions remained with State, Defense, and the CIA. And it is fair to say that Acheson, Dulles, and Marshall insisted on that.

Under Kennedy and Johnson, the NSC came to be less of a forum of discussion among principals, and more of a in-house vehicle for the president's personal direction of foreign policy. Kennedy wanted to be his own secretary of state; Johnson insisted on minutely directing the war in Vietnam. The NSC staff was expanded to provide backup for the president. That trend continued under Nixon and Carter. A succession of high-powered national security advisers—Bundy, Kissinger, Brzezinski—often supplanted the secretary of state as the president's principal adviser in foreign affairs. Even more serious, the NSC staff became the operating arm of presidential policy: an end run around the State Department and the Pentagon. In some respects, it was a throwback to the free-wheeling days of the Roosevelt White House that the Act of 1947 had been designed to prevent. Only now, with a burgeoning NSC staff, the impact of spontaneous presidential direction was far more immediate.

Under the loose management style of Ronald Reagan, the NSC staff became not only the operating arm of presidential policy, but the formulator of that policy as well. George Shultz and Defense Secretary Caspar Weinberger were often excluded. The president's national security advisers, Bud McFarlane and John Poindexter, made policy; Oliver North and his minions executed it, and eventually the system went off the rails.

To Scowcroft's credit, he had restricted the operational bent of the NSC staff, but he had failed to restore its original function. The principals rarely met. A deputies committee chaired by Robert Gates handled the technical nitty-gritty of coordination, but systematic discussion among the statutory members of the NSC rarely occurred. When the principals did meet, Bush liked to keep the atmosphere jovial: jokes, camaraderie, the conviviality of old friends. Formality was eschewed. Interruptions were common. Such casualness would not have occurred under Truman or Eisenhower. The records of those administrations, now public, make clear that NSC meetings were tightly structured. Discussions were crisp and decisions firm. It was not that Marshall and Dulles were not fun guys (they were not), but that both Truman and Eisenhower understood the gravity of the issues with which they were dealing and the importance of providing clear direction.

By contrast Powell and Cheney often returned to the Pentagon unsure of what, if anything, had been decided at meetings of Bush's NSC. "What are we supposed to do?" they asked.[34] Instead of focusing discussion and allowing the State and Defense Departments to present reasoned briefs, Scowcroft, in Powell's opinion, "had become the First Companion and all-purpose playmate to the president on golf, fishing and weekend outings. He was regularly failing in his larger duty to ensure that policy was carefully debated and formulated."[35] It was FDR redux—except that Roosevelt had Fleet Admiral William Leahy (also not a fun guy) and the White House "map room" to at least maintain a semblance of order.

Meanwhile, in Kuwait, Saddam continued to dig in; Schwarzkopf pressured Powell for guidance; and, to judge from press reports, the president was becoming increasingly testy and frustrated. More important, the National Security Council did not meet. But on Friday, October 5, Powell was afforded an unexpected opportunity to make his case for sanctions to the president. Secretary Cheney, who had an appointment with Bush that afternoon, invited the chairman to go along. "Why don't you come over with me and we'll see what the man thinks about your idea?" said Cheney.[36]

As reported by Bob Woodward, Powell despaired of those informal Oval Office meetings with the president even more than the NSC. The setting was too relaxed. Things were done too casually. People would "kick the ball around. Feet would

be up on the table, cowboy boots gleaming."[37] Fifty years earlier, General Marshall had felt the same way. He habitually
declined to meet with FDR except under the most formal circumstances, lest he be carried away by the president's charm.[38]

Powell laid two options before the president that afternoon.
Option one was to reinforce Schwarzkopf's troops and prepare
for offensive action to drive Saddam from Kuwait. The second
option was to stay the present course of maintaining sanctions.
That would take longer, but in Powell's view it would ultimately be successful.[39]

Powell did not say which option he preferred. Having placed
two winning possibilities before the president, he deferred to
the commander in chief to make the choice. Woodward, who
interviewed Powell at length, reports that the chairman told
those assembled that "he could live with either containment
or an offensive option."[40] Insofar as Powell was concerned, it
was the president's call.

Critics may argue that was an abdication of responsibility. By statute, the chairman of the joint chiefs of staff is the
president's senior military adviser. He has a legal as well as a
moral obligation to speak frankly. If he felt it was best to stick
with sanctions, he should have said so. General Marshall never
left Roosevelt in doubt as to his opinion,* nor for that matter
did Truman ever doubt where Bradley stood during the Korean
war. The military leaders of World War II and Korea prided
themselves on their forthrightness. It was an article of faith in
the military that one was obliged to say what one thought up
to the point that a decision was made. Then, regardless of one's
opinion, he loyally carried out that decision. Or he resigned.
General Marshall, who always placed the Army's interests above
the president's, provided a model for future chiefs. Later, as
secretary of state, Marshall also gave the president forthright

---

*Historians of World War II would point out that only once, on the question of
Marshall's own preference for the command of OVERLORD, the invasion of Europe,
did the general decline to express an opinion. Since that issue involved Marshall
personally, it does not diminish General Marshall's deserved reputation for frankness.

advice, but acquiesced once the president had decided against him. For example, Marshall was bitterly opposed to American recognition of Israel, but when Under Secretary of State Robert Lovett reminded him that it was Truman's decision, Marshall never raised the matter again.

As chairman of the joint chiefs of staff, Powell failed in his obligation to give the president his best advice. It was a serious but not a fatal flaw. Powell did insist that offensive action not be undertaken until the forces deployed were sufficient to guarantee success. In that sense, he was acting in the professional tradition of refining and executing the president's policy. Yet on the crucial issue of war and peace, he pulled his punches. That, too, may say something about the American military of the 1990s. Faithful, reliable, and professionally accomplished, the officers of Powell's and Schwarzkopf's generation have acquired high rank through an accelerated promotion system that rewards the accomplishments of goals set by one's superior. The system is highly personal and occasionally capricious. Catering to the whims of a superior officer is sometimes essential to acquire that "outstanding" rating upon which future promotions depend. Such a system militates against independent advice. There are few rewards for speaking frankly, and the smothering blanket of professional conformity dictates a successful officer's career.

By contrast, the officers of Marshall's time were promoted strictly on the basis of seniority, at least through the rank of colonel. That delayed advancement, but it encouraged independence and forthrightness. A superior officer's predilections did not have to be catered to, and there was no penalty for speaking one's mind. It is difficult to blame Powell for not speaking more openly. The system in which he lived, and in which he had thrived, did not encourage it. Marshall, Eisenhower, and Nimitz were products of a different system, and a different set of values.

When given the options by Powell, George Bush did not flinch. "I don't think there is time politically" to stay with sanctions, he said.[41] It is not clear what Bush was referring to. If he meant the fragility of the coalition he had put together, he may have made the right call. No one knew better than the president the daily toll of keeping such disparate partners together. Bush may also have been referring to potential pressure to bring the troops home: a genuine possibility if the forces were kept in the desert too long. Would the American public tolerate an extended deployment under the unforgiving Saudi sun? Though there would be no body bags, it smacked of the endless struggle in Vietnam, and that did not give the White House much comfort.

It is equally possible that Bush was referring to the impact of a prolonged stalemate on his own political fortunes—a partisan political judgment that presidents are prone to make. Bush's term was almost half over. Could he go before the electorate with 230,000 troops deployed in Saudi Arabia and Saddam still sitting in Kuwait? Even worse, if it ultimately became clear that sanctions would not work, would war at a later date be any easier? Either that, or back down and crawl back? Both possibilities were even less attractive for Bush.

Regardless of which political aspect Bush had in mind— they are not mutually exclusive—his decision was firm. Whether the United States should have gotten itself into that position in the first place; whether a quarter of a million troops should have been deployed in the Saudi desert; whether Baghdad's overtures to compromise should have been so rudely rejected— these are questions that can be answered either way. But by early October, those questions had been foreclosed. By deciding to intervene on a massive scale in early August, Bush had crossed the military Rubicon. By unilaterally, perhaps flippantly, escalating American goals to include the liberation of Kuwait ("This will not stand"), Bush had already dictated the offensive option. The administration skillfully concealed that choice. Perhaps it had not been made consciously. But having made the liberation of Kuwait his goal, and being unwilling to compromise with Saddam, Bush ultimately had no choice but to take offensive action.

For George Bush, the military outcome could not have been more fortuitous. The armed services, the United States, and our allies benefited handsomely from the awesome display of force unleashed by Desert Storm. Leaving aside the long-term consequences of such action on the region, the allied attack, in military terms, was an outstanding success.

Serious problems remain. The most difficult of those problems involve the process by which American decisions were taken and the unilateral authority that Bush asserted. From the days of the Caesars, the personalization of power has led to regrettable excess. The elaborate system of checks and balances designed by the Constitution's framers was intended to prevent that. But as the American escalation in the autumn of 1990 indicates, that system has eroded badly.

Ultimately, General Powell was given the opportunity to lay the sanctions option before the president. That he failed to rise to the occasion is regrettable but understandable. What is less acceptable is the total failure of the National Security Council to provide a means for sustained policy direction. There was no formal meeting of the NSC to consider whether to stick with sanctions or to move to the offensive option. There was no routine canvassing of policy alternatives, no departmental analyses, and no debate or discussion by the principals themselves. The president, arguably, enjoys the constitutional authority to direct the executive branch as he sees fit, within the broad confines of legislative enactment. Whether Bush's method of personal leadership was a wise one is open to doubt. In the end, U.S. policy was determined by presidential fiat: the personal predilection of elected kingship. It survived the military test in the Gulf, thanks partially to Saddam's ineptness, but it is fraught with peril for the future.

On Saturday, October 6, the day following the White House meeting, Scowcroft informed Cheney that the president wanted the details of an offensive option to drive Saddam from Kuwait. On Sunday Powell notified Schwarzkopf. Central Command was instructed to prepare plans immediately for a move against the Iraqi forces. Powell told Schwarzkopf to send someone to Washington within forty-eight hours with the details. No one expected a finished product, just a preliminary plan of attack.[42]

Schwarzkopf was dumbfounded. It seemed like Vietnam all over again. The politicians were giving the military a task they could not accomplish. In August at Camp David, he had told the president that it would require three-quarters of a million men to attack Saddam, and that it would take until August 1991 to assemble them. Iraq now had 430,000 troops in Kuwait, and they were well dug in. That was a four-fold increase since August. Central Command had half that many. To attack under those circumstances spelled disaster. It was an impossible task. And whether by design or necessity, Schwarzkopf would prove it.

On Wednesday, October 10, Central Command's chief of staff, Marine Major General Robert Johnston, was in Washington with Schwarzkopf's plan. That afternoon he briefed Powell, Cheney, and others at the Pentagon. If the White House wants to attack, here's what it will look like, said Johnston.

The plan was divided into four phases. Phase One called for an air attack on Iraqi command posts and communications facilities. A simultaneous assault would be launched against Iraq's air force and air defense system. Additional strikes would knock out Saddam's chemical, biological, and nuclear facilities.

In Phase Two, the air bombardment would turn its attention to Iraqi supply lines and munition depots. The support elements of the Iraqi army would be systematically destroyed.

Phase Three involved an air attack on the entrenched Iraqi forces in Kuwait and on Saddam's republican guard.

The final phase, which Johnston indicated could commence as early as one week after the air bombardment began, was the ground assault. Schwarzkopf proposed a three-pronged frontal attack. The Marines would launch an amphibious assault from the Gulf, the Army would move directly forward against the Iraqi lines, and the Egyptians, located to the west, would also drive straight at the enemy forces while protecting the Army's flank.

Johnston's Pentagon audience was stunned. The first three phases—the air war—were plausible and well thought out. General Horner, Schwarzkopf's air commander, had been working on that strategy since arriving in Saudi Arabia, and the plan had few rough edges. But everyone present recognized that the air assault alone was not going to drive Saddam's forces out of Kuwait. The ground would have to be taken, or the Iraqi army would have to be outflanked and cut off. Johnston said that Central Command had insufficient forces for a flanking movement. The only alternative was to go straight at the enemy and hope that the air bombardment would have softened the Iraqis to such an extent that they would not put up much of a fight.

As Schwarzkopf had been betting, no one in the Pentagon war room was prepared to believe that. Cheney, above all, proved to be skeptical. United States ground forces were to be launched against a numerically superior Iraqi army in well-prepared defensive positions. Even if the air bombardment was effective, one didn't need to be a graduate of the War College to see that meant trouble. Also, the American troops, especially the airborne divisions, were lightly armed. There was little artillery and even less armor. They would be up against the T-72s of the Iraqi army, now deployed in strength in Kuwait. And the Iraqi artillery was formidable. In addition, there were no allied reserves and no provisions for resupply. Schwarzkopf, with too few troops and too little backup, had thrown everything into the initial assault.

Powell and the military chiefs added their concerns to those of Cheney. They sympathized with Schwarzkopf and recognized that the plan of attack would not survive serious scrutiny. General Johnston concluded the briefing with Schwarzkopf's frank assessment: "We do not have the capability on the ground to guarantee success."[43] Schwarzkopf was telling it like it was. Six months away from retirement, he was not going to say he could do something he could not. He was not going to tell Washington what it wanted to hear. Central Command said it needed three more armored divisions before it could launch a credible assault. There was a window of opportunity between January 1 and February 15 when conditions would be most favorable. The weather would be temperate, and heavy rains would not set in until March. After that, the desert heat and the Moslem holy days would make an attack difficult.

Johnston's briefing punctured whatever optimism there may have been for a quick military move against Saddam. To complicate matters further, *L'Express*, the French weekly newsmagazine, printed a garbled version of Central Command's plan.[44] Pentagon denials were so carefully phrased that they raised more questions than they answered.[45] Whether someone in Central Command had leaked the plan or not, the cover had been blown.

On October 11, Johnston presented Schwarzkopf's plan to Bush and his advisers at the White House. The president's reaction was similar to that of Cheney and the military chiefs. It was obvious that Schwarzkopf did not have the forces to do the job. Johnston repeated Schwarzkopf's desire for three additional armored divisions if a ground attack was to be launched. Bush asked how long it would take. Johnston said two to three months. After two hours, the briefing ended. Schwarzkopf had thrown a monkey wrench into any plans for an immediate attack. Nevertheless, Bush remained determined. He pressed Cheney for an offensive option, and Cheney leaned on Powell. Could existing U.S. forces flank the Iraqi positions by moving four hundred miles to the west? Powell said no. It was too far for the limited forces that Central Command possessed, and it would leave Saudi Arabia open for an easy Iraqi move south.

Schwarzkopf's gambit gave the Pentagon breathing room. But it was now apparent that Bush would not be satisfied until the military had found a way to wrest Kuwait from Saddam's clutches. On Sunday, October 21, Powell flew from Washington to Central Command headquarters in Saudi Arabia to discuss the situation with Schwarzkopf firsthand. There was no decision from Bush about the next stage, but both Powell and Schwarzkopf anticipated what was in store.

When Powell arrived, Schwarzkopf was still smarting over the order to send Johnston to Washington on such short notice. Central Command had built an effective defensive force literally from scratch in the Saudi desert, but it was incapable of offensive action.

Powell was sympathetic. A commander with less stamina than Schwarzkopf would have wilted under the pressure. Powell said that the White House was pressing for an offensive option. Schwarzkopf replied that to dislodge the Iraqi army from Kuwait would be costly and bloody. "Do they know this back in Washington?" he asked.[46]

In numerous press interviews that autumn, Schwarzkopf had indicated that his personal heroes were Grant and Sherman. Like both, Schwarzkopf was a reluctant warrior. "These generals who say they love to fight scare the living hell out of me," he once said.[47] If war came, Schwarzkopf, like Grant and Sherman, would fight it with everything he had and wreak massive destruction on the enemy. But, if possible, he preferred to avoid it.

Powell commiserated with Schwarzkopf. Nevertheless, the chairman said they had to be ready with a viable plan. Bush was determined to go ahead. As a former military hero himself—Bush had flown fifty-eight missions as a Navy fighter pilot in World War II—the president appeared to be aware of the price that would have to be paid. Powell asked Schwarzkopf what he would need and encouraged him not to underestimate Central Command's requirements.

Schwarzkopf said that to take the offensive against Iraq, he needed twice as much of everything. Twice as many planes and missiles; six carrier groups instead of three; twice as many ground troops. Double the Marine divisions, and add three armored divisions from Germany. "I want VII Corps," said

Schwarzkopf.[48] He was determined to avoid the piecemeal escalation that took place in Vietnam and thought it best to go through the front door with a realistic estimate. That would serve two purposes. It would immediately bring home to Washington the enormity of the task ahead, and it would ensure that if hostilities did break out, Schwarzkopf would have what it required to end them quickly.

Powell was stunned by Schwarzkopf's request. Not only would it mean that well over half of the surface Navy and more than half of the Air Force would be deployed in the Gulf, but so would VII Corps, which was the centerpiece of NATO's defense of Western Europe. For forty years, the troops and heavy armor of VII Corps had been constantly replenished and modernized. Headquartered in Stuttgart, the corps maintained a perpetual state of combat readiness. At a moment's notice it was prepared to go against Soviet armor pouring through the fields and forests of central Germany and Czechoslovakia, and, with luck, hurl it back. In months of field training at NATO's major training center at Grafenwöhr, VII Corps had perfected the Army's tactical doctrine of AirLand Battle. It was the best the United States had: the cream of the professional Army, and Schwarzkopf said he needed it in the Gulf.

Aside from the logistical problems of disengaging and transporting three heavy divisions that were scattered in small kasernes along a front that stretched from Regensburg to Hof, the move would shatter NATO's defensive posture in Europe. Before 1990, such a request would have been inconceivable. But the more Powell thought about it, the more plausible it became. German unification and the collapse of the Warsaw Pact had made the threat from the East negligible. The reduction of conventional forces in Europe was at hand, and VII Corps had, in fact, been slated to be withdrawn into NATO's mobile reserve at some undetermined future date. All things considered, Powell thought Schwarzkopf was right. He said he would back the request, if the president wanted to pursue an offensive option. In addition, Powell said he would add the 1st Mechanized Infantry Division from Fort Riley, Kansas—the Big Red One, another of the Army's elite units that had often trained with VII Corps. Powell shared Schwarzkopf's desire to make the assault as massive as possible. In retrospect, it was that determination by the military high command that made Desert Storm the pushover that it ultimately proved to be.

When Powell returned to Washington, the military's game plan was clear. Central Command would remain in a defensive posture. If the president chose to escalate, Schwarzkopf's requirements would be unveiled. Bush could then go forward and give Central Command what it needed, or, recognizing the magnitude of the effort involved, he could decide to stick with sanctions. Powell and Schwarzkopf hoped it would be the latter. Schwarzkopf's caution did not win universal approval. "McClellan lives," wrote fire-eating *New York Times* columnist William Safire—a reference to Lincoln's reluctant commander of the Army of the Potomac. "Send for Grant," he advised Bush.[49]

Despite the difficulties of launching an immediate offensive against Iraq, Bush continued to escalate the crisis. Warning of possible "war crimes trials" for Iraq's leaders, the president told a Republican fund-raising luncheon on October 15 that the confrontation involved more than the question of oil. "What is at stake is whether the nations of the world can take a common stand against aggression. Whether we live in a world governed by the rule of law or by the law of the jungle."[50]

Baker fell into line. Speaking at a news conference in Washington, the secretary dismissed "the siren song of appeasement." The administration, said Baker, categorically rejected any compromise with Saddam.[51] State Department officials said Baker's remarks "were deliberately planned to puncture the trial balloons being floated by Baghdad."[52] When Baker testified on Capitol Hill the following day, he ran into a blast of criticism from the Senate Foreign Relations Committee, which warned against a unilateral move by the administration to initiate hostilities. As the hearing opened, committee chairman Claiborne

Pell of Rhode Island held up a newspaper bearing the headline SHEVARDNADZE PROMISES TO CONSULT PARLIAMENT ON GULF IN- VOLVEMENT, referring to the assurances given by the Soviet for- eign minister to consult with the Supreme Soviet before Moscow committed any forces to the Gulf. Pell asked Baker whether he would "be prepared to be as forthcoming as Mr. Shevardnadze in informing Congress of any military action against Iraq prior to the takeoff?"[53]

Baker demurred. The administration would "consult" with the congressional leadership if military action was called for, said Baker, but he did not believe the president was obliged to get advance approval for the use of force against Iraq.[54]

Democrat Paul Sarbanes of Maryland objected immediately. "There is a difference between consultation and authoriza- tion," said Sarbanes. If the president intended to launch a ma- jor assault to drive Saddam from Kuwait, that "would require an authorization from the Congress." Sarbanes focused on the constitutional issue.

> If you get a declaration of war, you lose the element of surprise. But the notion that the president alone would be able to commit American forces in a major assault without receiving a shared decision by the Congress . . . is contrary to what the Constitution calls for.[55]

Baker remained obdurant. "I cannot give you a blank check commitment that we will, in every case, do nothing until we have consulted with all 535 members of Congress." Baker ar- gued that to require advance congressional approval would in- fringe the president's authority as commander in chief. The following day, Baker repeated that message to the House For- eign Affairs Committee. "I really think it would be self- defeating if we have days and days of discussion about what we should or should not do," said the secretary. "What Iraq is doing to Kuwait is indecent and inhumane and absolutely outrageous."[56]

Bush also stayed on the attack. On October 23, during a campaign swing through New Hampshire, the president told a GOP rally in Manchester that there could be no compromise with Saddam. "I am more determined than ever to see that this invading dictator gets out of Kuwait with no compromise of any kind whatever," he said.[57] "It isn't oil we're concerned about, it is aggression, and this aggression is not going to stand." As had been the case throughout the autumn, Bush took his lead from Martin Gilbert's *The Second World War*. "I'm reading a book, and it's a book of history, a great, big, thick history about World War II. And there is a parallel between what Hitler did in Poland and what Saddam Hussein has done in Kuwait."[58] The president's proclivity to use the first-person singular in describing U.S. policy had now become glaringly apparent. Not since Woodrow Wilson's quest for a League of Nations had a president so personalized foreign policy.

The following day, October 24, Bush summoned Cheney to the White House. The budget standoff with Congress had been resolved, and the president told Cheney he was leaning toward reinforcing Central Command in order to pursue an offensive option. How much would be required? he asked. Cheney told the president that Powell was on his way back from Saudi Arabia and that they should wait until he arrived home. With that simple conversation, American policy was effectively set. The offensive option would be put in place. If Saddam did not withdraw from Kuwait, Bush intended to force him out. No one questioned the president's decision. More important, no one questioned his authority to make it. The constitutional scheme of checks and balances yielded to the power of the commander in chief.

Later that day, Cheney and Baker briefed the congressional leadership on the situation in the Gulf. In keeping with the administration's arms-length approach in dealing with Congress, neither mentioned what Bush was contemplating.[59] Instead, Cheney went public. That, too, was typical of the Bush administration's approach. If the public was supportive, Congress would have no choice but to follow.

After returning to the Pentagon from Capitol Hill, Cheney and his press chief, Pete Williams, met with selected reporters off-the-record. The following morning, Thursday, October 25, the *Washington's Post*'s lead story quoted senior Pentagon officials as saying more troops, "perhaps as many as 100,000," would be needed in the Gulf "to provide a credible option for potential offensive action."

The *Post* article was a setup. Cheney had arranged to appear on all of the television morning shows that day, and each of the questioners wanted to know what was happening. That gave Cheney the opportunity to prepare public opinion before any announcement of the reinforcement was made.

Taping NBC's "Today" show at 6:30 A.M., Cheney said, "We are not at the point yet where we want to stop adding forces." On CBS's "This Morning," Cheney was asked whether a hundred thousand additional troops would be sent to the Gulf. Cheney replied that "it's conceivable that we'll end up with that big an increase . . . but we've never set an upper ceiling on it." The lesson was repeated on ABC. Again, it was the policy of minimum candor. Cheney's rehearsed answers opened the door to an even larger augmentation.[60] According to subsequent press reports, Pete Williams was quick to amplify the secretary's remarks by saying that no upper limit had ever been placed on the U.S. deployment in Saudi Arabia.[61] Since Schwarzkopf already had his full complement of 230,000 troops necessary for an effective defense against Iraq, the inescapable conclusion was that the administration was planning an offensive option.

Sam Nunn and the congressional leadership were stunned. If the administration was planning an offensive option, why hadn't Cheney said so when he briefed them the day before? The military were even more surprised. General Powell saw

Cheney's comments on television during a stopover in Europe. He had not been consulted. Nor had any of the joint chiefs. Nor had Schwarzkopf. "What's going on?" Powell asked an aide. "I haven't seen the president on this. Goddammit, I'll never travel again."[62]

Powell knew how Washington worked. He knew that Cheney would not have spoken of another massive deployment without White House approval. There was nothing accidental in Cheney's comments. Just as with Bush's "This will not stand" comment in August, Powell had learned of the administration's decision after the fact. Once more, it seemed that George Bush was shooting from the hip. As chairman of the joint chiefs of staff, Powell would be called upon to implement that decision. Yet his views had not been requested beforehand.

In Saudi Arabia, Schwarzkopf was equally surprised. So, too, were the Saudis and America's other allies. What was Washington up to? they wanted to know. Like Powell, Schwarzkopf was angry at having had no advance warning, let alone input. Field commanders should not have to learn of the government's policy by watching television. More important, Schwarzkopf questioned the wisdom of the decision. A massive augmentation of the forces under his command could mean but one thing: Bush was going for the offensive option.

Later that week Schwarzkopf granted a long interview to the *Atlanta Constitution*. "We are starting to see evidence that sanctions are pinching," he said. "So why should we say, 'Okay, [we] gave 'em two months, didn't work. Let's get on with it and kill a whole bunch of people? That's crazy. . . . If the [alternative] to going to war is sitting out here in the desert another summer, that's not a bad option."

With congressional elections set for November 6, there was no urgency to announce the president's decision. To the contrary, political wisdom suggested that it was best to let matters rest until the votes had been counted. There was no reason to interject the question of attacking Iraq into the campaign, especially since it was not clear how the voters would react.

Nevertheless, the administration continued to lay the groundwork for going public. At a campaign rally in San Francisco, Bush told newsmen that he thought he had ample authority to take the nation into war without asking Congress for approval. "History is replete with examples where the president has had to take action. . . . I've done this in the past," he said, an apparent reference to Panama, "and certainly would have no hesitancy [to do it again]."[63]

On October 30, with Powell back from Saudi Arabia, Bush was ready to act. That morning he met with the congressional leadership to secure their support for his policy in the Gulf, but held back from informing them about the possible reinforcement of Central Command. The meeting went badly. Pressed by the lawmakers to promise that he would not take military action without congressional approval, Bush declined. The president said he could not rule out unilateral action. "I will continue to seek your advice and support as we proceed," Marlin Fitzwater quoted the president as saying, but "we must all understand any such commitment must be hedged, given the unpredictable and dynamic circumstances of this crisis."[64]

The meeting produced little agreement as to the respective roles of the president and Congress. "There is obviously a difference of opinion in terms of whether the power to start hostilities rests with the executive branch or the congressional branch," Senator Cohen of Maine said afterward.[65]

That afternoon, Bush met with Baker, Cheney, Scowcroft, and Powell. Despite his failure to win the support of the congressional leaders, the president was going ahead. The meeting was another of those informal White House sessions among men who had worked together for years. No agenda, no position papers, no formality. Once again, Bush made it clear that he was not prepared to accept anything less than the liberation of Kuwait.[66]

Powell was asked to report on his meeting with Schwarzkopf. What did Central Command require to make an offensive option credible? Reports of the meeting that have been generally accepted indicate that when Powell said that Schwarzkopf wanted twice as much of everything, everyone present, except Bush, was shocked that so much would be required. The president seemed neither surprised nor dissuaded.[67] Powell said he supported Schwarzkopf's request. He estimated that it would take another three months to deploy the troops, and that it was going to be expensive.

Cheney backed Powell. He urged Bush to go forward with the buildup. Powell was right, said Cheney, to ask for what he needed up front, rather than have to come back later and ask for more.

Finally, the president said, "If that's what you need, we'll do it."[68] The official presidential order authorizing the doubling of the forces of Central Command was signed the next day. No public announcement was made. Congress was not informed.

Following the president's decision to reinforce Central Command, Baker was dispatched to inform the allies. That took precedence, and the Soviets, in particular, appeared to need stroking. Gorbachev had recently called for a new Arab peace initiative,[69] and, to Washington's discomfiture, Yevgeny Primakov continued to exude optimism about the possibilities of settlement. In addition, Baker hoped to lay the groundwork for a new Security Council resolution authorizing the use of force. "The threat of armed conflict is not just words," Baker told reporters accompanying him.[70] He claimed that the administration had "the requisite authority" for military action under Article 51 of the United Nations Charter. That provision permits the "collective self-defense" of other nations.[71] But the argument was weak and had been repeatedly criticized by legal scholars.[72] Kuwait no longer existed, and the right of self-defense had long expired. Baker indicated that he would seek Soviet support for a new resolution, and he hoped that China would at least abstain if it could not support the measure.

Arriving in Jidda on November 3, Baker said that "a new phase" of the crisis had begun in which "the global community is prepared to resort to force" if a peaceful settlement is not found.[73] "I don't think that we can, nor should we, rule out resort to force, if that should be necessary." Given the extensive press coverage of Baker's trip, his comments served two purposes. They increased the pressure on Saddam, and at the same time they helped to prepare public opinion for the buildup that the president had ordered but not yet announced.

Bush also kept up the pressure. Speaking to reporters on his way to a political fund-raising breakfast in Alexandria, Virginia, the president said "I've had it" with Iraq's efforts to starve out the American embassy in Kuwait City. "The people out there are not being resupplied. The American flag is flying over the Kuwaiti embassy and our people inside are being starved by a brutal dictator. And do you think I'm concerned about it? You're damned right I am. And what am I going to do about it? Let's just wait and see."[74]

Bush's continued personalization of the crisis had a serious downside. The confrontation took on the earmarks of a struggle of wills with Saddam Hussein, and it was difficult to prevent an element of waspish vindictiveness from creeping into the president's remarks. Also, Bush risked a further alienation of congressional support. To go to war because America's vital interests were threatened was one thing. To fight because of a president's impatience was quite another. Also, as American policy became personalized, it appeared to lack consistency and continuity. "We seem to be zigzagging because sometimes it's less a matter of a game plan and more a matter of the president's moods," said one White House official.[75]

Nevertheless, the steady drumbeat from the White House was having its effect. On November 6, a *Washington Post*–ABC News poll revealed that for the first time a majority of Americans favored attacking Iraq if economic sanctions failed to dislodge Saddam from Kuwait.[76] Seven out of ten people believed the United States was headed for war, another significant increase from the time U.S. troops were dispatched to Saudi Arabia in August. And while more than two-thirds said that Bush should get permission from Congress before going to war, a plurality said they would support the president if there was insufficient time to notify Congress. Overall, 65 percent said they approved of the way Bush was handling the crisis—unchanged since early October.

It was not until November 8, two days after the congressional elections, that Bush announced his decision to reinforce Central Command. The prior speculation by Cheney and others that an additional hundred thousand men would be dispatched to the Gulf had prepared the way. Just as with the initial deployment in August, the number of troops had been deliberately understated. If the public accepted the principle of sending more soldiers to the Gulf, which they did, few would quibble about the number. Or so the administration thought. Cheney had placed the camel's nose under the tent two weeks earlier on the morning talk shows; now Bush inserted the whole animal.

Bush's news conference was originally scheduled for 3 P.M. It was delayed three times as he awaited word from Baker in Moscow that the Soviets were on board. Eventually the call came in, and Baker, who had met with both Shevardnadze and Gorbachev, announced that the United States and the Soviets "were together" on Gulf policy. "We're on the same wave length in terms of objectives," said Baker.[77] Shevardnadze added cautiously that the "use of force . . . probably could not be ruled out," although he made it plain that was not the Soviet Union's preference.[78]

The president's comments were brief. Bush said that "I have today directed the Secretary of Defense to increase the size of U.S. forces committed to Desert Shield to insure that the coalition has an adequate offensive military option, should that be necessary to achieve our common goals."[79] He did not specify the number of troops involved or the units designated. Nor did he indicate that the presidential order authorizing the move had been signed eight days earlier. America's allies had been informed. Saudi approval had been obtained. But the American public and Congress had been kept in the dark. The congressional leadership had been notified shortly before the president spoke. It had not been consulted.* Legislative approval had not been sought. Bush, as commander in chief, was acting unilaterally. His constitutional authority to do so had been stretched to the limit. If Congress objected, he would have to pull back. That risk seemed small. Most legislators were back in their districts, and the new session of Congress would not commence until January. In addition, the constitutional issue was abstract, with substantial precedents on both sides. And the public was behind the president. The spin control placed on Bush's announcement was designed to minimize whatever anxieties might be aroused. Again, no figures were provided. By increment, by stealth, the United States was inching toward war at the president's direction.

At the press conference that followed, Bush was asked whether he was prepared to use military force to drive Saddam from Kuwait. The question was framed in such a way to suggest that the issue was one for the president to decide on his own authority without reference to Congress.

"I don't want to say what I will or will not do," said Bush, furthering the impression that the question of war or peace was the president's call. "I have not ruled out the use of force at all, and I think that's evident by what we are doing today."[80]

Once again Bush stressed that the primary issue was not oil or jobs, but the need "to see that aggression is unrewarded." He closed his remarks with another vow that "this aggression simply will not stand."[81]

At a follow-up briefing at the Pentagon, Cheney and Powell fleshed out the president's announcement. Powell ticked off the units being sent. Cheney emphasized that "the additional military capability that's now being added clearly will give us the ability to conduct offensive military operations should that be

*Representative Les Aspin, chairman of the House Armed Services Committee, and Senator Sam Nunn, chairman of the Senate Armed Services Committee, were informed of the president's pending announcement one hour beforehand by Dick Cheney.

required." But he warned that it would be well into the new year before all of the forces could be assembled and made ready for battle, in effect allowing several additional months for economic sanctions to take their bite.[82] Cheney also said that the military's plans for rotating the forces in Saudi Arabia had been scrapped. Asked whether the 230,000 troops presently in the Gulf were there for the duration of the crisis, Cheney said, "That's correct." A Pentagon official later reaffirmed Cheney's comments.

As soon as Bush spoke, senior administration officials were off and running to place the appropriate twist on his remarks. Scowcroft told the *Washington Post* that the president had ordered the escalation because Saddam was not "taking us seriously" and that a greater show of strength was needed to convince him that the United States would not wait indefinitely for him to evacuate Kuwait.[83]

Cheney, in a subsequent off-the-record briefing, told the *Post* that "there's a lot to be said for not dragging this out. [Something] more than sanctions is needed, and if you know you will end up at a certain point anyway, it is better to get there sooner rather than later."[84]

But if the administration was preparing the nation for war, the soldiers continued to downplay the imminence of conflict. "There are many elements of the equation," a senior military official, presumably General Powell, told the *Washington Post*. "It doesn't mean, however, that just because we will have a larger force in place before bad weather [sets in] or a religious celebration that we should do something. We are not going to war based on weather forecasts."[85]

From Riyahd, Schwarzkopf again exhibited the caution that had become his hallmark. In an hour-long interview with Youssef Ibrahim of *The New York Times*, the commander of Desert Shield suggested that the destruction of Iraq was not necessarily "in the interest of the long-term balance of power in this region."[86] Hinting once again that he preferred to stick with economic sanctions, Schwarzkopf observed that war with Iraq "would cause thousands and thousands of innocent casualties. . . . I do think there are other alternatives to having to drive on to Baghdad and literally dig out the entire Baathist regime and destroy them all in order to have peace and stability in the region." On the other hand, Schwarzkopf made it clear that if war came, he was going to launch massive assault to end the struggle as quickly as possible. "Now why do I do that? I do that because I want to minimize the casualties in my troops and the way to do that is to make the enemy pay dearly."[87]

Bush's sudden announcement that the forces in Saudi Arabia would be doubled caught the country by surprise. The very boldness of the move was breathtaking. Another 230,000 troops were going to the Gulf, and possibly into action. The significance of the president's action sank in slowly. Congressman William Broomfield of Michigan, ranking Republican on the Foreign Affairs Committee, reflected the rising concern on Capitol Hill. "While the president has taken great pains to consult with the Soviets, the Syrians, the Egyptians, the Saudis, the French, the Germans, the British, and many others at the United Nations," said Broomfield, "his administration has failed adequately to consult with the American Congress."[88] Sam Nunn was skeptical of the president's move,[89] annoyed that he had been informed, not consulted. Foreign Relations Committee Chairman Claiborne Pell chastised Bush for acting unilaterally. Pell said once again that the president lacked authority to initiate hostilities "without clear prior expression of congressional support."[90]

By Sunday, the Democrats had their ducks in a row and opened an attack on Bush's buildup. Appearing on CBS's "Face the Nation," Nunn questioned the move and suggested that sanctions be given more time to work. "I think that the president has a real obligation here to explain why liberating Kuwait is in our vital interest," he said.[91] Nunn, who was especially close to Powell and the other joint chiefs and who often reflected their thinking, also questioned why the Pentagon's rotation schedule had been scrapped.

Senate Majority Leader Mitchell said much the same on ABC's "This Week with David Brinkley." He acknowledged that the president had the authority to deploy the troops, but again insisted that only Congress could authorize an attack on the Iraqi forces in Kuwait. Paraphrasing Justice Brandeis in *Myers v. United States*, Mitchell asked, "Isn't that inconvenient for the president? Of course it is. The Constitution imposes a great many inconveniences on those in power in this country."[92]

House Armed Services Committee Chairman Les Aspin, who supported the president's decision to send more troops to the Gulf, agreed. Aspin said that a decision to go to war should be made by formal vote of Congress, not just an informal consultation between the president and congressional leaders.[93]

A large part of the administration's problems stemmed from its failure to take Congress and the public into its confidence. That was Bush's style in foreign policy. It prompted Archbishop Roger Mahony of Los Angeles to write that "our country needs an informed and substantive discussion of the human and ethical dimensions of the policy choices under consideration in the Gulf."[94] Mahony's statement was subsequently supported by America's Catholic bishops during their annual meeting in Washington.[95] In a joint statement sounding the same note, Speaker Foley and House Majority Leader Richard Gephardt said, "We urge the President to explain fully to the American people the strategy and aims that underlie his decision to dispatch additional forces to the region."[96]

Meanwhile, efforts to resolve the crisis through negotiation continued, much to the Bush administration's displeasure. On Sunday, November 11, Saddam told an interviewer from Britain's Independent Television News that he was ready for a "deep dialogue" on Middle East security issues.[97] At the same time, Tariq Aziz said, "The decision of Mr. Bush is not going to help find a peaceful solution. Instead of sending more troops he should send diplomats and send people who could understand the situation in the region . . . and try to open peace talks."[98]

Morocco's King Hassan, an early supporter of American intervention, warned that a conflict was drawing near and urged an immediate Arab summit "to give peace a last chance. The drums of war are beginning to throb."[99] Iraq did not reject Hassan's suggestion but insisted that the Arab-Israeli dispute be included on the agenda. Following a late-night meeting of the Revolutionary Command Council in Baghdad, a government spokesman said, "You can look on it as a qualified rejection or a qualified acceptance, depending on how [the other Arab nations] react."[100] But the possibility of an Arab summit died when Egypt, Saudi Arabia, and Kuwait dismissed Hassan's proposal.

In the United States, public criticism of Bush's policy intensified. On the political right, Pat Buchanan, Jeane Kirkpatrick, and Edward Luttwak joined liberals such as Arthur Schlesinger, Jr., in questioning whether America's vital interests were at stake in the Gulf. Further left, Ramsey Clark, David Dellinger, and George McGovern joined in decrying the rush to war. New York's Daniel Patrick Moynihan told ABC's "Good Morning America" that Bush was rushing into war without consulting the Congress, the American people, or the United Nations. "It's as if that great armed force which was created to fight the Cold War is at the president's own disposal for any diversion he may wish, no matter what it costs," said Moynihan.[101] For once, the administration had overplayed its hand, and public support was hemorrhaging badly.

On Tuesday, November 13, Senate Democrats turned up the heat by announcing joint hearings of the Foreign Relations and Armed Services committees to review U.S. policy in the Gulf. In a joint statement, Mitchell, Pell, and Nunn said that "if it is the president's intention to ask the American people to stand behind a military mission that goes beyond deterring Iraq from attack on Saudi Arabia, the president owes the American people the fullest possible explanation of what our military mission is in that region and how he hopes to achieve that goal."[102]

Two days later, in an effort to head off increasing congressional criticism, Bush met with two dozen congressional leaders at the White House. Afterward, Speaker Foley said that Bush had assured them that U.S. policy in the Gulf had not changed: that American troops were in Saudi Arabia "for defensive purposes." That particular policy had "very, very strong bipartisan support," Foley said.[103] Bush also assured the lawmakers that no decision had been made about how long to stick with sanctions. "I have not crossed any Rubicon," the president was reported as saying.[104] In a literal sense that was true. But the military were already making preparations to attack.

The problem that the congressional leadership wrestled with was that the mobilization in the Gulf had assumed a momentum of its own. Just as military mobilization drove the Great Powers of Europe toward war in August 1914, the escalation of force levels in Saudi Arabia appeared to be producing the same effect.

Few problems were solved by the White House meeting. Bush complained that congressional criticism of his policy was encouraging Saddam to sit tight. He maintained that as commander in chief the decision to use force was his. Bush said he was "willing to consult Congress," but that he was still commander in chief.[105] Reflecting on the meeting afterward with Baker and Scowcroft, the president decided that a U.N. resolution offered the best solution. If China and the Soviet Union were prepared to authorize the use of force, surely Congress could not refuse.[106]

The day after meeting the congressional leadership, Bush told CNN's Frank Sesno that the time for a peaceful solution to the crisis was running out. "There is a ticking of the clock," the president said, that would soon make military action inevitable. "I don't think this matter is going to go on forever. As far as I'm concerned, it's not."[107]

Bush also sought to provide a broader rationale for American policy. "If I haven't done as clear a job as I might on explaining this, then I've got to do better in that regard, because I know in my heart of hearts that what we are doing is right. . . . I know that we have to stand up against aggression: An aggression that goes rewarded today means instability and horror tomorrow."

As for the possibility of a negotiated settlement, Bush remained uncompromising. "When you rape, pillage, and plunder a neighbor, should you then ask the world, hey, give me a little face? The answer is no, there isn't going to be any compromise with this kind of naked aggression."

The president was equally unyielding as to his authority as commander in chief. "I've read the Constitution," he told Sesno. Congress has "the right to declare war, and I have the right, as commander in chief, to fulfill my responsibilities, and I'm going to safeguard those executive powers. . . . My job is to make tough decisions and to hold this coalition together and to drive forward to see that this aggression is not rewarded."[108]

Saddam responded to Bush's tough talk with another call for negotiations. Interviewed once again by ABC's Peter Jennings, Saddam said that the United States and Iraq should conduct "dialogues toward the achievement of a comprehensive peace in the region. . . . We have been ready for negotiations all along. We are ready to talk to the parties concerned." Although he dismissed the possibility of a prior Iraqi pullout from Kuwait as "preconditions for capitulation," Saddam's tone was less confrontational than previously. "The right way to go is the course of peace and that peace should be complete and final," he told Jennings.[109]

Washington quickly dismissed Saddam's overture. Marlin Fitzwater called it "another propaganda speech" and said that Iraq should not be rewarded in any way for its aggression.[110]

On November 18, with the war clouds gathering, Bush began a weeklong trip to Europe and the Middle East to rally international support. Stopping first in Prague, the president evoked the memory of Munich. "You know from your own bitter experiences that the world cannot turn a blind eye to aggression," said Bush. "You know the tragic consequences when nations, confronted with aggression, choose to tell themselves it is no concern of theirs, just a 'quarrel in a faraway country between a people of whom we know nothing.' "[111] The quote was from Neville Chamberlain, and referred to Hitler's claim to the Sudetenland in 1938.

From Prague, Bush went on to Germany and then to Paris, where he, along with other world leaders, was to attend a three-day, thirty-four-nation conference on Security and Cooperation in Europe. In Germany, Bush spent five hours with Chancellor Kohl, who had become visibly skeptical of the president's policy. Warning of the possibility of high casualties, Kohl said, "Those who believe you can solve this militarily have to think about the consequences of a military operation." Afterward, Bush said that the chancellor had "made very clear he'd like to see a peaceful resolution to this question, and so would I." Apparently, the president took note of Kohl's views, but remained determined to forge ahead. "We're not ruling out any options; we're not ruling any options in," he said as the presidential party departed for Paris.[112]

Gorbachev, also en route to Paris, appeared to share Kohl's doubts about a military solution. The Soviet leader said in Rome that he remained convinced that the situation in the Gulf could be settled without war.[113]

The following day, Monday, November 19, Bush met with Gorbachev in Paris for a lengthy dinner at the American embassy. Afterward, *The New York Times* reported that Bush had failed to secure a commitment from Gorbachev that would authorize the use of force in the Gulf. The two agreed that Iraq must relinquish Kuwait, but when Bush canceled a much ballyhooed joint news conference, it became clear that the Soviets still were not on board for military action against Saddam. The most the administration could point to was an undertaking to continue consultations at the level of foreign ministers, and a mild acknowledgment that "force cannot be ruled out."[114] According to Soviet spokesman Valery Ignatenko, "Both sides agreed that it is time for the Security Council to discuss this situation further."[115]

The differences between the U.S. and Soviet positions were not as great as they at first appeared. The problem related to the wording of any Security Council resolution that might authorize the use of force, rather than to the concept itself. "The French and the Russians aren't willing to buy a pig in a poke," said one European diplomat. "They want to see the resolution first. The Americans have been looking for commitments before [submitting] a resolution, and Jim Baker tried to force the pace a little bit last weekend. So there's a certain amount of circling going on."[116]

Soviet support did not come cheaply. In addition to the prospect of Western economic aid, the United States rallied behind Gorbachev to keep representatives from Latvia, Lithuania, and Estonia from attending the Paris conference. No United States representative turned up at Latvia's National Day celebration in Paris on November 19, nor did Bush make a single reference to Baltic demands for self-determination in his Paris speech about the new world of freedom that he said he was trying to create in Europe. Similarly, a long-scheduled trip by Assistant Treasury Secretary Bruce Bartlett to Vilnius, the capital of Lithuania, to discuss economic matters was abruptly canceled as "inappropriate."[117]

From Paris, Bush flew to Saudi Arabia to spend Thanksgiving with the troops of Desert Shield. "We won't pull punches," he told a Marine outpost less than eighty miles from the Kuwait border. "We are not here on some exercise. This is a real world situation. And we are not walking away until the invader is out of Kuwait." For the first time in his public statements, the president emphasized the threat posed by Saddam's nuclear weapons program. Although technical experts believed it would be five to ten years before Iraq could develop such a capability, recent opinion polls in the U.S. indicated that the nuclear argument resonated strongly. "No one knows precisely when this dictator may acquire atomic weapons or who they may be aimed at down the road," said Bush. "But we do know this for sure: He has never possessed a weapon he has not used."[118]

Scowcroft and Cheney moved quickly to reinforce the president's rationale of denying Saddam access to nuclear weaponry. Appearing on the Sunday-morning talk shows, both suggested a much shorter time frame for Iraq's nuclear development than that predicted by scientific experts. Scowcroft, on ABC's "This Week with David Brinkley," said disingenuously that it might be "a matter of months." According to the president's NSC adviser, waiting for sanctions to work "raises the possibility that we could face an Iraq armed with nuclear weapons, which would dramatically change the character of any conflict." Virtually all experts agreed that the administration was crying wolf, and that recent opinion polls indicating public concern about a potential Iraqi nuclear capability had affected the administration's judgment. As Richard Cohen pointed out in the *Washington Post*,[119] following the opinion polls came naturally to the White House. After all, it was "the way Bush got to be president: Willie Horton, the Pledge of Allegiance and all that jazz."[120]

As was so often the case that autumn, the military put as much daylight as possible between the go-for-broke attitude in the White House and their own much more cautious assessment. Schwarzkopf told CBS's Dan Rather that "nobody wants to rush into war. I think that first of all we have to wait and see if sanctions work."[121]

Schwarzkopf's caution reflected not only the U.S. military's traditional reluctance to initiate hostilities, but the relative unpreparedness of Central Command for offensive action. Foley had it right. The military mission of the forces in Saudi Arabia had been to deter and defend. Not only were there too few troops, too little armor, and not enough artillery for anything but a defensive mission, but supplies of every kind were woefully inadequate. Spare parts and ammunition of all caliber were in critical short supply. Already the Air Force had cannibalized its aircraft in the United States to find parts for Central Command.[122]

General Gray, the Marine commandant, suggested that Bush was moving too quickly. "We ought to let this thing unfold and stay behind sanctions," he told an audience of military contractors in Washington. "What's the hurry here?" Gray asked. "Time is on our side, not Saddam's."[123] Like Schwarzkopf, Gray was concerned that the forces in the Gulf were not sufficient for an offensive move against Iraq. "We don't have as much there as we ought to," he said.[124] Marine Lieutenant General Ernest Cook, the head of training, was even more outspoken. "We ought to all be sitting and praying that the sanctions and the diplomatic process win out," said Cook.[125]

Meanwhile, there was increasing evidence that the efforts of Bush and Baker to mobilize the U.N. for a resolution authorizing the use of force were about to bear fruit. After a hastily arranged meeting in the northwestern Chinese city of Urumqi, Soviet Foreign Minister Shevardnadze and his Chinese counterpart, Qian Qichen, issued a brief statement demanding that Iraq "withdraw its army from Kuwait unconditionally and immediately."[126] The two went on to say that there was "still hope for a peaceful solution," although it was now apparent that neither the USSR or China would veto a U.S. proposal to use force.[127]

The administration's pressure for Security Council action reflected its growing unease with Congress. An anonymous White House official repeated the administration's strategy to R. W. Apple of The New York Times. "Those guys on the Hill aren't going to vote against a war if the U.N. has already voted for it."[128]

The fact was, congressional support for Bush was ebbing fast. In an attempt to head off the administration, Congressman Ron Dellums of California and fifty-three House colleagues filed suit in United States District Court challenging Bush's authority to launch offensive military action without explicit Congressional approval. Despite the unhappy history of such court challenges to presidential authority, the lawmakers requested an injunction to bar the president from ordering U.S. forces to attack. As Dellums observed, "War is a very solemn act, and the decision to go to war should not be granted to one person." Congressman Don Edwards of California, another sponsor of the suit, told reporters on the courthouse steps that "there is no necessity for quick action here. We are not being invaded. There is no reason why the Constitution in this case should not be honored."[129]

Dellums's suit was supported by eleven of the nation's most respected legal scholars. In a brief filed with the court, they urged the trial judge to rule that President Bush could not initiate an attack on Iraq unless he received explicit permission from Congress. Drafted by Professor Harold Koh of Yale, the signatories reflected a wide ideological spectrum, including such conservative legal voices as Philip Kurland of Chicago, Erwin Griswold, former dean of the Harvard Law School and former solicitor general under Nixon, and Gerald Gunther and John Hart Ely of Stanford. They, together with Louis Henkin of Columbia and Lawrence Tribe of Harvard, argued that the Constitution unequivocably vested Congress, not the president, with the authority to initiate war. Professor Koh said that those signing the brief wanted to demonstrate that "you could hold different views about politics but share a similar view about the Constitution."[130]

On Tuesday, November 27, the Senate Armed Services Committee began hearings on U.S. policy in the Gulf. "The question is not whether military action is justified," said Chairman Sam Nunn. "It is. The question is whether military action is wise at this time and in our own national interest."[131]

Throughout the crisis, the administration underestimated Sam Nunn, just as it had during the hearings on the nomination of John Tower to be secretary of defense. "Nunn can make it bumpier or smoother along the way," said one White House official, "but in the end he really doesn't matter."[132]

That assessment, apparently from John Sununu, was immediately rapped by a GOP spokesman on the Hill. "Anyone that doesn't know that Nunn is the vote that counts most up here can't count votes," he said.[133]

And it was true that with the 101st Congress adjourned *sine die*, the Senate hearings provided the most effective means of challenging administration policy. The White House did its best to minimize the effect by charging Nunn with political partisanship. The problem was that Bush's massive escalation on November 8 had alarmed many on the Hill that the president was leading the nation into war. In Nunn's view, that move by Bush, together with the scrapping of a rotation policy for U.S. troops in the Gulf, placed enormous pressure on the White House to find a swift end to the crisis. The equation was simple, Nunn thought. The more troops in Saudi Arabia, the less patience in Washington.

Worse still, from the legislators' perspective it appeared that Bush intended to launch an attack on his own authority as commander in chief without asking Congress for an explicit vote of approval. Even those senators firmly behind Bush's policy were sensitive to their constitutional responsibilities. Finally, the hearings reflected the concerns of the military establishment. The staff of the Senate Armed Services Committee had worked hand in glove with the military for decades, and no one in Washington was closer to the uniformed services than Sam Nunn.

The committee's first witness, former Defense Secretary and CIA chief James Schlesinger, testified that economic sanctions were proving to be far more effective than had been thought. An early "official estimate," he said, was that it would require a year for the sanctions to take effect. "It is now apparent that they are working much more rapidly than originally anticipated."[134] Schlesinger was also critical of the White House for raising the nuclear weapons issue, and suggested that it had more to do with recent opinion polls than with scientific reality. "That's no accident, Comrade," he told the committee.

But the blockbuster testimony came on the committee's second day of hearings. The two most recent chairmen of the joint chiefs of staff, Admiral William Crowe and Air Force General David C. Jones, sitting side by side, lambasted the administration's concentration on a military solution to the crisis. Jones said that his concern with the massive reinforcement ordered by the president "isn't that we might choose to fight, but rather that the deployment might cause us to fight prematurely and perhaps unnecessarily." Jones told the committee he "would have stayed with the lower number [of troops] until we gave sanctions a little more time to work."[135]

Admiral Crowe was equally outspoken. "War is not neat," he said. "It's not tidy. And once you resort to it, it's a mess." Crowe said the issue "is not whether an embargo will work but whether we have the patience to let it take effect."[136] He noted that stability in the Middle East was America's primary national interest in the region. "It is not obvious to me that we are looking at the crisis in that light. Our dislike for [Saddam] Hussein seems to have crowded out many other considerations."[137] Like Schlesinger, Crowe dismissed the Iraqi nuclear threat as exaggerated. "It's a long-term issue. It isn't a justification to attack Iraq today."

Without criticizing the president directly, Crowe suggested that Bush was moving too fast. "We are selling our country short by jumping to the conclusion that we can't stare down our opponent. . . . It is curious that just as our patience in Western Europe has paid off and furnished us the most graphic example in our history of how sanctions is sometimes the better course in dealing with thorny international problems, a few armchair strategists are counseling a near-term attack on Iraq. It is worth remembering that in the 1950s and '60s, individuals were similarly advising an attack on the USSR. Wouldn't that have been great?"

The White House was undeterred. Scowcroft told the *Washington Post* that "the bottom line on sanctions is when does it cause Saddam enough heartburn to decide he's had enough? We don't see that happening anytime soon." Spring would be optimistic, he said. "It could be next fall."[138] For Powell and Schwarzkopf, next fall did not sound too bad, but that would be too late for George Bush.

Another senior administration spokesman said, "We're not prepared to give this guy [Saddam] unlimited time, whoever's side time is on. Clearly, sanctions are not at the point where he is seriously constrained."[139]

Bush was even more outspoken. "We're getting tired of the status quo," he said at a luncheon meeting in Washington, "and so is the rest of the world."[140]

With the Senate on the verge of mutiny, Bush and Baker left no stone unturned in their efforts to secure passage of a Security Council resolution authorizing the use of force. On Monday, November 26, China announced that it had been invited by the United States to send a high-level trade delegation to Washington in mid-December to discuss economic issues. That signaled an easing of the U.S. sanctions against China that had been imposed after the 1989 massacre of pro-democracy demonstrators in Tiananmen Square. Chinese officials did not say how China would vote on the proposed U.S. resolution in the U.N., but indicated that it would not veto the measure.[141]

In addition, the difference between the Soviet Union and the United States appeared to have been resolved. Speaking at a press conference in Moscow, Gorbachev said there was "absolutely" no difference between him and Washington on the issue of Iraqi withdrawal. "This is not Vietnam. This is not Afghanistan. This is extremely serious," he said.[142]

Three days later, on Thursday, November 29, the weeks of intense diplomatic activity by Bush and Baker paid off as the Security Council voted 12–2, China abstaining, to approve the use of force. According to the text of U.S.-sponsored Resolution 678, member states were authorized "to use all necessary means" to liberate Kuwait if Iraq did not withdraw by January 15.

The resolution marked a major victory for George Bush. By leaving responsibility for enforcement to "member states," the Security Council authorized each country to act on its own, independent of further U.N. control. That gave the United States and its allies carte blanche to take military action if Iraq did not withdraw. In effect, the Russians and Chinese had signed off, leaving the control of policy to the president.

In deference to the Soviets, the U.N. resolution did not explicitly authorize the use of military force, but instead used the phrase "all necessary means"—a euphemism that satisfied Moscow. To underscore the importance of the occasion, the Security Council session was chaired by Secretary Baker and was attended by the foreign ministers of twelve of the other fourteen members. In announcing the vote, Baker, by prearrangement, referred to the possible "use of force" if Iraq "does not reverse its course peacefully."[143]

By making January 15 the effective date of the resolution, the Security Council was providing Iraq a forty-seven-day respite during which it was hoped that Saddam would withdraw. Indeed, most of the foreign ministers who spoke at the U.N. stressed that the resolution was intended to promote the peaceful settlement of the crisis by convincing Saddam that he must give up Kuwait unconditionally.

The Security Council did not act under Article 42 of the Charter. That article enables the Security Council to authorize military action to deal with aggression or other threats to world order. Invoking Article 42 would have required a unified U.N. command over the forces engaged against Iraq. Instead, the Council's action followed the pattern set on August 25 when it authorized individual countries to enforce the naval blockade. By leaving the responsibility up to each country, the United States retained a free hand to act as it wished.

The U.N. action had little effect on Baghdad. After stressing the importance of negotiations and dialogue for the past month, a defiant Saddam told an Iraqi television audience that he was "determined not to kneel down to injustice." "If war breaks out," he said, "we will fight in a way that will make all Arabs and Muslims proud."[144]

The morning after the U.N. vote, Bush delivered what appeared to be another tactical masterstroke. With domestic support unraveling and the Nunn hearings providing the first effective forum for a debate on Gulf policy, Bush disarmed his critics by announcing that Baker would go to Baghdad to try to resolve the crisis. In addition, Bush said he was inviting the Iraqi foreign minister, Tariq Aziz, to Washington.

Bush made the announcement during a quickly called news conference at the White House. Once again, the move reflected Bush's style. America's allies were neither informed nor consulted. The State Department, the Pentagon, the intelligence community, and Central Command—where Schwarzkopf was still wrestling with delicate command problems—were taken by surprise. The congressional leadership, gearing up for a showdown with the president, were caught flatfooted. The National Security Council drew a blank. Cheney, Quayle, Sununu, and Powell were informed after the decision had been made. Only three persons had been involved: Bush, Baker, and Scowcroft. The decision was made at one of their customary 8 A.M. meetings in the White House. Baker argued strongly that with the U.N. now on record, the administration had to stop the domestic political bleeding, recapture public support, and deflect the criticism that Bush was leading the nation into war. The best way to do that, Baker suggested, was for him to go to Baghdad and meet with Saddam. Such an overture, coming on the heels of the U.N. vote, would demonstrate to critics that the administration was doing everything possible to find a peaceful solution.

Baker suggested it was a "no lose" proposition. By sending the secretary of state, Bush would confound his critics, undercut Sam Nunn, and reestablish his command of public opinion. If the mission succeeded and Saddam agreed to withdraw from Kuwait, the United States would have won a bloodless victory.

On the other hand, if Saddam still chose to sit tight, no one could accuse Bush of not having made that last effort to secure a peaceful solution. The Russians, the Chinese, and the French would be mollified, and Congress would have no option but to grant Bush the authority to launch an attack. Best of all, public opinion would be strongly supportive regardless of how the effort turned out.

Bush quickly agreed. As a tactical device, the move was brilliant. Though Fahd, Assad, and Mubarak were initially caught off guard, fast footwork reassured them that they were not being sold out. The dramatic suddenness with which the offer was announced mobilized public support. That permitted the administration to reverse the erosion that had occurred. *The New York Times* bannered BUSH OFFERS TO SEND BAKER ON A PEACE MISSION TO IRAQ. A *Washington Post* opinion poll published two days later showed that 90 percent of those contacted supported the president's proposal. January oil prices dropped $4.06 a barrel on the New York Mercantile Exchange (12.3 percent); the Dow jumped 41 points. The fear of war subsided, and Bush regained control of the situation. Paradoxically, the announcement was a decisive turning point on the road to war. Baker's analysis proved correct. Merely having made the offer was sufficient to justify recourse to the military option.

It would be a harsh judgment to conclude that Bush's peace overture was a sham. If Saddam had acquiesced and folded his tent in Kuwait, war would have been avoided. But there was little likelihood of that. And the available evidence suggests that the president's initiative was a public relations gambit and nothing more. It re-cemented the alliance, revived domestic support, and undercut congressional opposition. It was a demonstration of the agility of the Bush team at its best. Minimum candor remained the order of the day.

The downside of Bush's offer was that it was read differently in Baghdad than in Washington. Saddam thought Bush had blinked, and was encouraged to hold fast. Immediately prior to Bush's announcement, Iraqi troops in Kuwait City had suddenly and without explanation appeared at the U.S. embassy bearing fuel, fruit, vegetables, and cigarettes for the besieged legation. The Iraqi ambassador to the U.N. had requested an urgent meeting with Prince Bandar, presumably to discuss the terms of a settlement. At least that was Bandar's view.[145] With Bush's proposal to send Baker to Baghdad, all bets were off. The Iraqi ambassador canceled out, and no further gestures were made by Saddam. That reading of Bush's intentions in Baghdad made war inevitable.

On Capitol Hill, response to the president's announcement was enthusiastic. House Majority Leader Gephardt said Bush had done the right thing by "using yesterday's U.N. vote as an opportunity for diplomacy."[146] A White House meeting with the congressional leadership later that day turned jocular, even boisterous. Participants reported that the atmosphere "was like a men's club house, with much backslapping and joking."[147] But when the president once again asked for a blank check, the mood turned serious. Speaker Foley cautioned that the president should consult the new Congress in January. "If you decide to go to war, you'll have to come to Congress," said the Speaker. Senate Majority Leader Mitchell concurred. A vote was not only necessary, it was constitutionally required, he said. Despite the euphoria that greeted Bush's announcement that Baker would go to Baghdad, the congressional leadership was unwilling to surrender its constitutional mandate.

6.

DESERT STORM

I have announced time and time again that
I will never be guilty of any kind of action
that can be interpreted as war until
Congress, which has the constitutional
authority, says so . . . and I am not going to
order any troops into anything that can be
interpreted as war until Congress directs it.
President Dwight D. Eisenhower
April 4, 1956

With the passage of U.N. Resolution 678 and the announcement of Baker's visit to Baghdad, the White House regained
the initiative. The impact of the Senate hearings was lessened,
and Bush reasserted his control over public opinion. The U.N.
resolution indicated broad international support for the president's policy. That was reassuring after the go-it-alone years in
Vietnam. And the suggestion for Baker to meet with Saddam
pulled the teeth of those critics who charged that Bush was

rushing the nation into war. The situation had not changed, nor had Bush's determination flagged. But public confidence in the president's leadership—which had been slipping badly—was restored virtually overnight.

Dick Cheney reports that the passage of the United Nations resolution authorizing the use of force was a watershed for Bush. Cheney was convinced that if Saddam did not withdraw from Kuwait by January 15, the president would instruct Central Command to drive him out.[1] If Congress concurred, that would be helpful. But with the U.N. on record, neither Bush nor Cheney worried about the administration's authority to order U.S. forces into combat. *Time* reported that in private White House conversations Bush insisted that he could ignore Congress so long as it remained divided; so long as there was no consensus for or against his Gulf policy.[2]

Bush was equally uninterested in negotiating with Saddam. From the beginning, Baker's proposed visit to Baghdad (and the invitation for Aziz to come to Washington) was a public relations gambit and nothing more. "Basically the president has made up his mind," Scowcroft told Prince Bandar in early December. "These are all exercises"—meaning that the invitation had been designed for its domestic impact.[3]

Sununu went on record to the same effect. The offer was simply "part of a checklist from which the president is ticking off diplomatic and domestic moves the administration thinks it must make . . . before considering military force."[4] In the end, the president scuttled the exchange, blaming Saddam for refusing to set a date sufficiently in advance of the January 15th U.N. deadline. In reality, Bush had moved the goal posts. The original offer had given Baghdad the choice of any date between December 15 and January 15. But when Baghdad evidenced interest in the talks, Washington quickly aborted them.

In fact, no sooner was Baker's proposed trip announced than the president redefined its terms to make it difficult for Saddam to accept. "I'm not in a negotiating mood."[5] "There can be no face-saving."[6] "They must withdraw without condition."[7]

"There will be no give."[8] Eventually it was agreed that Baker and Aziz would meet in Geneva on January 9. But each was kept on a short leash. Bush explicitly ruled out a subsequent trip to Baghdad for Baker, and there was no suggestion that Aziz might come to Washington. From a negotiating standpoint, the meeting was little more than a formality, although once again, Iraqi obtuseness played into the administration's hands. When Aziz declined to accept a bluntly worded letter from President Bush to Saddam ("Anything less than full compliance with U.N. Security Council Resolution 678 and its predecessors is unacceptable"),[9] it appeared that Iraq, not the United States, was being intransigent.

Middle East specialist William Quandt dismissed the entire episode as a political sideshow. "At first I felt they were seriously looking for a political dialogue," said Quandt. "In retrospect, it seems they never intended to have a serious diplomatic outcome—only to affect the domestic debate. The whole thing looked as if it wasn't meant to work in the first place."[10]

On Saturday, December 1, Bush met with the joint chiefs of staff at Camp David. It was the president's first meeting with America's top brass since the crisis began, and the chiefs were none too pleased with having been shut out from White House decision-making. That reflected Bush's operating style. Decisions were narrowly held. Throughout the buildup, and later, during the war itself, the president dealt primarily with four people: Baker, Cheney, Powell, and Scowcroft. That maximized Bush's personal control. All four men were immensely capable and had worked together for years. They knew what was effective; they understood how to turn the bureaucracy to the president's purpose. On the other hand, such tight control insulated the president from a broad spectrum of advice. In particular, it screened out technical expertise—whether that involved area specialists or, in this case, the nation's senior military officers. If the war had gone badly, critics would point to that as a major failing. Since the war went well, at least from a military standpoint, Bush's style may not have been that bad.

Certainly, it prevented him from becoming bogged down in the trivia that can sink a presidency. It also allowed the military to get on with their job without the distraction of endless White House meetings. Finally, by keeping the circle tight, security was maximized. There were no leaks.

The chiefs' principal concern that December morning was where they were heading. They were not in the operational chain of command in the Gulf, although each was in charge of his particular service. Reinforcements to Central Command were their responsibility. All had been planning to rotate their forces and had been caught off guard by the president's sudden announcement that another 230,000 troops would be deployed in Saudi Arabia.[11]

Each of the chiefs briefed the president on their forces in the area. General "Tony" McPeak, the Air Force chief of staff, indicated that if Bush chose to launch an attack, the air bombardment phase should last about thirty days. McPeak said they would lose about five planes a day. A total of 150. Those present at the briefing report that the president took the news with no show of emotion.[12] All agreed that if hostilities began, American forces should be used massively in order to secure victory as quickly as possible.[13]

The use of massive force had become an article of faith in the Pentagon. Some described it as the "doctrine of invincible force,"[14] and Colin Powell had become Pope in a church of true believers. Essentially, it was a rejection of the limited-force doctrine that had dominated American strategic thinking during the Vietnam period. Spawned in numerous think tanks and academic seminars, limited force had become fashionable during the Kennedy era and, in turn, had been a reaction to the doctrine of massive retaliation espoused by Eisenhower and Dulles. Supposedly, the United States should have a choice between surrender or nuclear war, and by employing force gradually on a calibrated basis, the degree of involvement could be matched to the particular crisis.

That concept read well on the Charles River, but it proved

to be a disaster for the fighting men who had to implement it in Vietnam. Conflict is not an abstraction. Casualties are real, and, regardless of the number, they inflict great pain and suffering. Old soldiers like Eisenhower knew that war was not an instrument of everyday policy. It was something to be undertaken only when all else had failed. And something to be ended as quickly as possible. The men who fought in Vietnam came to share that sentiment and now, fifteen years after the fall of Saigon, shaped American military policy in light of their experience.

The invasion of Panama was the first application of the doctrine of invincible force. Unlike Carter's tentative approach to Desert One (the disastrous and undermanned effort in 1980 to rescue the hostages in Tehran), or Reagan's dispatch of an outgunned detachment of Marines to Lebanon, Operation Just Cause stressed the shock action of overwhelming military force—a force so formidable that opposition is defeated quickly. That was not a new idea or a revolutionary concept. For centuries successful commanders have sought to marshal their forces for maximum effect on the battlefield. But few pursued it quite as relentlessly as General Powell.

As formal military doctrine, the idea of invincible force gained credence during the tenure of Caspar Weinberger as secretary of defense. In a 1984 speech entitled "The Uses of Military Power," Weinberger laid out rigorous criteria for sending U.S. troops into combat. If it was ever necessary to do so, said Weinberger, "we should do so wholeheartedly, and with the clear intention of winning." Powell was Weinberger's military assistant at the time and had helped shape that speech. But Weinberger had stopped short of saying that overwhelming force should be committed to guarantee success. That was Powell's embellishment, and it had been fully accepted by both Bush and Cheney.

Cheney signed on early. Despite his lack of military experience, Cheney recognized the political futility of an extended conflict in the desert. "It would be morally irresponsible for us to send our men and women into battle without every advantage we can give them," he announced on September 12. To do otherwise would be "a sin," he said privately. "This will not be a protracted, drawn-out war. The only acceptable outcome is absolute, total victory."[15]

Bush agreed fully. "The president belongs to what I call the 'don't screw around' school of military strategy," Cheney declared on another occasion. Indeed, Bush was as adamant as Powell that a war with Iraq not become another Vietnam. "If there must be a war, we will not permit our troops to have their hands tied behind their backs," he said. "If one American soldier has to go into battle, that soldier will have enough force behind him to win and then get out as soon as possible. . . . I will never, ever agree to a halfway effort."[16]

The initial deployment in August, and the massive reinforcement announced in November, conformed to the doctrine of invincible force. Despite the dislocations it entailed, the military was reassured that Bush meant business. As one senior admiral expressed it, the November announcement "shivered the timbers of the whole military system. It was a helluva signal" of the administration's willingness to deploy as much military firepower as needed to prevail in the Gulf.[17]

"Today's war may be quick and clean, or it may be quick and dirty, but above all it will be quick," said Lieutenant General Walter Boomer, the Marine Corps commander in the Gulf.[18]

The downside of the doctrine of invincible force, particularly in the context of the Saudi desert, was that the massive deployment became a factor driving the nation toward war. If the U.S. goal was merely to defend Saudi Arabia, victory could have been declared and the troops withdrawn. But once Bush fixed on the liberation of Kuwait, the enormous force in the desert had to be used—assuming Saddam did not back down. Its very size, and the concomitant problems of resupply and combat effectiveness, militated against keeping it there indefinitely.

On December 3, Cheney and Powell went before Senator

Nunn's committee. Powell took advantage of the opportunity to lay out the doctrine of invincible force for public view. If war came, he said, it would be fought all out. "We will use our strengths against their vulnerabilities, and we will avoid their strengths." Powell implied that the greatest tank battle in history might follow. The use of massive air, ground, and naval forces, he said, enjoyed the unanimous approval of the joint chiefs of staff.

To ensure the lesson was clear, Powell castigated those strategists who urged "alleged low-cost, incremental, may-work" strategies, such as relying solely on U.S. airpower. Powell said "such strategies are designed to hope to win; they are not designed to win." Instead, he said the allies would employ such overwhelming force that "the only question the Iraqis will have to consider is, do they move it, or do they lose it?"[19]

Cheney, in his testimony, put the senators' backs up when he claimed the president could initiate hostilities without congressional approval. "I do not believe the president requires any additional authority from Congress," he said. "Of the more than two hundred occasions in American history when presidents have committed U.S. military force, on only five of those occasions was there a prior declaration of war."[20]

The following day, House Democrats responded to Cheney's assertion of prerogative power by adopting (177–37) a caucus resolution declaring that President Bush should not initiate military action in the Gulf without the formal approval of Congress. That vote marked the most explicit position taken by congressional Democrats thus far and suggested that despite Security Council Resolution 678 and Baker's pending visit to Baghdad, the administration was in for some rough sledding. In effect, the issue of the president's authority had been joined.

Any doubts on that score were laid to rest when Baker himself came before the Senate Foreign Relations Committee two days later. The secretary of state normally had excellent relations with the committee and was considered an icon of sorts on Capitol Hill. But when he too articulated the doctrine of unilateral executive authority, the senators pounced on him with vengeance. Once again, it was the usually soft-spoken Sarbanes of Maryland who led the charge. On constitutional issues Sarbanes is formidable. A graduate of the Harvard Law School, he had, as a member of the House of Representatives, helped draft the articles of impeachment against President Nixon. Now he laid into Baker for rushing the nation into war. The administration's decision to double the forces committed to Desert Shield, he said, "almost irresistibly takes you down the path of going to war. I cannot say to a family that loses a son or daughter in a conflict that may well take place in the next sixty to ninety days, that we exhausted every possibility for a peaceful resolution before this happened, because the sanctions option has not been exhausted."[21]

Senator Bob Kerrey of Nebraska, a holder of the Medal of Honor from Vietnam, reminded Baker of the shared responsibility between the president and Congress. "As important as it is for us not to restrict the president's ability to threaten the use of force, it is equally important for Congress to represent the country's hesitancy about using that force. We each have a role to play."[22]

The Senate's mood was reflected by Sam Nunn, who said that at some point he would support military action in Kuwait. "The question is whether that is wise at this time. I don't think that it's vital that Kuwait be liberated with 95 percent American forces and 95 percent American casualties between now and February."[23]

As if to complicate matters further, on the day of Baker's testimony, the United States District Court heard oral argument in the suit brought by Congressman Dellums and other House members to enjoin the president from taking military action against Iraq without a declaration of war.[24] Presiding Judge Harold Greene said he was troubled by the political nature of the dispute. "No court," he told the plaintiffs, "has ever issued an injunction [such as the one] you are asking for." Nevertheless, Judge Greene reserved his sharpest queries for the administration's attorneys. "If a declaration of war is not called for in this case, when would it be?"[25] he asked. The judge said he would study the case and rule sometime in the future, disappointing the Justice Department lawyers who had hoped for a quick dismissal.

But the following week Judge Greene did, as predicted, dismiss the suit. The issue, he held, was "not ripe" for judicial decision. Court action, said Judge Greene, could not be triggered by individual congressmen. For the court to accept jurisdiction, Congress would have to request it by majority vote.

> It would be both premature and presumptuous for the Court to render a decision on the issue of whether a declaration of war is required at this time or in the near future when the Congress itself has provided no indication whether it deems such a declaration necessary, on the one hand, or imprudent, on the other.[26]

Greene went on to say, much to the administration's discomfiture, that the Constitution gave to Congress alone the power to declare war. He also said that the history of Article I of the Constitution left no doubt that the framers intended that a president could not go to war without the explicit approval of Congress.

What was most surprising was that Judge Greene dismissed the administration's arguments that the issue was a nonjusticiable political question, and that the congressmen lacked standing to sue. Greene said the government's claims were "far too broad to be accepted by the courts." If an impasse developed between the president and Congress, "action by the courts would appear to be the only available means to break the deadlock." The political questions doctrine did not apply, said Judge Greene, because courts "have historically made determinations about whether the country was at war." The congressmen were entitled to standing because the Constitution gave to them the right to vote for or against a declaration of war. If the president preempted that right, they would have sustained an injury that the court was authorized to prevent.

Those findings, though buttressed by precedent, marked a departure from recent judicial decisions on the subject.*[27] They suggested that if the full Congress approved a resolution insisting that President Bush seek a declaration of war before launching an attack, the court would consider the case. "To put it another way," said Judge Greene, "this Court is not prepared to read out of the Constitution the clause granting to Congress, and to it alone, the authority 'to declare war.' "

Judge Greene's ruling left the situation unchanged. No injunction was granted, but the tenor of his comments served as a warning shot to the Bush administration. The constitutional authority of Congress to declare war could not be ignored.

Indeed, the growing congressional opposition to war with Iraq was the most serious problem Bush faced. With the possible exception of Baker and Powell, the president's team instinctively slighted Congress and resisted sharing power. George Wilson, the dean of Washington's military correspondents, expressed it best when he wrote, "Many of Bush's potential troubles stem from following LBJ's handbook, which could be entitled 'How to Go to War Without Anybody Knowing It Until Too Late.' Both Johnson and Bush treated Congress like a doormat, getting lawmakers aboard early on by not saying how big a war they were prepared to fight."[28]

But with the 101st Congress adjourned, the *Dellums* case dismissed, and the Nunn hearings completed, Capitol Hill grew

---

*In an unrelated case decided the same day, Judge Royce Lambeth, also of the United States District Court for the District of Columbia, dismissed a suit brought by a National Guardsman who had been ordered to the Gulf and who challenged the president's authority, citing the War Powers Act. Contrary to Judge Greene, Lambeth held the issue was a political question. The judiciary, he said, "is neither equipped nor empowered to intrude into the realm of foreign affairs where the Constitution grants operational powers only to the two political branches and where decisions are made based on political and policy considerations." Lambeth took the traditional view, suggesting that if Congress objected to the president's actions, it could withhold appropriations or even impeach him. *Ange v. Bush*, 752 F. Supp. 509 (D.D.C. 1990).

quiet. Senate Majority Leader Mitchell and Speaker Foley agreed to keep the new 102nd Congress in session after it convened on January 3 (in past years, it had recessed for two weeks immediately afterward), and the hiatus until then provided a period of watchful waiting. The leadership was unsure whether Congress should go on record before the U.N. deadline expired on January 15. If the president lost the vote, Saddam would have no incentive to pull out. If Bush won, war seemed inevitable.

"I believe that the president is trying to use the threat of war to prevent war," said Mitchell. The president "does not need the approval of the Congress to threaten war. But he does need the approval of the Congress to make war."[29] Whether Congress would vote that approval was unclear.

The president also seemed uncertain how to proceed. Questioned at his press conference on December 14 as to whether he intended to ask Congress for authority to take offensive action, Bush avoided giving a direct answer. He would continue talking to the leaders, he said, but had made no decision about sending a specific request up to the Hill.[30]

As the deployment grew, and more and more troops arrived in the Gulf, the momentum worked to the president's advantage. In the absence of sustained congressional criticism, the balance of public opinion shifted once more toward the administration. The week before Christmas, Bush invited to the White House the ambassadors of the twenty-eight nations that comprised the coalition. The president told them that if he had to make a decision to go to war, he hoped he would have the support of Congress and the American people. If he didn't have the support of Congress, Bush said he hoped he would have the support of the American people. If he didn't have either, he said he would not be deterred from going to war if it was the right thing to do.[31]

Afterward, he told Prince Bandar that if Saddam did not withdraw from Kuwait by January 15, "we'll just have to implement the [U.N.] resolutions." Bandar said he realized at that point that Bush was "going to do it."[32] Whether the president had the authority to lead the nation into war was not questioned by either Bush or Bandar.

Meanwhile, from Baghdad, the ruling Revolutionary Command Council continued to send mixed signals. The military buildup in Kuwait continued, but on December 17 the Council issued a formal statement that "we want peace. . . . We want a dialogue for peace. We respect legitimacy, and we want international law to be applied to the issues of our nation, but we refuse capitulation."[33] If that was a tentative offer to negotiate, it was again dismissed by Washington. Speaking in Brussels at the close of a two-day NATO conference, Secretary Baker rejected any compromise with Baghdad and called for the full implementation of all U.N. resolutions on Kuwait. To do otherwise, said Baker, "would reward aggression. I think it is important that we not do that."[34]

Bush was more emphatic. He continued to see the conflict as a confrontation between himself and Saddam: a rerun of an old Western movie with George Bush leading the sheriff's posse. "The entire world [is] against this man," he said at his press conference on December 18. "And he's got to understand it. No concession. No negotiation for one inch of territory. And Mr. Saddam Hussein, simply do what the world is calling upon you to do: Get out. We have to keep repeating it. Some people are slow to get the word."[35] Two days later, he told a group of congressmen recently returned from the Gulf that if it came to war, Saddam "is going to get his ass kicked."[36] Congressman George Durden of Georgia quoted the president as saying he had "crossed the Rubicon" in his Gulf policy. That meant war could not be far off. "My sense is he's very impatient," said Representative Michael McNulty of New York.

Bush's hectoring rhetoric (he habitually mispronounced Saddam's name)* was scarcely conducive to levering Iraqi forces

---

*According to the April 1991 *Washingtonian* magazine, the CIA advised Bush that by accenting the first syllable (SAD-dam), the meaning of the word changed from "one who confronts" to "a little boy who cleans the shoes of old men."

from Kuwait by peaceful means. To the contrary, it seemed intentionally designed to provoke Saddam into a showdown. How else could the military balance in the region be rectified? How else could Baghdad's nuclear and chemical warfare capability be checked? By badgering Saddam, Bush foreclosed the possibility of an Iraqi pullout. "Never spit on a man's mustache unless it's on fire," is a common saying in the Arab world,[37] an admonition not to insult an opponent's dignity. Yet for the past three months, Bush had been doing exactly that.

The fact is, Bush personalized the confrontation up to the very end. In his speech to the country on January 16 announcing that war had begun, he mentioned Saddam twenty times.[38] If at any point during the crisis the White House had sought a settlement, it would not have focused on Saddam, nor would Bush have been so unrelenting in his attacks. Saddam had been a head of state for twelve years; he was exceptionally touchy about his dignity. To talk about kicking ass (a phrase that gains strength in Arabic), Bush provoked all of Saddam's macho instincts. The phrase had boomeranged on Bush following his 1984 debate with Geraldine Ferraro, and it simply provided another indication that the White House was uninterested in a peaceful settlement. "You don't talk to Arabs like they're dogs in the street," said one Pentagon official. "You don't say you're going to kick ass. This is not to say [Saddam] would have backed down, but that level of discourse isn't conducive to a diplomatic solution."[39]

Some believed that Bush's swagger had a darker side. That he was proving to himself that he could stand up to Saddam. That despite the characterization of *Newsweek* (and George Will), he was not a wimp.[40] When he personalized the issue, when he lapsed into his Clint Eastwood routine, when he said that Saddam was going to get his ass kicked, he was demonstrating how tough he was.

That explanation becomes more plausible when one realizes how out of character it was for George Bush to speak of himself publicly. As a child, Bush had been drilled by his parents not to brag. "I don't want to hear any more about the Great I Am," his mother would chide him.[41] At Greenwich Country Day School, which he attended before Andover, he was graded on a category called "Claims no more than his fair share of time and attention," a category his father always inquired about when report cards came home.[42] Those habits were deeply ingrained and strongly reinforced. At the age of eighty-six, Bush's mother occasionally called her vice president son to say, "You're talking about yourself too much, George."[43] Peggy Noonan, Reagan's gifted speechwriter, reports how difficult it was to craft a speech for Bush because he would invariably delete all of the "I" 's—a throwback to his early training.[44]* To pick a fight with Saddam, as Bush was doing, and to personalize it to the extent he did, strongly suggested a pressing need to prove himself as president. "We all know instinctively this is not a strong man," a senior senator told Elizabeth Drew. "I try not to think about it. I don't know anyone who's honest with himself who doesn't think this."[45]

On December 19, with the reinforcement of Central Command moving full tilt, Cheney and Powell arrived in Riyadh to review Schwarzkopf's planning for an allied assault. Each, in his own way, was aware that the die was cast: If Saddam was not out of Kuwait by January 15, the president very likely would order an attack. None questioned his authority to do so. None reflected on the constitutional role of Congress. None doubted the determination of the commander in chief. The chain of command linked each of them to Bush's purpose.

Schwarzkopf's new strategy took advantage of VII Corps' superior mobility and firepower. The preliminary air campaign remained unchanged, but instead of a frontal attack against the

---

*Noonan said she became adept at writing pronounless sentences. "Instead of 'I moved to Texas and soon we joined the Republican party,' it was "Moved to Texas, joined the Republican Party, raised a family." But she worried about Bush's Inauguration speech: " 'Do solemnly swear, will preserve and protect. . . .' " Peggy Noonan, *What I Saw at the Revolution* (New York: Ballantine Books, 1990), pp. 312–313.

Iraqi fortifications, Schwarzkopf proposed to send his armor wide to the left, around the enemy flank. The Marines would go forward to hold the Iraqis in place, and the amphibious force offshore would threaten to land, but the main assault would be mounted two hundred miles to the west. VII Corps would skirt the enemy front, drive deep into Iraq, take on the republican guard with a crushing tank attack, and generally wreak massive destruction. XVIII Corps, farther west, would strike toward the Euphrates and block the enemy's retreat. Additional elements of XVIII Corps would launch a helicopter-borne air assault far behind the Iraqi lines and set up a supply base. Like Grant's crossing of the James in 1864, or his flanking of Vicksburg the year before, Schwarzkopf would deceive the enemy as to his main point of attack. Most believed that the sand of the western Iraqi desert was too fine to support an armored attack. Schwarzkopf's own staff had concluded as much. But as Grant often did, Schwarzkopf made his own reconnaissance. Poking in the sand like a junior officer, he concluded that the terrain offered no obstacle.[46] At that point, his strategy was set.

Schwarzkopf explained the plan to Cheney and Powell. There were no elaborate options from which Washington could choose. Stormin' Norman was doing it his way, based on the guidance he had received to make it massive and make it quick.[47] It was a daring concept. The logistical challenge was formidable. Central Command had to slip 250,000 troops—two full corps, plus the British and French divisions—and a mountain of supplies down a single highway past the enemy front and reassemble them several hundred miles to the west, all within a matter of days, and all without being detected by Iraqi surveillance. Air supremacy was imperative. There could be no slipup. Schwarzkopf anticipated heavy casualties. Possibly as many as twenty thousand, including seven thousand killed.[48] But it would be over quickly. "It's going to be a tough fight. I do not envision a protracted war [but] you can always get a stalemate."[49]

After assuring themselves that what Schwarzkopf proposed could be done, Cheney and Powell signed on. "Be ready for war," Powell told the troops as he headed back to Washington.[50] "If we go in, we go in to win, not to fool around."[51] Cheney said, "It's far better to deal with [Saddam] now than it would be five or ten years from now."[52]

A slight glitch occurred when Schwarzkopf's deputy, Lieutenant General Calvin Waller, told members of the press accompanying Cheney and Powell that the Army would not be ready to attack until mid-February.[53] "What's so special about January fifteenth?" he asked. That rocked the war hawks in Washington, who thought Waller's candor was misplaced, but Cheney took it in stride. Waller, a veteran tank commander with thirty-one years of distinguished service in the Army, was inexperienced in the techniques of spin control practiced by the Bush men. Besides, what he said was no secret. Powell had said the same thing in congressional testimony the week before, but the press had not picked up on it.[54] "Welcome to the NFL," Cheney told the general as he departed.[55] Bush also remained stoic. He dismissed the incident as "rabbit trails in the snow," meaning that it would soon be forgotten.[56]

On Christmas Eve, Cheney and Powell briefed the president at Camp David. It was true that the Army would not be ready to move until mid-February (the 1st Division would not arrive in Saudi Arabia until late January), but Schwarzkopf, they told Bush, was prepared to launch the air-assault phase immediately following the U.N. deadline of January 15. That would provide thirty days of uninterrupted air bombardment before the ground war began. Bush appeared satisfied and said they should "think seriously about starting the air campaign" as soon after January 15 as possible.[57] Powell was instructed to ask Schwarzkopf for the optimal date based on the moon and weather forecasts. The order to go had not been given, but when Cheney and Powell left Camp David that evening, they understood what lay ahead.

Christmas Day Powell called Riyadh. Based on the recommendation of his air commander, General Horner, Schwarzkopf said that 3 A.M. desert time on January 17 was best. That would be 7 P.M. in Washington the day before—just nineteen hours after the U.N. deadline expired. It would be a moonless night, perfect for a surprise attack: too late for many Iraqi defenders to be up, too early for them to be awake. Powell passed the word and put the final touches on a warning order instructing Schwarzkopf to make ready. On Saturday, December 29, the president authorized Powell to go ahead. The warning order to prepare for attack was flashed to Schwarzkopf shortly before noon.[58] If Saddam did not withdraw from Kuwait prior to the U.N. deadline, war would begin at 3 A.M., January 17. The United States would launch a surprise attack on a country with which it was not at war. Congress had not been consulted, and there were no plans to obtain a declaration of war. The White House was going it alone. The commander in chief had decided on war and the military complied. The Constitution was held in abeyance. *Inter arma silent leges.* In times of war, the laws are silent.

On New Year's Day Bush returned to Washington from Camp David. Whatever doubts he may have had, had been resolved.[59] Over the holidays, in the quiet of the Catoctin Mountains, the president had steeled himself for what lay ahead. That evening he met with Baker, Cheney, Powell, Scowcroft, and Sununu in the family quarters of the White House. Over dinner, Bush held a council of war. How to handle Congress? What about the Israelis? Would the coalition stick together? The military aspects, having been settled, were largely passed over.

Bush repeated his resolve to liberate Kuwait and punish Saddam. Choosing words similar to those he used when he spoke to the allied ambassadors before Christmas, he said that "it boils down to a very moral case of good versus evil, black versus white. If I have to go [to war], it's not going to matter to me if there isn't one congressman who supports this, or what happens to public opinion. If it's right, it's gotta be done."[60]

As was now his habit, Bush discussed the crisis in the first-person singular. By implication, he dismissed Congress's constitutional role. Insofar as he was concerned, the question of peace or war was the president's decision. No objections were entered. The question the Bush team wrestled with was how Congress could be cajoled into going along. Its prerogative to declare war was viewed as a tactical impediment—not a constitutional imperative. In the guise of punishing aggression, the Bush administration was repeating what the Reagan team had attempted in Iran-contra. Foreign policy, including the war powers, was seen as an executive monopoly. The only difference was that Bush was going through the front door.

James Baker, still unhappy with the war option, urged one last effort to meet with Saddam.[61] Cheney was skeptical. He thought the coalition was too shaky. In the end Bush agreed to send Baker to Geneva to meet with Aziz, but there would be no negotiations. Baker would not go to Baghdad. The meeting was another sop to public opinion. No progress was anticipated. Perhaps none was desired.

The following evening, PBS aired a presidential interview with David Frost that had been taped before Christmas. Bush discussed at length a report from Amnesty International dealing with human-rights violations perpetrated by the Iraqis and told Frost that a great moral principle was at stake. "It's that big. It's that important. Nothing like this since World War II. Nothing of this moral importance since World War II."

Those remarks by Bush illustrate the extent to which he had become mesmerized by the crisis. To call the invasion of Kuwait, which was initially unopposed, the greatest moral issue since World War II was patently absurd. The forty-year standoff between East and West in central Europe, Korea in 1950, Vietnam—certainly for those who fought there—raised deep and troubling moral concerns that were far more profound than the replacement of one Middle Eastern despotism by another. In fact, domestic critics of the Bush team might argue that the end of racial segregation in the 1950s and '60s, the quest for equal rights, and the admission of blacks and other minorities as full participants in American society had a moral content at least the equal of anything that has happened in North America since the Civil War. Bush's hyperbole, his blinkered view of the crisis with Iraq, propelled American policy into an unyielding position that made conflict inevitable.

The fact was, the Amnesty International report on Iraq differed little from similar Amnesty documents on Syria, Iran, Turkey, and Saudi Arabia (to say nothing of pre-August 2 Kuwait), but Bush, who was unfamiliar with the genre, had been powerfully impressed. "No price is too heavy to pay" to reverse the Iraqi aggression, he told Frost.[62]

On the morning of January 3, Bush invited the congressional leadership to the White House for a breakfast conference. The 102nd Congress would be sworn in at noon that day, and the president wanted to test the water for his policy in the Gulf. That was long overdue. Senate Democrats, led by Mitchell and Nunn, appeared determined to prevent the president from sidling into war without congressional authorization. Kennedy, Kerrey, and North Carolina's Terry Sanford were against war under any circumstances, and even Bob Dole, the Senate's minority leader, seemed to have wandered off the reservation. Never close to the president, particularly after the bruising primary season in 1988, Dole told NBC's "Meet the Press" that putting the emir of Kuwait back on his throne was "not worth one American life, as far as I'm concerned."[63]

One advantage of sending Baker to Geneva was that it offered the White House an opportunity to forestall congressional action. At 7:30 A.M. on January 3, thirty minutes before Bush was scheduled to meet with the legislators, Marlin Fitzwater broke the news that Baker would meet Aziz on January 9. Just as had been the case on November 30 when the first Baker visit to Baghdad was announced, the news had a euphoric effect. The congressional leaders, who had been loaded for bear, waxed eloquent about the proposal. Representative Lee Hamilton of Indiana said "a new chapter" had begun. "It is difficult for me to think that indepth talks will not slide imperceptibly into negotiations."[64] Bush told the lawmakers he would like congressional endorsement for his policies in the Gulf, but that he would rather forgo it if it could not be "an overwhelming endorsement without a messy debate."[65] Messy debates are what democracy is all about, and the leadership declined to oblige the president. Nevertheless, rather than compromise Baker's negotiating position in Geneva, they agreed to hold off.[66]

When Mitchell spoke to the newly installed Senate that afternoon, he urged that no resolutions on the crisis be introduced until January 23. Since the warning order to Schwarzkopf set the attack for January 16, the Senate would have been excluded. In effect, it would, by silence, have acquiesced to Bush's decision to go to war. When Mitchell made his proposal, he was not privy to Schwarzkopf's instructions. But the president's men were fully aware of what was in store, and above all, so was George Bush. As had happened so often since August 2, the president had dissembled and Congress had been taken in. By dangling Baker's trip before the leadership, the White House had short-circuited congressional debate.

But the victory was short-lived. Mitchell's colleagues would have no part of the deal. Led by Tom Harkin of Iowa, Brock Adams of Washington, and Quentin Burdick of North Dakota, the Senate rejected Mitchell's proposed moratorium and demanded an immediate debate. The exchange was sharp, and the historic Senate chamber was packed. The Republicans sat silent as the Democrats ripped into their leader.

The following day, yielding to the pressure from his colleagues, Mitchell placed the Gulf crisis on the agenda for January 10, the day after Baker would meet with Aziz in Geneva. Dole supported the move. He was not the president's man. "For months we've been standing on the sideline, making all kinds of speeches but not casting a single vote. Congress had been AWOL," Dole said.[67] Mitchell expected the Senate to "dispose of the issue by January 15"—the date of the U.N. deadline.[68]

On Sunday, January 6, Speaker Foley indicated that the

House, too, would take up the issue, and that it would face an up-or-down vote before the U.N. deadline expired. Appearing on ABC's "This Week with David Brinkley," Foley said he thought the House would "narrowly" support a decision by President Bush to use force. Personally, he opposed it.[69]

Taken aback by the newfound congressional assertiveness, the administration shifted gears. James Baker, appearing on the same program with Foley, led the way. Of all the Bush team, Baker had been the most solicitous of Congress, and the most eager to bring it along. "We, frankly, are welcoming the fact that there will be a debate in the Congress," he told Foley. Baker was signaling that the administration did not want a constitutional crisis on top of a diplomatic and military crisis in Kuwait.[70]

That evening, the Bush team assembled once again in the living quarters of the White House. Baker, who had departed for Europe that afternoon, was not present. Bush took charge. With debates scheduled in both the House and the Senate, and final votes likely, the president said he wanted a favorable outcome. They needed a resolution to authorize the use of force. Quayle agreed. So, too, did Powell and Scowcroft. Powell believed it was important to have Congress behind them. He did not want the troops left in the lurch. A nation at war had to say it was at war. Not like Korea. Not like Vietnam.

Dick Cheney held back. Obsessively partisan himself, he attributed those motives to others. He was suspicious that the Democrats, especially Sam Nunn, would use a floor debate to seek political advantage. Why go to Congress and risk a "no" vote, he asked? Cheney was impatient with constitutional arguments. If the war was successful and over quickly, the president would be acclaimed. If the war went badly or dragged on, Bush would be blamed regardless of what Congress had done. Why take the chance?[71]

Cheney was alone. That night Bush began calling House and Senate Republicans to get a head count. The telephone technique that the president had used to build the coalition was turned on Capitol Hill. Bush personally typed out the letter he would send requesting Congress to endorse the U.N. resolution.[72]

Tuesday morning, January 8, the president met again with his top advisers and their legal staffs. The congressional liaison teams were brought in. Bush distributed copies of his draft letter. He said he was inclined to send it. The question was whether to support it actively or stand back and let events take their course. Most thought the president would win a vote, but it would be close.

Bush asked about his constitutional authority. If Congress voted no, could he still carry out the U.N. mandate? Deputy Attorney General William P. Barr, the senior lawyer present, thought that he could. The war power was a shared power. Obviously the president's authority would be strongest if Congress agreed. But as commander in chief, the president could order the forces into combat.* "An inconsistent resolution," said Barr, "could not take your power away."[73] Congress could cut off the funds. "They can put you in a difficult political position." Barr hedged his advice. He thought it was best for

---

*Strongest support for the president to use force on his own authority lies in two Supreme Court decisions, the *Prize Cases* in 1863 (2 Black 635), and *Martin v. Mott* in 1827 (12 Wheaton 19).

In the *Prize Cases*, Justice Grier, speaking for a sharply divided Court, upheld President Lincoln's imposition of a naval blockade on Southern ports without prior congressional sanction. In *Mott*, Justice Story, with a unanimous Court behind him, sustained President Madison's order calling the New York militia to Federal service during the war of 1812. Both instances involved judgment calls by the president, and both can be easily distinguished from the situation Bush confronted in 1991.

In the *Prize Cases*, Lincoln was dealing with active rebellion in the Southern states and was trying desperately to preserve the Union. Before the Supreme Court heard the case, Congress had retroactively approved the president's actions. In *Mott*, the country also was at war, and Madison acted in the face of what he thought to be an impending British invasion from Canada.

Unlike the situation in the Gulf, Lincoln and Madison were acting to defend the United States under circumstances in which hostilities had already begun. In both instances the president was acting pursuant to his authority as commander in chief to defend the nation from attack. Neither case would support a unilateral decision by the president to initiate hostilities against a country with which the United States was at peace.

Bush to try to gain Congress's support. So too did Scowcroft. Even if Bush had the authority to initiate conflict, Scowcroft thought the president's position would be enhanced with an affirmative vote. Sununu agreed. "We've got to. We've got to try to shape it."[74]

Cheney again dissented. If the president sent the letter, it would be interpreted as meaning he needed congressional authorization. Cheney thought the risks were too great. He urged Bush to stand aside.[75] It is curious that Cheney, the only member of the Bush team (aside from Quayle) with significant legislative experience, should take such a dim view of Congress's role. Part of that is attributable to excessive partisanship: the take-no-prisoners syndrome of the GOP's far right. But part reflected executive hubris, the pride that accompanied the power of command. For Cheney, a Vietnam dropout, to preside over the nation's defense establishment was a heady experience. Why share it with "my former colleagues," as he sarcastically labeled them?

Bush decided to send the letter. That afternoon identical copies were dispatched to Foley, Mitchell, Dole, and House Minority Leader Bob Michel. "The current situation in the Persian Gulf," the president wrote, "threatens vital U.S. interests. [It] also threatens the peace." Bush said it would improve the chances for peace if Congress would support "the position adopted by the U.N. Security Council." He stressed the impact congressional support would have on Iraq. Throughout the letter, Bush emphasized his desire for a peaceful solution. The fact that he was asking Congress for a mandate to go to war was glossed over. Bush's style had not changed. He was asking for the functional equivalent of a declaration of war and calling it a vote for peace.

I therefore request that the House of Representatives and the Senate adopt a Resolution stating that Congress supports the use of all necessary means to implement U.N. Security Council Resolution 678. Such action would send the clearest

*possible message to Saddam Hussein that he must withdraw
without condition or delay from Kuwait. . . .*[76]

The day after Bush's letter was sent, Baker met with Aziz
in Geneva. After six hours of unproductive discussion, the
meeting broke up. Looking back, Aziz believes it was preor-
dained. "The West was unwilling . . . to accept Iraq as an equal
partner in a negotiation," he told Milton Viorst of *The New
Yorker*.[77]

From Geneva, Baker flew to Saudi Arabia for a prearranged
meeting with King Fahd. The purpose was to ask Fahd's permission to launch an attack. Under the agreement negotiated
by Cheney in August, that was required. Fahd immediately
agreed, asking only that he be informed beforehand.[78] Baker's
immediate flight to Riyadh after meeting Aziz leaves little
doubt that the Geneva overture was never taken seriously
by Washington. It was simply another box that had to be
checked off.

On January 10, the congressional debate began. It was apparent that the vote would be close, especially in the Senate,
where Sam Nunn, rock-solid on national security, provided
cover for liberal Democrats instinctively opposed to the use of
force. On the president's side, the Committee for Peace and
Security in the Gulf, a bipartisan coalition of Middle East hawks
headed by defense specialist Richard Perle and including such
prominent Democrats as Robert Strauss, Ann Lewis, and Representative Stephen Solarz of New York, provided effective support for those who favored military action. The committee
"made a real difference on the Hill," said Scowcroft afterward.
"People like Solarz were very good as a balance to Nunn because it showed that some of the smartest, most knowledgeable
people in this area were on our side of the issue."[79] Solarz, in
fact, helped draft the administration's resolution, and cospon-
sored it in the House. The American Israel Public Affairs Committee (AIPAC) and prominent defense contractors worked

vigorously on the president's behalf.[80] AIPAC, one of America's most influential lobbies, unleashed its nationwide network of contributors, prominent businessmen, and social friends of House and Senate members in a last-minute effort to corral the undecided. How effective that was is problematic. The issue was so important, and the feelings so deep, that most members voted their conscience. For example, Jewish members in both chambers, usually sympathetic to an AIPAC appeal, divided almost evenly in support and opposition to the president's policy.[81]

In both the House and the Senate, two separate resolutions were introduced. In the House, opponents of the president's policy, led by Majority Leader Dick Gephardt and Representative Lee Hamilton, offered a measure that would continue economic sanctions against Iraq. In the Senate, Nunn and Mitchell proposed a similar resolution, adding an explicit reference to the exclusive authority of Congress to declare war. The administration's measure was introduced by Solarz, Foreign Affairs Committee Chairman Dante Fascell, and Minority Leader Michel in the House, and Senator John Warner of Virginia in the Senate, the ranking Republican on the Armed Services Committee. It authorized the president "to use United States Armed Forces pursuant to United Nations Security Council Resolution 678" to liberate Kuwait and enforce all other U.N. resolutions dealing with the crisis. As required by the War Powers Act, the resolution provided explicit statutory authorization for the president to use force. Representative Fascell called it the "practical equivalent of a declaration of war."[82] Dick Cheney told members not to vote for it "if you are reading this as another diplomatic lever."[83] Baker said that if Iraq was not out of Kuwait when the U.N. deadline expired, the United States "would not wait very long to go to war to force the Iraqis out."[84]

The debate lasted three days, much of it carried live on network television. In the House, 223 of the 435 members spoke on the issue. So many senators wanted to speak on Friday, January

11, that the Senate remained in session until 2:40 A.M. There were moments of heartfelt eloquence, as when Representative Barbara Vucanovich, a Republican from Nevada, recounted how she came from a military family.

> *Two of my brothers were West Point graduates. My Dad, a career Army officer, taught at West Point. And my grand-father, also a career Army officer, was in the Medical Corps. One of my brothers gave his life at Anzio, and I can remember the day my mother was notified of my brother's sacrifice. It was a day that was permanently etched in my memory. . . . [But] there can be no reward for brutal aggression. If we do nothing, and Saddam Hussein pays no price for swallowing up the country of Kuwait . . . we are as guilty as he is.*[85]

Senator Joseph Lieberman, Democrat from Connecticut, who worked hard for the administration's resolution, spoke for many when he called on his colleagues to "stand shoulder to shoulder with our president at this critical moment of confrontation."[86]

The Senate opposition was led by Mitchell and Nunn. Mitchell said, "This is not a debate about whether force should ever be used. No one proposes to rule out the use of force. . . . The question is should war be truly a last resort when all other means fail or should we start with war before other means have been fully and fairly exhausted."[87]

Edward Kennedy, always eloquent and often right, said, "Our policy in the Persian Gulf is not broken, and it cannot be fixed by war. There is still time for the Senate to save the president from himself—and save thousands of American soldiers . . . from dying in the desert in a war whose cruelty will be exceeded only by the lack of any rational necessity for waging it."[88]

At times there was an air of testiness, as when Moynihan

accused Bush of moving secretly "to create the ongoing permanent Orwellian crisis,"[89] or when Dole, warming to the debate, allowed how "the Republican strategy is to get Saddam Hussein out of Kuwait. Some of the Democrats' strategy appears to be to get George Bush out of the White House."[90]

As the debate wound to a close early Saturday morning, it became increasingly apparent that the president had the votes. As the roll calls neared, both chambers were jammed with members. The mood was solemn, the galleries hushed. There was little bravado or chest-thumping. Speaker Foley may have captured the mood best as he closed the House debate with a rare floor speech:

> Let me offer a public prayer for this House, for all of us, for Congress, for our president—and for the American people, in particular, those young Americans who stand ready to make the supreme sacrifice. May God bless us and guide us and help us in fateful days that lie ahead. However you vote, let us come together after this vote without recrimination. We are all Americans here—not Democrats, not Republicans.[91]

Across the chamber, Minority Leader Michel dabbed tears from his eyes. "In thirty-five years of legislating, no vote has affected me more emotionally. There can't be anything more profound," he said.[92]

Despite the drama that stalked Capitol Hill, and the occasional eloquence of the debate, it had come too late. The president, through his resolute action, had foreclosed the issue. Once a half-million U.S. troops were deployed in Saudi Arabia, it was too late to second-guess administration policy. By remaining silent earlier, by failing to challenge the president promptly, Congress had no option but to ratify the war that was all but certain.

The Gephardt-Hamilton resolution to stick with sanctions

was voted first. It lost 183–250, a surprisingly wide margin. The administration's measure authorizing the use of force passed by exactly the same total, 250–183. Eighty-six Democrats, including the chairmen of Appropriations (Jamie Whitten), Ways and Means (Dan Rostenkowski), Armed Services (Les Aspin), and Foreign Affairs (Dante Fascell), supported Bush. Only three Republicans voted against. Two members, both ill, did not vote.*

In the Senate, the count was much closer. "It was an hour of doubt, an hour of destiny," said Maine's William Cohen. Nunn closed the debate. "We are playing a winning hand," he said. "I see no compelling reason to rush to military action."[93] His proposal for sanctions was voted first. Each senator rose at his desk to cast his vote as the clerk called his name. That procedure was rarely used. Those who followed Congress closely could remember only three other occasions in their lifetimes. Forty-six senators voted in favor of Nunn's resolution, fifty-three opposed. Then the vote on the administration's proposal. Fifty-two voted yes, forty-seven voted no. The measure had carried by just three votes. Senator Cranston, undergoing treatment for cancer, did not vote. Two Republicans, Hatfield of Oregon and Grassley of Iowa, voted against the president. Ten Democrats voted in favor. The Joint Resolution had passed. The constitutional issue had been resolved. Congress had granted Bush the authority to initiate hostilities if Saddam did not withdraw by January 15—three days away. There was no applause in the chamber when the result was announced.

Moments after the congressional action, President Bush made a brief statement. The vote, he said, "unmistakably dem-

---

*As a historical footnote, there were twenty-seven members of Congress who had been present in 1964 when the Gulf of Tonkin Resolution had been passed. All had voted in favor. Of the twenty-seven, twelve voted to authorize the use of force in Kuwait, and fourteen voted against. One was ill. One member of Congress, Jamie Whitten of Mississippi, the dean of the House, had been present on December 8, 1941, to vote for the declaration of war against Japan.

onstrates the United States' commitment to the international demand for a complete and unconditional withdrawal of Iraq from Kuwait. This clear expression of the Congress represents the last, best chance for peace."[94]

Bush signed the resolution into law Monday morning, January 14.[95] As he did so, he restated the administration view of prerogative power. That view had been muted during the congressional debate.

> As I made clear to congressional leaders at the outset, my request for congressional support did not, and my signing of this resolution does not, constitute any change in the longstanding positions of the executive branch on either the President's constitutional authority to use the Armed Forces to defend vital U.S. interests or the constitutionality of the War Powers Resolution.[96]

Bush, who little more than a week earlier had not wanted a messy debate, eagerly accepted the victory. Nevertheless, he was not backing away from the pretensions of the imperial presidency. Passage of the Joint Resolution temporarily quelled the constitutional debate. The White House was free to proceed with what was still euphemistically described as the offensive option. Only the military seemed less than elated. On the eve of battle, it was General Powell who sounded a note of caution. "War is a terrible thing with unpredictable consequences," he reminded an audience in Washington.[97] "Many, many people are going to die. And it's important for people to understand that it's not inconceivable we could lose." It is ironic that in the last days of peace, it fell to America's soldiers to warn the nation of the horrors of war.

Late Monday afternoon, the president held an urgent briefing for congressional leaders. Senator Dole said afterward that "there has been absolutely no ray of hope coming from Saddam Hussein."[98] Congressman Michel said the tone was somber. War appeared inevitable. The nation rallied round. Sam Nunn said, "It's time for America to stand together."[99]

Wednesday morning, January 16, the first flight of B-52s took off from Barksdale Air Force Base in Louisiana. Flying time to their targets in the Gulf was eighteen hours. They could still be recalled should Saddam begin his withdrawal. At 4:50 in the afternoon, the first F-15 Eagles were launched from bases in Saudi Arabia. They too could be recalled, but the clock was ticking down. Forty minutes later, 5:30 P.M. Eastern Standard Time, the cruiser *Bunker Hill* fired the first of its Tomahawk cruise missiles at a target deep in Iraq. Its flight time was ninety minutes. It could not be recalled. The war had begun. The massive air attack, in the planning stage for months, would eventually launch more sorties in a single day against Iraq than Iran had mounted during its entire eight-year war. The awesome might of Desert Storm had been unleashed. The president, backed by Congress, the United Nations, and the American people, had ordered it.

At eight minutes after 7 P.M., as the first missiles hit their targets, Marlin Fitzwater read a brief statement to the press. Paraphrasing Dwight Eisenhower's famous radio address on June 6, 1944, Fitzwater said, "The liberation of Kuwait has begun."[100]

Two hours later, President Bush addressed the nation. "Tonight the battle has been joined," the president said. "We are determined to knock out Saddam Hussein's nuclear bomb potential. We will also destroy his chemical weapons facilities. Much of Saddam's artillery and tanks will also be destroyed."[101]

Bush said he had instructed the military "to take every necessary step to prevail as quickly as possible. . . . This will not be another Vietnam. . . . Our troops . . . will not be asked to fight with one hand tied behind their back."

Finally, the president said the United States had no quarrel with the people of Iraq. "Our goal is not the conquest of Iraq. It is the liberation of Kuwait."

Forty-three days later, that goal was achieved. More than

half a million Iraqis had been killed or wounded. The destruction was massive. Iraq had not surrendered, Saddam still held power, but George Bush called a halt. The slaughter ceased. Kuwait had been set free. Or perhaps more accurately, it had been returned to the control of the al-Sabah dynasty.

EPILOGUE

And everybody
praised the Duke,
Who this great fight
did win.
"But what good came
of it at last?,"
Quoth little Peterkin.
"Why that I
cannot tell," said he,
"But 'twas a famous
victory."
Robert Southey
The Battle of Blenheim

America's forty-three day war with Iraq was fought to punish aggression. It was also fought to destroy Iraq's military potential. It may have been fought to remove Saddam Hussein from power. Certainly it was fought because President Bush decided there was no other option. The United Nations sanctioned the conflict, Congress approved it, and the American people supported it. But in the final analysis, this was George Bush's war, and, inevitably, whatever passes for peace in the region is George Bush's peace.

For the first time in its history, the United States finds itself deeply embroiled in the muddled affairs of the Middle East. An Army support force remains in Saudi Arabia, unsure of its mission yet hesitant to withdraw. A mighty armada stands offshore, poised to intervene should that be required. More than 20 percent of the Air Force is still deployed in the Gulf, combat-loaded and ready for action, while a mountain of military supplies, all properly accounted for, too valuable to be abandoned but too expensive to move, lies moldering in the heat.

In Iraq and Kuwait, the destruction unleashed by Desert Storm has been massive. More than half a million Iraqis lie dead or wounded. An additional hundred thousand—Kurds and Shiites—perished in the civil strife that followed. Five million people have fled their homes, a refugee exodus that has spawned enormous suffering and deprivation.[1] In many localities, water treatment and sewage facilities no longer function. Red Cross health officials despair of cholera, typhoid, and a host of water-borne diarrheal diseases.[2] Eight months after the war, 80 percent of Iraq's power grid was still out of service, aggravating the crisis in health care and retarding economic recovery. Epidemic and famine lurk menacingly as the embargo continues to take its toll.[3] The U.N. Children's Fund reports that "malnutrition, which had not been seen in Iraq in the last decade, is now widely reported in pediatric wards and health clinics across the country."[4] The situation, in short, is a human catastrophe of incalculable proportions. General Powell was right. "War is a terrible thing."[5]

In Baghdad, Saddam Hussein remains in power, and the Baathist regime appears as firmly entrenched as ever. True, Iraq's military threat to the region has been diminished, its armaments industry curtailed and its nuclear program apparently nipped in the bud. But whether any of that will remain the case is open to doubt. Victorious coalitions quickly lose interest in the affairs of a defeated nation, while among the vanquished, resentment festers and a desire for revenge often gains ascendancy.

In retrospect, it is far from clear that the war was necessary or that the coalition's victory will bring stability to the region. The responsibility for that lies with President Bush. Rather than seek a consensus solution that would include Iraq, Bush disdained to deal with Baghdad. Throughout the crisis, he escalated American aims and made war all but inevitable. In early August 1990, Washington's announced goal was to defend Saudi Arabia. By September, it had become the liberation of Kuwait and the return of the emir to power. In October, Bush advocated war crimes trials for Iraq's leadership. Then, in November, he altered the defensive configuration of Desert Shield, adding another 230,000 troops to provide an "offensive option." By December, the policy of economic sanctions had been rejected, and a U.N. ultimatum for Iraq's withdrawal from Kuwait had been imposed. That was accompanied by new demands that Iraq's chemical and nuclear weapons be destroyed. Throughout that period, Bush remained in personal control of American policy. Baghdad's overtures for settlement, often garbled in the double-talk of the Middle East, were abruptly dismissed. George Bush, it seems, wanted a fight, and, as future historians will point out, he provoked Saddam into obliging him.

Throughout the crisis, Bush dissembled. American forces were ordered to the Gulf ostensibly to thwart an Iraqi attack on Saudi Arabia. Supposedly, the initiative had come from King Fahd. But Saudi Arabia was never directly threatened, and Fahd acted only after being subjected to enormous pressure from Washington. Early efforts to implement an "Arab solution" that would have effected an Iraqi withdrawal from Kuwait were deliberately torpedoed by the White House. At the same time, Bush publicly castigated Saddam for his intransigence.

In the United States, presidential impatience determined the rate of march. For whatever political reasons may have been involved, Bush discarded economic sanctions and, over the visible reluctance of the military high command, selected war as the preferable option. That, too, was disguised. Not until eight days after signing the presidential order doubling the size of Central Command did Bush inform the Congress and the American people. The doubts of the joint chiefs of staff and of General Schwarzkopf were never publicly acknowledged. The preference of the diplomatic and military communities to stick with sanctions was ignored.

Most important, Bush's original order to General Powell to commence hostilities on January 16 was a singular, unilateral decision made by the president based on his authority as commander in chief. It, too, was not initially revealed to Congress or to the public. A declaration of war was not requested. In fact, the White House sought to mislead the legislators into postponing a debate on American policy in the Gulf until after war had begun. In that sense, Secretary of State Baker's meeting with Tariq Aziz in Geneva was a red herring.

Throughout the crisis, Bush acted with a small coterie of subordinates. Expert opinion was screened out, and the National Security Council rarely met in structured fashion. Means and ends were never reconciled, policy alternatives were not canvassed, structured analysis was not rendered. The executive branch of government moved at the president's command, and no institutional checks were provided. Ultimately, it was George Bush's personal preferences that determined American policy. A constitutional crisis was narrowly averted when the White House, at the eleventh hour, sought congressional approval to make war, but as soon as that had been obtained, Bush again proclaimed prerogative powers.

Congress itself merits little credit. The tradition of bipartisanship in foreign policy deterred most members from criticizing the president's actions. In addition, the White House concealed its hand effectively. Congress was kept in the dark as to administration motives until it was too late to offer effective criticism. The initial deployment in August, the massive reinforcement in November, and the final orders to Schwarzkopf on December 29 were cloaked from congressional oversight. The president made policy and Congress acquiesced. Only rarely did the congressional leadership assert its constitutional authority. And it usually did so because it was pushed by the legislative rank and file. In a sense, the leadership wanted to have it both ways. They sought to protect Congress's war powers, but they ducked responsibility for the substance of American policy. Instinctively, they deferred to the president's judgment.

Bush's coalition diplomacy was impressive. But the costs were high. Independence movements in Estonia, Latvia, and Lithuania became hostages to U.S.-Soviet cooperation. China was forgiven the brutal repression of pro-democracy forces in Tiananmen Square, Egypt's loyalty was assured through debt write-offs at the ultimate expense of the American taxpayer, and Syria was forgiven virtually every crime of which Iraq stood accused—including the occupation of small neighboring countries (vide Lebanon). The bottom line was that American power was used capriciously. Opportunism, not principle, determined the administration's policy.

Conventional wisdom to the contrary, the role of the United Nations is also troubling. The original Security Council resolutions condemning Iraqi aggression, calling on Baghdad to withdraw, and imposing economic sanctions, are fully consistent with the organization's Charter. But the passage of Resolution 678, permitting each member country to proceed as it wished against Iraq, represented an abdication of international responsibility. In effect, the United States was given a blank check to go to war, independent of U.N. control. That is a dangerous precedent. It legalizes military action by nations acting individually, subject to no restraint except their own good judgment. Equally disturbing is the failure of the Security Council to seek a negotiated settlement. Article 33 of the Charter imposes an obligation to attempt a peaceful solution of any situation that is war threatening. Was military conflict the only way to restore an independent Kuwait? Should the Security Council have played a more active role? Should it have opened a dialogue with Saddam instead of simply issuing ultimatums? Did the Security Council become a tool of American foreign policy, thus compromising its future credibility?

It is an ill wind that blows no good. By insisting on massive force, the American military has made its point. War is not an instrument of everyday policy. The abstractions of academia to the contrary, the longings of defense contractors notwithstanding, war is something to be resorted to only when all else has failed. In a world shrouded in cynicism, that, historically, has been an American tradition. From Washington's farewell address, through Sherman's grim reminder that "war is hell," to President Eisenhower's heartfelt admonition about the pernicious influence of the military-industrial complex, the United States, by and large, has eschewed foreign adventures except when national survival was at stake. But the Cold War lowered the threshold of military intervention. Korea and Vietnam provide stark reminders. And the eagerness with which popular opinion embraced American intervention in the Gulf is an unfortunate legacy. The destructive consequences of the conflict, the enormous toll of human suffering, the unsolved problems of the region that remain, combined with the long agenda of domestic needs unattended to, make clear the utter folly of George Bush's war.

John Quincy Adams may have said it best:

Wherever the standard of freedom and independence has been unfurled, there will be America's heart, her benedictions, and her prayers. But she goes not abroad in search of monsters to destroy.

July 4, 1821

APPENDIX

RESOLUTIONS AUTHORIZING USE OF FORCE

United Nations Security Council
November 29, 1990—Resolution 678
UN approves "All necessary means" to end crisis.
Vote 12–2 (China abstaining).

The Security Council,

Recalling and reaffirming its Resolutions 660 (1990), 661 (1990), 662 (1990), 664 (1990), 665 (1990), 666 (1990), 667 (1990), 669 (1990), 670 (1990), 674 (1990) and 677 (1990),

Noting that, despite all efforts by the United Nations, Iraq refuses to comply with its obligation to implement Resolution 660 (1990) and the above subsequent relevant resolutions, in flagrant contempt of the Council,

Mindful of its duties and responsibilites under the Charter of the United Nations for the maintenance and preservation of international peace and security,

Determined to secure full compliance with its decisions,

Acting under Chapter VII of the Charter of the United Nations,

1. Demands that Iraq comply fully with Resolution 660 (1990) and all subsequent relevant resolutions and decides, while maintaining all its decisions, to allow Iraq one final opportunity, as a pause of goodwill, to do so;

2. Authorizes Member States cooperating with the Government of Kuwait, unless Iraq on or before January 15, 1991 fully implements, as set forth in paragraph 1 above, the foregoing resolutions, to use all necessary means to uphold and implement Security Council Resolution 660 (1990) and all subsequent relevant resolutions and to restore international peace and security in the area;

3. Requests all states to provide appropriate support for the actions undertaken in pursuance of paragraph 2 of this resolution;

4. Requests the states concerned to keep the Council regularly informed on the progress of actions undertaken pursuant to paragraphs 2 and 3 of this resolution;

5. Decides to remain seized of the matter.

Congressional Joint Resolution
January 12, 1991
(Public Law 102–1)

House Action   Senate Action
Yeas 250; Nays 183   Yeas 52; Nays 47

Whereas the Government of Iraq without provocation invaded and occupied the territory of Kuwait on August 2, 1990; and

Whereas both the House of Representatives (in H.J. Res. 658 of the 101st
Congress) and the Senate (in S. Con. Res. 147 of the 101st Congress) have
condemned Iraq's invasion of Kuwait and declared their support for international action to reverse Iraq's aggression; and

Whereas Iraq's conventional, chemical, biological, and nuclear weapons
and ballistic missile programs and its demonstrated willingness to use weapons
of mass destruction pose a grave threat to world peace; and

Whereas the international community has demanded that Iraq withdraw
unconditionally and immediately from Kuwait and that Kuwait's independence and legitimate government be restored; and

Whereas the U.N. Security Council repeatedly affirmed the inherent right
of individual or collective self-defense in response to the armed attack by Iraq
against Kuwait in accordance with Article 51 of the U.N. Charter; and

Whereas, in the absence of full compliance by Iraq with its resolutions,
the U.N. Security Council in Resolution 678 has authorized member states
of the United Nations to use all necessary means, after January 15, 1991, to
uphold and implement all relevant Security Council resolutions and to restore international peace and security in the area; and

Whereas Iraq has persisted in its illegal occupation of, and brutal aggression against Kuwait: Now, therefore be it

*Resolved by the Senate and House of Representatives of the United States of
America in Congress assembled,*

SECTION 1. SHORT TITLE

This joint resolution may be cited as the "Authorization for Use of Military Force Against Iraq Resolution".

SEC. 2. AUTHORIZATION FOR USE OF UNITED STATES ARMED FORCES.

(a)   AUTHORIZATION.—The President is authorized, subject to subsection (b), to use United States Armed Forces pursuant to United Nations
Security Council Resolution 678 (1990) in order to achieve implementation
of Security Council Resolutions 660, 661, 662, 664, 665, 666, 667, 669, 670,
674, and 677.

(b)   REQUIREMENT FOR DETERMINATION THAT USE OF MIL-
ITARY FORCE IS NECESSARY.—Before exercising the authority granted
in subsection (a), the President shall make available to the Speaker of the

House of Representatives and the President pro tempore of the Senate his determination that

(1)   the United States has used all appropriate diplomatic and other peaceful means to obtain compliance by Iraq with the United Nations Security Council resolutions cited in subsection (a); and

(2)   those efforts have not been and would not be successful in obtaining such compliance.

(c)   WAR POWERS RESOLUTION REQUIREMENTS.—

(1)   specific statutory authorization.—Consistent with section 8(a)(1) of the War Powers Resolution, the Congress declares that this section is intended to constitute specific statutory authorization with the meaning of section 5(b) of the War Powers Resolution.

(2)   APPLICABILITY OF OTHER REQUIREMENTS.—Nothing in this resolution supersedes any requirement of the War Powers Resolution.

SEC. 3 REPORTS TO CONGRESS

At least once every 60 days, the President shall submit to the Congress a summary on the status of efforts to obtain compliance by Iraq with the resolutions adopted by the United Nations Security Council in response to Iraq's aggression.

NOTES

Introduction

Admiral Crowe's quote cited in Bob Woodward, *The Com-manders* (New York: Simon & Schuster, 1991), p. 39.
1. News conference remarks, November 30, 1990. *Weekly Compilation of Presidential Documents, Administration of George Bush*, 1990, p. 1948. (Hereinafter WCPD.)
2. Television address, August 8, 1990. "I ask for your support in a decision I've made to stand up for what's right and condemn what's wrong, all in the cause of peace." WCPD, 1990, p. 1216.
3. News conference remarks, October 31, 1990. "The American flag is flying over the Kuwaiti Embassy, and our people inside are being starved by a brutal dictator. And do you think I'm concerned about it? You're damned right I am. And what am I going to do about it? Let's just wait and

see. Because I've had it with that kind of treatment of Americans." *WCPD, 1990,* p. 1707.

4. News conference remarks in Cairo (with President Mubarak), November 23, 1990. "And I can tell you, sir [to a U.S. reporter], I am getting increasingly frustrated about the treatment of the U.S. Embassy [in Kuwait] and the treatment of innocent hostages." *WCPD, 1990,* p. 1912.

5. News conference remarks, November 30, 1990. "Consider me provoked when it comes to the United States Embassy [in Kuwait]. Consider me provoked when I see Americans without proper food and medical equipment." *WCPD, 1990,* p. 1951.

6. News conference remarks, November 1, 1990. "I've indicated we're prepared to give sanctions time to work, and I'll report that here again today. But I am not ruling out further options. . . ." *WCPD, 1990,* p. 1719.

7. News conference remarks, November 8, 1990. *WCPD, 1990,* p. 1791.

8. Speech, Mashpee Middle School, Orlando, Florida, November 1, 1990. "And today, I am more determined than ever in my life: This aggression will not stand." *WCPD, 1990,* p. 1718.

9. News conference remarks, November 8, 1990. "So, I have not ruled out the use of force at all, and I think that's evident by what we are doing here today." *WCPD, 1990,* 1791.

10. News conference remarks, November 21, 1990. "Well, the deadline [for Iraqi withdrawal] should have been the day the U.N. passed its first resolution or, in my view, the day he first went in [to Kuwait]. But I have no specific deadline in mind." *WCPD, 1990,* p. 1879.

11. News conference remarks, November 30, 1990. "And I pledge to you: There will not be any murky ending. . . . I will never—ever—agree to a halfway effort." *WCPD, 1990,* p. 1949.

12. The statement is implicitly attributed to General Powell in Woodward, *op. cit.*, p. 41.

13. Martin Gilbert, *The Second World War: A Complete History* (New York: Henry Holt and Company, 1989).

14. Arthur Schlesinger, Jr., "Iraq, War, and the Constitution," *The Wall Street Journal*, November 12, 1990.

15. Address to the Federalist Society, Washington, D.C., January 30, 1987. Cited in the *Washington Post*, January 31, 1987.

16. George Bush (with Douglas Weed), *Man of Integrity* (Eugene, Ore.: Harvest House, 1988), p. 75.

17. Exchange with reporters, San Francisco, California, October 29, 1990. "History is replete with examples where the president has had to take action. And I've done this in the past [Panama] and certainly . . . would have no hesitancy at all." *WCPD*, 1990, p. 1701.

18. For Baker's testimony, see the *Hearings* of the Senate Foreign Relations Committee (October 18, 1990) and the House Foreign Affairs Committee (October 19, 1990). Both are reported extensively in *The New York Times* and *Washington Post*, October 19 and 20, respectively.

19. *Hearings*, Senate Armed Services Committee, December 3, 1990. Cited in *The New York Times*, December 16, 1990.

20. *WCPD*, 1991, p. 25.

21. Garry Wills, ed. *The Federalist Papers* (New York: Bantam Books, 1982), p. 386 (Federalist 75).

22. *Ibid.*, p. 350 (Federalist 69).

23. *The Writings of James Madison*, ed. Gaillard Hunt (New York: G. P. Putnam's Sons, 1902), vol. 6, p. 179.

24. *Ibid.*, vol. 2, pp. 131-133.

25. Marshall's speech was delivered March 7, 1800. For the text, see *The Papers of John Marshall*, ed. Charles T. Cullen (Chapel Hill: University of North Carolina Press, 1974), vol. 4, pp. 83–109. For commentary, see Albert J. Beveridge, *The Life of John Marshall* (Boston: Houghton Mifflin,

1916), vol. 2, pp. 458–475; Edward S. Corwin, *The President: Office and Powers*, 4th rev. ed. (New York: New York University Press, 1957), pp. 177–178.

26. See, in particular, Marshall's Opinion for the Court in *Little v. Barreme*, 2 Cranch (6 U.S.) 170 (1804). Also see *Bas v. Tingy*, 4 Dallas (4 U.S.) 37 (1800); and *Talbot v. Seeman*, 1 Cranch (5 U.S.) 1 (1801).

27. 1 Cranch (5 U.S.) at 28.

28. Impromptu remarks on the South Lawn of the White House after returning from a weekend stay at Camp David, 3:05 P.M., August 5, 1990. "This will not stand. This will not stand, this aggression against Kuwait." *WCPD 1990*, p. 1209.

29. Woodward, *op. cit.*, p. 261.

30. *Newsweek*, January 28, 1991, p. 60.

31. The Iraqi transcript of Glaspie's interview with Saddam was published in *The New York Times*, September 23, 1990. With minor modifications, its authenticity appears genuine.

32. Woodward, *op. cit.*, p. 353.

33. *Ibid.*, pp. 41–42.

34. *Ibid.*, p. 342.

35. Winston Churchill. *The River War* (London: Longmans Green, 1899); Robin Hallett, *Africa Since 1875* (Ann Arbor: University of Michigan Press, 1974), p. 98.

36. The text of the U.N. report is reprinted in *The New York Times*, March 23, 1991.

37. Richard J. Barnet, "The Uses of Force," *The New Yorker*, April 29, 1991, p. 88.

38. Tom Wicker, "Smoke Over Kuwait," *The New York Times*, April 3, 1991; Wicker, "Kuwait Still Burns," *ibid.*, July 28, 1991.

1. Invasion

1. The best on-the-scene coverage of the Iraqi invasion is in *The Times* (London), August 3 and 4, 1990. The *Washington Post* and *The New York Times* carry related stories, the *Post* from Kuwait City, the *Times* from Washington.
2. Unless otherwise indicated, all military statistics are from *The Military Balance, 1990–1991* (London: Institute for Strategic Studies, 1990).
3. General Powell's press conference remarks were reprinted in *The New York Times*, August 9, 1990.
4. As reported by Caryle Murphy from Kuwait City, *Washington Post*, August 3, 1990.
5. For a lengthy obituary of Sheik Fahd, see *The Times* (London), August 4, 1990.
6. *Ibid.*, August 3, 1990.
7. *The New York Times*, August 4, 1990.
8. *The Times* (London), August 3, 1990.
9. *The New York Times*, August 4, 1990.
10. *The Times* (London), August 3, 1990.
11. *Washington Post*, August 3, 1990.
12. Alexander Cockburn, in *The Wall Street Journal*, September 6, 1990.
13. *Washington Post*, August 2, 1990.
14. *Ibid.*, August 3, 1990.
15. *Ibid.*, August 2, 1990.
16. *Ibid.*
17. Bob Woodward, *The Commanders* (New York: Simon & Schuster, 1991), p. 222.
18. *Time*, January 7, 1991, p. 20.
19. *Washington Post*, August 3, 1990.
20. *Ibid.*
21. *The New York Times*, August 4, 1990.
22. *Ibid.*, August 3, 1990.
23. *Ibid.*, August 4, 1990.
24. Security Council Resolution 660.

25. *The New York Times*, August 3, 1990.

26. *The Times* (London), August 3, 1990.

27. *The New York Times*, August 3, 1990.

28. *Ibid.*

29. *The Wall Street Journal*, December 26, 1990.

30. Quoted in Judith Miller and Laurie Mylorie, *Saddam Hussein and the Crisis in the Gulf* (New York: Times Books/ Random House, 1990), p. 8.

31. Don Oberdorfer, "Missed Signals in the Middle East," *Washington Post Magazine*, March 17, 1991, p. 21.

32. *Washington Post*, August 4, 1990.

33. *The Wall Street Journal*, August 10, 1990.

34. *Time*, August 6, 1990, p. 34.

35. Milton Viorst, "Report from Baghdad," *The New Yorker*, September 24, 1990, p. 90.

36. Kuwait's OPEC quota was 1.5 million barrels a day. For most of 1990, its daily production exceeded 2 million barrels. *Time*, August 6, 1990, p. 34.

37. *Washington Post*, July 31, 1990; *The Times* (London), August 2, 1990.

38. The quotation is from Mohammed al-Mashat, Iraqi ambassador to the United States. Cited in Miller and Mylorie, *op. cit*, p. 20.

39. *The Times* (London), August 2, 1990.

40. King Hussein interview, *The New York Times*, October 16, 1990.

41. Miller and Mylorie, *op. cit.*, p. 10.

42. Milton Viorst, "Report from Baghdad," *The New Yorker*, June 24, 1991, p. 66.

43. King Hussein interview, *op.cit.*

44. The World Bank, *World Development Report, 1990* (New York: Oxford University Press, 1990), pp. 178–179.

45. *The Times* (London), August 8, 1990.

46. Bernard Lewis, "The Roots of Muslim Rage," *Atlantic Monthly*, September 1990, p. 52.

47. Fouad Ajami, "The Summer of Arab Discontent," *Foreign Affairs*, Winter 1990/91, p. 3.
48. *Ibid.*, p. 9.
49. *Ibid.*, p. 18.
50. Miller and Mylorie, *op. cit.*, p. 202.
51. Richard F. Nyrop, ed, *Persian Gulf States: Country Studies*, Area Handbook Series (Washington, D.C.: Department of the Army, 1985), p. 91.
52. *Ibid.*, p. 35.
53. *Ibid.* p. 118.
54. *Ibid.*
55. *Washington Post*, August 31, 1990.
56. Nyrop, *op. cit.*, p. 93.
57. *The New York Times*, August 3, 1990.
58. *Time*, August 13, 1990, p. 14.
59. *The New York Times*, September 26, 1990.
60. *Ibid.*, August 8, 1990.
61. Ajami, *op. cit.*, p. 18.
62. Nyrop, *op. cit.*, p. 113.
63. Miller and Mylorie, *op cit.*, p. 22.
64. *Washington Post*, August 1, 1990.
65. Miller and Mylorie, *op. cit.*, p. 22.
66. Federal Research Division, Library of Congress, Helen Chapin Metz, ed., *Iraq: A Country Study*, Area Handbook Series (Washington, D.C.: Department of the Army, 1990), p. 5.
67. *Washington Post*, August 3, 1990.
68. *Ibid.*
69. Cited in *The New York Times*, September 30, 1990.
70. *Ibid.*, July 29, 1990.
71. *The Times* (London), August 3, 1990.
72. Miller and Mylorie, *op. cit.*, p. 11.
73. *The Times* (London), August 3, 1990.
74. Library of Congress, *op. cit.*, p. 59.
75. *The Wall Street Journal*, October 9, 1990.

76. Edward N. Luttwak, "Saddam and the Agencies of Disorder," *Times Literary Supplement,* January 18, 1991, p. 3.

77. Library of Congress, *op. cit.,* p. 70.

78. *Ibid.* p. 5.

79. George Ball, "The Gulf Crisis," *The New York Review of Books,* December 6, 1990. p. 16.

80. *The New York Times,* October 24, 1990.

81. Phoebe Marr, *The Modern History of Iraq* (Boulder, Colo.: Westview Press, 1985), p. 181.

82. *Ibid.*

83. Abdul-Reda Assiri, *Kuwait's Foreign Policy* (Boulder, Colo: Westview Press, 1990), p. 70.

84. *Washington Post,* July 26, 1990. See also *The Times* (London), July 23, 1990.

85. Miller and Mylorie, *op. cit.,* p. 11.

86. Saddam's concern was not misplaced. The VOA editorial was introduced by an announcer who said, "Next, an editorial reflecting the views of the U.S. government." Another voice read the editorial, which strongly condemned the secret police in Eastern Europe. It concluded as follows:

Secret police are also entrenched in other countries, such as China, North Korea, Iran, Iraq, Syria, Libya, Cuba, and Albania. The rulers of these countries hold power by force and fear, not by the consent of the governed. But as East Europeans demonstrated so dramatically in 1989, the tide of history is against such rulers. The 1990s should not belong to the dictators and secret police, but to the people.

Announcer: "That was an editorial reflecting the views of the U.S. government." Voice of America, Editorial 0-03982, February 15, 1990.

87. Oberdorfer, *op. cit.,* p. 22.

88. The details of U.S. activities in Iraq were revealed by the

House Select Committee on Intelligence Activities in their report of January 1976. The decision to intervene apparently originated following a conversation between the Shah and Henry Kissinger, then President Nixon's national security adviser. President Nixon authorized a covert-action budget for the project and sent John Connelly to Tehran to inform the Shah. In this connection, see Christopher Hitchens, "Why We Are Stuck in the Sand," *Harpers*, January 1991, pp. 71–72.

89. Hitchens, *ibid.*, p. 72.

90. *Ibid.*

91. Miller and Mylorie, *op. cit.*, p. 143.

92. *Ibid.* p. 144.

93. Hitchens, *op. cit.*, pp. 73–74.

94. William Safire, "I'll Remember April," *The New York Times*, March 22, 1991.

95. Miller and Mylorie, *op. cit.*, p. 148.

96. Oberdorfer, *op. cit.*, pp. 21–22.

97. *The Economist*, September 29, 1990, p. 19.

98. Miller and Mylorie, *op. cit.*, p. 12.

99. *Ibid.*, p. 13

100. *The Economist*, September 29, 1990, p. 20

101. *The Wall Street Journal*, October 1, 1990.

102. *The New York Times*, April 3, 1990.

103. Oberdorfer, *op. cit.*, p. 33.

104. *The New York Times*, April 10, 1990.

105. Woodward, *op. cit.*, pp. 199–204.

106. *Ibid.*, p. 204.

107. *Ibid.*

108. *Ibid.*

109. *The Wall Street Journal*, September 20, 1990.

110. *The Economist*, September 29, 1990, p. 20.

111. *Washington Post*, October 1, 1990.

112. *The Economist*, September 29, 1990, p. 20.

113. *Ibid.*

114. Miller and Mylorie, *op. cit.*, p. 15.

115. *The New York Times*, May 30, 1990.

116. *Financial Times* (London), July 14, 1990.

117. Milton Viorst, "Report from Baghdad," *The New Yorker*, June 24, 1991, p. 66.

118. *The Economist*, September 29, 1990, p. 22.

119. Miller and Mylorie, *op. cit.*, p. 16.

120. *The Economist*, July 21, 1990.

121. *Financial Times* (London), July 18, 1990.

122. *Ibid.*

123. *Ibid.* July 20, 1990. Also see *The Wall Street Journal*, September 6, 1990.

124. *Washington Post*, July 19, 1990.

125. *Ibid.* July 25, 1990.

126. *Ibid.* July 20, 1990.

127. *The New York Times*, September 23, 1990.

128. *Ibid.*

129. *Washington Post*, July 20, 1990.

130. *Financial Times* (London), July 25, 1990.

131. *The New York Times*, July 25, 1990.

132. *Ibid.*

133. *Washington Post*, July 25, 1990.

134. *Ibid.*

135. *Ibid.*

136. Miller and Mylorie, *op. cit.*, p. 18.

137. The transcript of Saddam's conversation with Glaspie was released by the Iraqis and published in *The New York Times*, September 23, 1990.

138. *Ibid.*

139. *Ibid.*, September 12, 1990.

140. *Ibid.*

141. Glaspie's cables to and from Washington were reprinted in the *Los Angeles Times* and the *Washington Post*, July 13, 1991. Her congressional testimony in April 1991 appears to be at variance with those cables.

142. *Washington Post*, October 21, 1990. For the text of Bush's cable, see the *Washington Post*, July 13, 1991.

143. *Ibid.* July 26, 1990.
144. *Newsweek*, October 1, 1990, p. 25.
145. *Financial Times* (London), July 26, 1990.
146. *The New York Times*, July 28, 1990.
147. *The Wall Street Journal*, September 6, 1990.
148. *Washington Post*, August 19, 1990.
149. *The New York Times*, October 16, 1990.
150. *Ibid.* Also see Milton Viorst, "A Reporter At Large: After the Liberation," *The New Yorker*, September 30, 1991, pp. 64–66. Viorst confirms that the United States encouraged the Kuwaitis to hang tough. In addition to the testimony of Sheik Salim al-Sabah cited above, Viorst quotes Sheik Ali al-Khalifa, Kuwaiti's minister of oil and minister of finance, that Saddam "thought he could absorb Kuwait and bleed Saudi Arabia without invading, and that would solve everything. But we know the United States would not let us be overrun. I spent too much time in Washington to make that mistake, and received a constant stream of American visitors here. The American policy was clear. Only Saddam didn't understand it." Viorst reports that "even though it is unclear whether Kuwait deliberately bearded Saddam in the spring and early summer of 1990, there is little doubt that those who make Kuwait's decisions had ample reason to believe that, whatever they did, the United States would back them up."

2. This Will Not Stand

1. *Time*, January 7, 1991, p. 20.
2. *Ibid.*
3. *Ibid.*
4. *The New York Times*, October 16, 1990.
5. *Washington Post*, August 3, 1990.
6. *The New York Times*, October 16, 1990. For Bush's confirmation of that arrangement, see his press conference re-

marks of Sunday, August 5, 1990, reported in *The New York Times* the following day. Also see the *Washington Post*, August 6, 1990; *The New York Times*, August 7, 1990.

7. G. M. Dillon, *The Falklands: Politics and War* (London: Macmillan, 1989), p. 129.

8. *Maclean's*, May 14, 1990.

9. *Newsweek*, January 28, 1991, p. 58.

10. *Time*, January 28, 1991, p. 33.

11. *Washington Post*, August 3, 1990.

12. *Ibid.*

13. *The New York Times*, August 3, 1990.

14. *Washington Post*, August 3, 1990.

15. *Ibid.*

16. *The Times* (London), August 4, 1990.

17. *The Wall Street Journal*, August 6, 1990.

18. *The Times* (London), August 6, 1990.

19. *Newsweek*, January 28, 1991.

20. Martin Walker, "Dateline Washington: Victory and Delusion," *Foreign Policy*, Summer 1991, p. 167.

21. *The New York Times*, August 7, 1990.

22. *The Times* (London), August 23, 1990.

23. *Newsweek*, January 28, 1991, p. 64.

24. *Time*, January 7, 1991, p. 22.

25. *The Times* (London), August 4, 1991.

26. *The Tower Commission Report* (New York: Bantam Books, 1987), p. 6.

27. Anthony Lake, *The Tar-Baby Option: American Policy Toward Southern Rhodesia* (New York: Columbia University Press, 1976).

28. Michael Kinsley, "TRB from Washington," *The New Republic*, November 5, 1990, p. 4.

29. *Time*, January 7, 1991, p. 21.

30. *Ibid.*, January 4, 1962, p. 14.

31. *The New York Times*, October 16, 1990.

32. *Ibid.*

33. *Ibid.*, August 4, 1990.

34. *Ibid.*
35. *Ibid.*, August 9, 1990.
36. *Time*, January 7, 1991, p. 22.
37. *The New York Times*, August 9, 1990.
38. *Ibid.*, August 5, 1990.
39. *Ibid.*
40. *Ibid.*
41. *Washington Post*, August 6, 1990.
42. *Ibid.*, August 19, 1990.
43. *Ibid.*, August 6, 1990.
44. *The New Republic*, September 3, 1990, p. 14.
45. *The New York Times*, August 4, 1990.
46. *Ibid.*
47. *Washington Post*, August 19, 1990.
48. *The New York Times*, August 4, 1990.
49. *Washington Post*, August 19, 1990.
50. *Ibid.*
51. *Ibid.*
52. Foreign Broadcast Information Service, Near Eastern Service, 90–151, August 6, 1990, p. 55.
53. *The New York Times*, October 16, 1990.
54. *Time*, January 7, 1991, p. 22.
55. *The New York Times*, August 8, 1990.
56. Both the United Nations Charter, which is a binding treaty obligation, and the Panama Canal Treaty of 1979 preclude the introduction of military force by the United States, except to defend the Panama Canal. United Nations, *Treaty Series*, vol. 1280, no. 1-21086.
57. *Newsweek*, January 28, 1991, p. 58.
58. *Ibid.*, April 11, 1988, p. 42.
59. For Bandar's role in Iran-contra, see Ben Bradlee, Jr., *Guts and Glory: The Rise and Fall of Oliver North* (New York: Donald I. Fine, 1988), pp. 193–210.
60. *Newsweek*, April 11, 1988.
61. *The New York Times*, August 8, 1990.
62. *Time*, January 7, 1991, p. 22.

63. *The New York Times*, August 8, 1990.

64. *Ibid.*, August 4, 1990.

65. Judith Miller and Laurie Mylorie, *Saddam Hussein and the Crisis in the Gulf* (New York: Times Books/Random House, 1990), p. 192.

66. *Washington Post*, August 4, 1990.

67. Ronald Steel, *Walter Lippmann and the American Century* (Boston: Little, Brown, 1980), pp. 431 *ff.*

68. *Newsweek*, January 28, 1991, p. 58.

69. *Washington Post*, August 26, 1990; Bob Woodward, *The Commanders* (New York: Simon & Schuster, 1991), pp. 237 *ff.*

70. *Washington Post*, August 4, 1990.

71. *Newsweek*, January 28, 1991, p. 58.

72. *Washington Post*, August 4, 1990.

73. See especially Elizabeth Drew, "Letter from Washington," *The New Yorker*, September 24, 1990, p. 106.

74. *The New York Times*, August 9, 1990.

75. *Ibid.*

76. Mark Shields, "Bellicose Hypocrites," *Washington Post*, November 2, 1990.

77. *Atlanta Constitution*, February 17, 1991.

78. *Ibid.*, August 17, 1990.

79. *Ibid.*, October 28, 1990.

80. Woodward, *op. cit.*, p. 251.

81. Elizabeth Drew, *op. cit.*, p. 107.

82. *Ibid.*

83. *The New York Times*, August 17, 1990.

84. *Newsweek*, January 28, 1991, p. 59.

85. *Ibid.*

86. *The New York Times*, April 26, 1990.

87. *Ibid.*

88. *Ibid.*

89. *Time*, January 7, 1991, p. 22.

90. *Washington Post*, August 6, 1990.

91. *Ibid.*; *The New York Times*, August 6, 1990.

92. *The New York Times*, August 6, 1990.

93. *Ibid.*

94. Woodward, *op. cit.*, pp. 260–261.

95. *Ibid.*, p. 262.

96. *The New York Times*, May 20, 1991.

97. *Newsweek*, January 28, 1991, p. 59.

98. *Ibid.*

99. *The New York Times*, August 7, 1990.

100. *Newsweek*, January 28, 1991, p. 59.

101. Michael R. Gordon, "Cracking the Whip," *The New York Times Magazine*, January 27, 1991, p. 34.

102. *The New York Times*, August 7, 1990. See *Washington Post*, August 7, 1990.

103. *Newsweek*, January 28, 1991, p. 59.

104. *Ibid.*

105. *Ibid.*

106. *Ibid.*, p. 60.

107. *The New York Times*, August 7, 1990, Security Council Resolution 661.

108. *Washington Post*, August 7, 1990.

109. *Ibid.*

110. Foreign Broadcast Information Service, Near Eastern Service, August 7, 1990, p. 27.

111. *Ibid.*

112. *Washington Post*, August 7, 1990.

113. *Ibid.*

114. Woodward, *op. cit.*, p. 273.

3. HAIL TO THE CHIEF

1. For the full text of President Bush's speech, see *Weekly Compilation of Presidential Documents, Administration of George Bush, 1990* August 13, 1990, pp. 1216–1218. (Hereinafter *WCPD*.)

2. Judith Miller and Laurie Mylorie, *Saddam Hussein and the*

Crisis in the Gulf (New York: Times Books/Random House, 1990), p. 192.

3. *Washington Post*, August 10, 1990.

4. *Ibid.*

5. Foreign Broadcast Information Service, Near Eastern Service, August 7, 1990, p. 27.

6. *WCPD, 1990*, pp. 1218–1223.

7. *The New York Times*, August 9, 1990.

8. *Washington Post*, August 9, 1990.

9. *Ibid.*

10. *Ibid.*

11. *Ibid.*

12. *The New York Times*, August 8, 1990.

13. *Ibid.*, August 9, 1990.

14. *Washington Post*, August 9, 1990.

15. *Ibid.*, August 10, 1990.

16. *Ibid.*

17. *Ibid.*, August 9, 1990.

18. *Ibid.*, August 8, 1990.

19. *Ibid.*

20. *The New York Times*, August 9, 1990.

21. *Ibid.*

22. *Ibid.*

23. *Washington Post*, August 9, 1990.

24. Bob Woodward, *The Commanders* (New York: Simon & Schuster, 1991), p. 279.

25. *Washington Post*, August 9, 1990.

26. Woodward, *op cit.*, p. 279.

27. *The New York Times*, August 10, 1990.

28. *Washington Post*, August 11, 1990.

29. War Powers Resolution, Public Law 93-148; 87 Stat. 555; November 7, 1973.

30. *The New York Times*, August 10, 1990.

31. *WCPD, 1990*, pp. 1225–1226.

32. For a table of the incidents, see Loch K. Johnson, *America as World Power* (New York: McGraw-Hill, 1991), p. 278.

33. *Washington Post*, August 10, 1990.

34. *Ibid.*

35. *Atlanta Constitution*, November 10, 1987.

36. *Washington Post*, August 11, 1990.

37. *Ibid.*

38. *Fleming v. Page*, 9 Howard (50 U.S.) 603 (1850), Justice McLean dissenting.

39. *Ibid.*, p. 615. See also *Ex Parte Milligan*, 4 Wallace (71 U.S.) 2, 139 (1866).

40. *In re Neagle*, 135 U.S. 1 (1890).

41. *In re Debs*, 158 U.S. 564 (1895).

42. 135 U.S. at 64.

43. Theodore Roosevelt, *An Autobiography* (New York: Macmillan, 1913), pp. 388–389.

44. William Howard Taft, *Our Chief Magistrate and His Powers* (New York: Columbia University Press, 1916), p. 94.

45. *Myers v. United States*, 272 U.S. 52 (1926).

46. *Public Papers of the President, Lyndon B. Johnson, 1965*, vol. 2, p. 616.

47. *WCPD*, 1990, p. 597.

48. *Durand v. Hollins*, 8 Fed. Cas. 111 (C.C.S.D.N.Y., 1860). For a description of the bombardment, see Milton Offutt, "The Protection Abroad by Armed Forces of the United States," Johns Hopkins University Studies in History and Political Science, series XLIV, no. 4, pp. 32–34 (1928). Also see Raoul Berger, "Protection of Americans Abroad," 44 U. Cinn. L. Rev. 741–743 (1975).

49. 8 Fed. Cas. at page 112. Emphasis added. Justice Nelson was sitting as a circuit court judge.

50. *Slaughter-House Cases*, 16 Wallace (83 U.S.), 36, 79 (1873).

51. 15 Stat. 223 (1868); 22 U.S.C. 1732 (1982).

52. Oliver North, *Taking the Stand: The Testimony of Lieutenant Colonel Oliver L. North* (New York: Pocket Books, 1987), pp. 503–504.

53. Harold Hongju Koh, *The National Security Constitution* (New Haven, Conn.: Yale University Press, 1990), p. 197.

54. *Dames & Moore v. Regan*, 453 U.S. 654 (1981).

55. 453 U.S. at 677 (1981).

56. James D. Richardson, ed., *Messages and Papers of the President* (Washington D.C.: Government Printing Office, 1896), vol. 1, p. 315.

57. *State of the Union Messages of the Presidents, 1790-1966* (F. Israel, ed. 1966), vol. 1, p. 352.

58. *Congressional Globe*, 30th Congress, 1st Session, p. 95 (1848).

59. Richardson, *Messages and Papers*, vol. 7, p. 3225.

60. 12 Stat. 326 (1861).

61. Dorothy Schaffter and D. M. Mathews, *The Powers of the President as Commander in Chief*, House Doc. 443, 84th Congress, 2nd Session (1956), p. 61.

62. War Powers Legislation: Hearings Before the Committee on Foreign Relations, U.S. Senate, 92nd Congress, 1st Session (1971), p. 560.

63. Edward S. Corwin, *The President: Office and Powers* (New York: New York University Press, 1957), pp. 212–213.

64. *Congressional Record*, April 20, 1914, pp. 6908–6909.

65. Corwin, *op.cit.*, pp. 438–439.

66. 38 Stat. 770 (1914). See Robert E. Quirk, *An Affair of Honor: Woodrow Wilson and the Occupation of Vera Cruz* (New York: Norton, 1967).

67. *Background Information on the Use of United States Armed Forces in Foreign Countries*, Committee on Foreign Affairs, 91st Congress, 2nd Session, 1970, p. 18.

68. Corwin, *op. cit.*, p. 202.

69. For the September 2, 1940, exchange of notes between Secretary of State Hull and the British ambassador, Lord Lothian, see *Documents on American Foreign Relations* (Boston: World Peace Foundation, 1941), p. 203, *cf.* 34 U.S.C. (1940) 492, 493a, 546c; 18 U.S.C. 33.

70. *Ibid.*, *Documents*, p. 228.

71. Corwin, *op. cit.*, p. 202.

72. *The New York Times*, April 23, 1948.

73. *Department of State Bulletin*, July 31, 1950, pp. 173, 176–177.

74. Formosa Resolution of 1955. 84th Congress, 1st Session, H.J. Res. 159. January 29, 1955.

75. Joint Resolution to Support Peace and Stability in the Middle East. 85th Congress, 1st Session, H.J. Res. 117. March 9, 1957.

76. U.S. Congress, Senate Committee on Foreign Relations, *The Middle East*, 85th Congress, 1st Session, pp. 903–904.

77. 1 Cranch (5 U.S.) 137 (1803).

78. *Crockett v. Reagan*, 558 F. Supp. 893 (D.D.C. 1982), *aff'd*, 720 F 2d. 1355 (D.C. Cir. 1983).

79. *Conyers v. Reagan*, 578F. Supp. 324 (D.D.C. 1984).

80. *Lowery v. Reagan*, Civil Action No. 87-2196 (D.C. Cir. 1988) *aff'g* 676 F. Supp. 373 (D.D.C. 1987).

81. *Goldwater v. Carter*, 444 U.S. 996 (1979).

82. 444 U.S. at 998 (1979).

83. *Mora v. McNamara*, 389 U.S. 934 (dissenting opinion).

84. "Philadelphiensis," *The Independent Gazetteer* (Philadelphia), February 7, 1788, in *The Antifederalists*, Cecelia M. Kenyon, ed. (Indianapolis, Ind.: Bobbs-Merrill, 1966), p. 70. Emphasis in original.

85. *Ibid.*, April 11, 1788, in Kenyon, p. 87.

86. Patrick Henry, speech to the Virginia Ratification Convention, June 4, 1788, in Jonathan Elliot, ed., *The Debates in the Several State Conventions on the Adoption of the Federal Constitution*, vol. 3, p. 58.

4. Bush Takes the Helm

1. *Washington Post*, August 5, 1990.

2. *Ibid.*, August 6, 1990.

3. *Ibid.*

4. *Ibid.*, August 5, 1990.

5. John Newhouse, "The Diplomatic Round (Iraq)," *The New Yorker*, February 18, 1991, p. 73.

6. *The New York Times*, August 6, 1990.

7. *Ibid.*

8. *Ibid.*

9. *Washington Post*, August 7, 1990.

10. *Ibid.*

11. *Ibid.*, August 8, 1990.

12. *The New York Times*, March 13, 1991.

13. *Ibid.*, August 11, 1990.

14. *Ibid.*

15. *Washington Post*, August 10, 1990.

16. *The New York Times*, August 20, 1990.

17. *Newsweek*, January 28, 1991, p. 60.

18. *The New York Times*, August 12, 1990.

19. For the text of President Bush's statement, citing a letter from the emir requesting aid, see *ibid.*, August 13, 1990.

20. U.N. Resolution 665. For text, see *The New York Times*, August 26, 1990.

21. *Newsweek*, January 28, 1991, p. 60.

22. President Nixon called out reservists in March 1970 to handle the mail during a brief postal strike.

23. Bob Woodward, *The Commanders* (New York: Simon & Schuster, 1991), p. 296.

24. *Washington Post*, August 13, 1990.

25. *The New York Times*, August 15, 1990.

26. *Ibid.*, August 16, 1990.

27. *Ibid.*, August 24, 1990.

28. *Ibid.*, August 17, 1990.

29. *Washington Post*, August 18, 1990. For the text of Mahdi's remarks, see *The New York Times*, August 19, 1990.

30. *The New York Times*, August 20, 1990.

31. U.N. Resolution 664. For text, see *The New York Times*, August 19, 1990.

32. *Washington Post*, August 19, 1990.

33. *Ibid.*

34. *Ibid.*, August 20, 1990.

35. *Ibid.*, August 21, 1990.

36. *Ibid.*, August 22, 1990.

37. George Bush (with Douglas Weed), *Man of Integrity* (Eugene, Ore.: Harvest House, 1988), p. 9.

38. For a discussion of the Stimson Doctrine, see especially Robert Langer, *Seizure of Territory: The Stimson Doctrine and Related Principles of Legal Theory and Diplomatic Practice* (Princeton, N.J.: Princeton University Press, 1947), pp. 50–66.

39. Godfrey Hodgson, *The Colonel: The Life and Times of Henry Stimson, 1867–1950* (New York: Alfred A. Knopf, 1990), p. 214. Also see Elting Morison, *Turmoil and Tradition* (Boston: Houghton Mifflin, 1960), pp. 475–476; and Richard N. Current, *Secretary Stimson: A Study in Statecraft* (New Brunswick, N.J.: Rutgers University Press, 1954), pp. 4–17.

40. Hodgson, *op. cit.*, p. 214.

41. *Weekly Compilation of Presidential Documents, 1990,* p. 1334. (Hereinafter *WCPD.*)

42. *Washington Post*, August 22, 1990.

43. *The New York Times*, August 23, 1990.

44. *Ibid.*

45. *Ibid.*

46. *Ibid.*, August 24, 1990.

47. *Washington Post*, August 24, 1990.

48. *Ibid.*

49. *The New York Times*, August 18, 1990.

50. *Ibid.*, August 21, 1990.

51. *Washington Post*, August 24, 1990.

52. *The New York Times*, August 19, 1990.

53. *Ibid.*

54. *Ibid.*, August 22, 1990.

55. *Ibid.*, August 28, 1990.

56. *Ibid.*

57. *Washington Post*, August 28, 1990.

58. *The New York Times*, August 29, 1990.

59. *Ibid.*

60. *Ibid.*

61. *Ibid.*
62. *Ibid.*
63. *WCPD, 1990,* p. 1502.
64. *The New York Times,* August 29, 1990.
65. *Washington Post,* August 29, 1990.
66. *Ibid.*
67. *The New York Times,* August 31, 1990.
68. *Ibid.*
69. *Ibid.*
70. *Washington Post,* September 1, 1990.
71. *Ibid.*
72. *Ibid.,* September 3, 1990.
73. *Ibid.,* September 1, 1990.
74. *WCPD, 1990,* p. 1306.
75. *Public Report of the Vice President's Task Force on Combatting Terrorism, 1986* (Washington, D.C.: Government Printing Office, 1986).
76. *Ibid.,* p. 7.
77. *Ibid.*
78. *Washington Post,* September 1, 1990.
79. *Ibid.*
80. *Ibid.,* September 2, 1990.
81. *Ibid.,* September 1, 1990.
82. *Ibid.,* September 5, 1990.
83. *Ibid.,* September 8, 1990.
84. Roland Evans and Robert Novak, *Washington Post,* September 7, 1990.
85. *Ibid.*
86. *Washington Post,* September 8, 1990.
87. *Ibid.,* September 9, 1990.
88. *Ibid.*
89. *Ibid.,* September 10, 1990.
90. *Ibid.*
91. *Ibid.,* September 11, 1990.
92. *Ibid.*
93. *Ibid.*

94. *Ibid.*
95. *Ibid.*, September 16, 1990.
96. *The New York Times*, March 28, 1991.
97. *WCPD, 1990*, pp. 1381–1382.
98. *Washington Post*, September 12, 1990.
99. *WCPD, 1990*, p. 1417.
100. *Washington Post*, September 12, 1990.
101. *The New York Times*, March 28, 1991.
102. *Washington Post*, September 30, 1990.
103. *Ibid.*
104. Michael Massing, "The Way to War," *The New York Review of Books*, March 28, 1991, p. 20.
105. *Washington Post*, September 30, 1990.
106. *Ibid.*
107. *Ibid.*
108. *Ibid.*, September 29, 1990.
109. *Ibid.*
110. *Ibid.*
111. *Ibid.*
112. *Ibid.*, August 22, 1990.
113. *Ibid.*
114. *Ibid.*, September 11, 1990.
115. *The New York Times*, October 14, 1990.
116. See Theodore Draper, *A Very Thin Line* (New York: Simon & Schuster, 1991), pp. 580–598.
117. *Washington Post*, January 31, 1987.
118. Bush, *Man of Integrity, op. cit.*, p. 75.
119. Albert J. Beveridge, *The Life of John Marshall* (Boston: Houghton Mifflin, 1916), vol. 2, pp. 458–475. Professor Edward S. Corwin, the acknowledged dean of constitutional law scholars, states unequivocally that the phrase "sole organ" meant "simply the President's role as *instrument of communication* with other governments." (Corwin's emphasis.) *The President: Office and Powers*, 4th rev. ed. (New York: New York University Press, 1957), pp. 177–178.
120. 229 U.S. 304 (1936).

121. *Id.* at 309. Emphasis added.

122. For Justice Sutherland's views, see, in particular, his earlier writings on the subject. Senator George Sutherland, "The Internal and External Powers of the National Government," Sen. Doc. No. 417, 61st Congress, 2d Session (1911); Sutherland, *Constitutional Power and World Affairs* (New York: Columbia University Press, 1919). The language Sutherland used in *Constitutional Power* reappears in his decision in *Curtiss-Wright*, often verbatim.

123. *Carter v. Carter Coal Company*, 298 U.S. 238 (1936).

124. *Chinese Exclusion Case*, 130 U.S. 581 (1889).

125. Philip Kurland, "The Importance of Reticence," *Duke Law Journal* 1968: 619, 623; Michael J. Glennon, "Two Views of Presidential Foreign Affairs Power: *Little v. Barreme* or *Curtiss-Wright*," *Yale Journal of International Law*, 13 (1988): 5–32; Thomas M. Franck, "Courts and Foreign Policy," *Foreign Policy* 83 (Summer 1991) 69: *ff*; David M. Levitan, "The Foreign Relations Power: An Analysis of Mr. Justice Sutherland's Theory," *Yale Law Journal* 55 (1946): 467–497; C. Perry Patterson, "*In re The United States v. Curtiss-Wright Corporation*" (pts. 1–2), *Texas Law Review* 22 (1944): 286, 445; Raoul Berger, "The Presidential Monopoly of Foreign Relations", *Michigan Law Review* 71 (1972): 1–58.

126. Alexander M. Bickel, "Congress, the President, and the Power to Wage War," *Chicago-Kent Law Review* 48 (1971): 131, 138–139; Myres McDougal and Asher Lans, "Treaties and Congressional-Executive or Presidential Agreements: Interchangeable Instruments of National Policy, II," *Yale Law Journal* 54 (1945): 257–258; Louis Henkin, *Foreign Affairs and the Constitution* (New York: W. W. Norton, 1972), pp. 16–28; Michael J. Glennon, *Constitutional Diplomacy* (Princeton, N.J.: Princeton University Press, 1990), pp. 18–34; Charles A. Lofgren, "*United States v. Curtiss-Wright Export Corporation*: A Historical Reassessment," *Yale Law Journal* 83 (1973): 1–35; Raoul Berger, "War-Making by the President," *University of Pennsylvania Law Review* 121

(1972): 29, 69–75; Harold Hongju Koh, *The National Security Constitution* (New Haven, Conn.: Yale University Press, 1988), pp. 128–158.

127. *Iran-Contra Affair*, H. Rept. No. 100-433; S. Rept. No. 100-216, 100th Cong., 1st Sess., pp. 388–390 (November 1987).

128. *Youngstown Sheet & Tube Co. v. Sawyer*, 343 U.S. 579 (1952).

129. 453 US. 654 (1981).

130. *American Intern. Group v. Islamic Republic of Iran*, 657 F. 2d 430, 438 n.6 (D.C. Cir. 1981).

5. DESERT SHIELD

1. *The New York Times*, October 2, 1990.
2. For the text of Mitterrand's remarks, see *The New York Times*, September 28, 1990.
3. *Ibid.*, October 10, 1990.
4. *Washington Post*, October 10, 1990.
5. *Ibid.*, October 4, 1990.
6. *Ibid.*
7. *The New York Times*, October 11, 1990.
8. *Washington Post*, October 4, 1990.
9. *Ibid.*
10. *Ibid.*
11. *Ibid.*, October 6, 1990.
12. *Ibid.*, October 12, 1990.
13. *Ibid.*
14. *Ibid.*, October 16, 1990.
15. *Ibid.*
16. *The New York Times*, October 13, 1990.
17. *Washington Post*, October 14, 1990.
18. *The New York Times*, October 17, 1990.
19. *Ibid.*, October 8, 1990.
20. Elizabeth Drew, "Letter from Washington," *The New Yorker*, September 24, 1990, p. 106.

21. *Time*, January 7, 1991, p. 24.
22. Bob Woodward, *The Commanders* (New York: Simon & Schuster, 1991), pp. 302 *ff*.
23. Elizabeth Drew, "Letter from Washington," *The New Yorker*, February 4, 1991, p. 88.
24. *Ibid.*, May 27, 1991, p. 86.
25. Woodward, *op. cit.*, pp. 223 *ff*.
26. *The New York Times*, October 8, 1990.
27. *Ibid.*, October 12, 1990.
28. Woodward, *op. cit.*, p. 262.
29. *Ibid.*, p. 314.
30. *Ibid.*, p. 298–303.
31. *Ibid.*, p. 300.
32. *Ibid.*
33. *Ibid.*
34. *Ibid.*, p. 302.
35. *Ibid.*
36. *Ibid.*, p. 41.
37. *Ibid.*
38. Forrest C. Pogue, *George C. Marshall*, vol. 1 (New York: Viking Press, 1963), pp. 324–325.
39. Woodward., *op. cit.*, p. 42.
40. *Ibid.*
41. *Ibid.*
42. *Ibid.*, pp. 303–304.
43. *Ibid.*, p. 306. Also see Roger Cohen and Claudio Gatti, *In the Eye of the Storm: The Life of General H. Norman Schwarzkopf* (New York: Farrar, Straus and Giroux, 1991), pp. 215–216.
44. *L'Express*, October 12, 1990.
45. *Washington Post*, October 13, 1990.
46. Woodward, *op. cit.*, p. 310.
47. Jack Anderson and Dale Van Atta, *Stormin' Norman: An American Hero* (New York: Kensington, 1991), pp. 159–160.
48. Woodward, *op. cit.*, p. 310.
49. *The New York Times*, October 22, 1990.

50. *Washington Post*, October 16, 1990.

51. *Ibid.*, October 17, 1990.

52. *Ibid.*

53. *The New York Times*, October 18, 1990.

54. *Washington Post*, October 18, 1990.

55. *Ibid.*

56. *Ibid.*, October 19, 1990.

57. *The New York Times*, October 24, 1990.

58. *Ibid.*

59. Woodward, *op. cit.*, p. 311.

60. *Washington Post*, October 26, 1990.

61. *Ibid.*

62. Woodward, *op. cit.*, p. 311.

63. *Washington Post*, October 30, 1990.

64. *The New York Times*, October 31, 1990.

65. *The Wall Street Journal*, October 31, 1990.

66. Woodward, *op. cit.*, p. 311.

67. *Ibid.*, p. 312.

68. *Ibid.*, p. 319.

69. *Washington Post*, November 2, 1990.

70. *The New York Times*, November 2, 1990.

71. *Washington Post*, November 4, 1990.

72. See, for example, Abraham Chayes, "The Use of Force in the Persian Gulf," paper, U.S.-Soviet Conference on the Non-Use of Force, October 4–6, 1990.

73. *Washington Post*, November 6, 1990.

74. *Ibid.*, November 1, 1990.

75. *The New York Times*, November 2, 1990.

76. *Washington Post*, November 6, 1990.

77. *Ibid.*, November 9, 1990.

78. *Ibid.*

79. The text of the president's remarks is reprinted in both *The New York Times* and the *Washington Post*, November 9, 1990.

80. *Washington Post*, November 9, 1990.

81. *Ibid.*

82. *The New York Times*, November 9, 1990.
83. *Washington Post*, November 9, 1990.
84. *Ibid.*
85. *Ibid.*
86. *The New York Times*, November 2, 1990.
87. *Ibid.*
88. *Ibid.*, November 10, 1990.
89. *Ibid.*
90. *Ibid.*, November 11, 1990.
91. *Washington Post*, November 12, 1990.
92. *Ibid.*
93. *Ibid.*
94. *The New York Times*, November 12, 1990.
95. *Washington Post*, November 13, 1990.
96. *The New York Times*, November 12, 1990.
97. *Washington Post*, November 12, 1990.
98. *The New York Times*, November 12, 1990.
99. *Ibid.*
100. *Washington Post*, November 13, 1990.
101. *Ibid.*
102. *The New York Times*, November 13, 1990.
103. *Washington Post*, November 15, 1990.
104. *Ibid.*
105. *Ibid.*
106. *The New York Times*, December 2, 1990.
107. *Washington Post*, November 16, 1990.
108. *Ibid.*
109. *Ibid.*
110. *Ibid.*, November 17, 1990.
111. *Ibid.*, November 18, 1990.
112. *Ibid.*, November 19, 1990.
113. *The New York Times*, November 19, 1990.
114. *Ibid.*, November 20, 1990.
115. *Ibid.*
116. *Ibid.*, November 21, 1990.
117. *Washington Post*, November 26, 1990.

118. *The New York Times*, November 23, 1990.
119. *Washington Post*, November 26, 1990.
120. *Ibid.*
121. *Ibid.*, November 23, 1990.
122. *Ibid.*
123. *Ibid.*, November 9, 1990.
124. *Ibid.*
125. *Ibid.*
126. *Ibid*, November 24, 1990.
127. *The New York Times*, November 24, 1990.
128. *Ibid.*, November 21, 1990.
129. *Ibid.*
130. *Ibid.*, November 27, 1990.
131. *Washington Post*, November 28, 1990.
132. *Ibid.*, December 16, 1990.
133. *Ibid.*
134. *The New York Times*, November 28, 1990.
135. *Washington Post*, November 29, 1990.
136. *Ibid.*
137. *Ibid.*
138. *Ibid.*, November 23, 1990.
139. *The New York Times*, November 25, 1990.
140. *Ibid.*
141. *Ibid.*, November 30, 1990.
142. *Washington Post*, November 27, 1990.
143. *The New York Times*, November 30, 1990.
144. *Ibid.*
145. *Woodward, op. cit.*, pp. 335–336.
146. *The New York Times*, December 1, 1990.
147. Woodward, *op. cit.*, pp. 337–338.

6. DESERT STORM

1. Bob Woodward, *The Commanders* (New York: Simon & Schuster, 1991), p. 341.

2. *Time*, January 7, 1991, p. 24.

3. Woodward, *op. cit.*, p. 345.

4. *Washington Post*, December 2, 1990.

5. *Weekly Compilation of Presidential Documents, Administration of George Bush, 1990,* December 5, 1990, p. 1926. (Hereinafter *WCPD*.)

6. *Ibid.*, November 30, 1990, p. 1952.

7. *Ibid.*, December 27, 1990, p. 2069.

8. *Ibid.*, December 18, 1990, p. 2047.

9. For the text of the president's letter, see *WCPD, 1991*, January 12, 1991, pp. 43–44.

10. Michael Massing, "The Way to War," *The New York Review of Books*, March 28, 1991, p. 22.

11. *Washington Post*, December 2, 1990.

12. Woodward, *op. cit.*, p. 340.

13. *Washington Post*, December 2, 1990.

14. *Ibid.*

15. *Ibid.*

16. *Ibid.*

17. *Ibid.*

18. *Ibid.*, December 23, 1990.

19. *Ibid.*, December 4, 1990.

20. *Ibid.*

21. *Ibid.*, December 6, 1990.

22. *Ibid.*

23. *The New York Times*, December 8, 1990.

24. *Dellums v. Bush*, 752 F. Supp. 1141 (D.D.C., 1990).

25. *Washington Post*, December 5, 1990.

26. 752 F. Supp. 1141, 1143 (D.D.C., 1990).

27. *Lowery v. Reagan*, 676 F. Supp. 333 (D.D.C. 1987); *aff'd*, No. 87-5426 (D.C. Cir. 1989); *Conyers v. Reagan*, 578 F. Supp. 324 (D.D.C. 1984); *Crockett v. Reagan*, 558 F. Supp. 893 (D.D.C. 1982); *aff'd*, 720 F. 2d 1355 (D.C. Cir. 1983).

28. *Washington Post*, December 2, 1990.

29. *Ibid.* December 11, 1990.

30. *The New York Times*, December 15, 1990.

31. *Washington Post*, December 30, 1990.

32. Woodward, *op. cit.*, p. 351.

33. *The New York Times*, December 18, 1990.

34. *Ibid.*, December 19, 1990.

35. WCPD, 1990, p. 2047.

36. *Washington Post*, December 21, 1990.

37. John Newhouse, "The Diplomatic Round (Iraq)," *The New Yorker*, February 18, 1991, p. 72.

38. *WCPD, 1991*, January 16, 1991, pp. 50–52.

39. Elizabeth Drew, "Letter from Washington," *The New Yorker*, February 4, 1991, p. 84.

40. *Newsweek* (cover story), October 19, 1987.

41. *Ibid.*, p. 32.

42. *Ibid.*, p. 28.

43. *Ibid.*, p. 32.

44. Peggy Noonan, *What I Saw at the Revolution* (New York: Ballantine Books, 1990), pp. 312–313.

45. Elizabeth Drew, *op. cit.*, February 4, 1991, p. 82.

46. *Newsweek*, "America at War," Spring/Summer 1991, p. 97.

47. Woodward, *op. cit.*, pp. 346–347.

48. *Ibid.*

49. *Washington Post*, December 17, 1990.

50. Woodward, *op. cit.*, p. 350.

51. *Washington Post*, December 22, 1990.

52. *The New York Times*, December 20, 1990.

53. *Newsweek*, January 28, 1991, p. 65.

54. *Washington Post*, December 18, 1990. "Our offensive capability is not where we would want it to be yet," Powell told the House Armed Services Committee.

55. *WCPD, 1990*, p. 2068.

56. Woodward, *op cit.*, p. 352.

57. *Ibid.*, p. 353.

58. *Newsweek*, January 28, 1991, p. 65. See also *The New York Times*, January 2, 1991.

59. *Newsweek*, January 28, 1991, p. 65.

60. Woodward, *op. cit.*, p. 353.

61. *Ibid.*, p. 65.

62. *Ibid.*, pp. 343–344. In a little-noted press release, John G. Healey, executive director of Amnesty International USA, stated that he was "deeply distressed by the selective use" of Amnesty's report by President Bush, and of the president's "opportunistic manipulation of the international human-rights movement." Martin Yant, *Desert Mirage: The True Story of the Gulf War* (Buffalo, N.Y.: Prometheus, 1991), p. 54.

63. *Washington Post*, December 31, 1990.

64. *The New York Times*, January 3, 1991.

65. *Ibid.*

66. *Ibid.*, January 7, 1991.

67. *Ibid.*, January 5, 1991.

68. *Ibid.*, January 7, 1991.

69. *Ibid.*

70. *Ibid.*

71. Woodward, *op. cit.*, p. 355.

72. *Ibid.*, p. 356.

73. *Ibid.*, p. 357.

74. *Ibid.*, p. 358.

75. *Ibid.*

76. *WCPD, 1991*, January 8, 1991, pp. 17–18.

77. Milton Viorst, "Report from Baghdad," *The New Yorker*, June 24, 1991, p. 68.

78. Woodward, *op. cit.*, p. 361.

79. Massing, *op. cit.*, p. 22.

80. Elizabeth Drew, "Letter from Washington" *The New Yorker*, February 4, 1991, p. 86.

81. *Ibid.*

82. *The New York Times*, January 11, 1991.

83. Woodward, *op. cit.*, p. 362.

84. *The New York Times*, January 12, 1991.

85. *Congressional Record*, 102nd Congress, 1st Session, vol. 137, Daily Edition, January 12, 1991, p. H-169.

86. *Ibid.*, p. S-377.
87. *Ibid.*, January 10, 1991, p. S-101.
88. *Ibid.*, January 11, 1991, p. S-249.
89. *Ibid.*, January 10, 1991, p. S-110.
90. *Ibid.*, January 11, 1991, p. S-127.
91. *Ibid.*, January 12, 1991, p. H-441–442.
92. *Washington Post*, January 13, 1991.
93. Congressional Record, *op. cit.*, January 12, 1991, p. S-367.
94. WCPD, *1990*, January 12, 1991, p. 39.
95. Public Law 102-1 (1991).
96. WCPD, *1991*, January 14, 1991, pp. 48–49.
97. *Washington Post*, January 13, 1991.
98. *The New York Times*, January 15, 1991.
99. *Ibid.*
100. WCPD, *1991*, January 16, 1991, p. 50.
101. *Ibid.*, pp. 50–52.

Epilogue

1. *The New York Times*, June 16, 1991.
2. *Ibid.*, June 3, 1991.
3. *Ibid.*, June 24, 1991.
4. Murray Kempton, "The Wake of the Storm," *The New York Review of Books*, July 18, 1991, p. 45.
5. *Washington Post*, January 13, 1991.

BIBLIOGRAPHY

War Powers and the Constitution

Agee, William P. "The War Powers Resolution: Congress Seeks to Reassert Its Proper Constitutional Role as a Partner in War-Making." *Rutgers Law Journal* 18 (Winter 1987).

Berger, Raoul. "The Presidential Monopoly of Foreign Affairs." *Michigan Law Review* 71 (1972): 1–58.

———. "Protection of Americans Abroad." *University of Cincinnati Law Review* 44 (1975): 741–743.

———. "War-Making by the President." *University of Pennsylvania Law Review* 121 (1972): 29–85.

Beveridge, Albert J. *The Life of John Marshall.* Boston: Houghton Mifflin, 1916.

Bickel, Alexander M. "Congress, the President, and the Power to Wage War." *Chicago-Kent Law Review* 48 (1971): 131–147.

Blechman, Barry M., and Kaplan, Stephan S., *Force Without War.* Washington, D.C.: Brookings Institution, 1978.

Borchard, Edwin. "The Attorney General's Opinion in the Exchange of Destroyers for Bases. *American Journal of International Law* 34 (1940): 690.

Bush, George (with Douglas Weed). *Man of Integrity*. Eugene, Ore.: Harvest House, 1988.

Chayes, Abram. "The Use of Force in the Persian Gulf." Paper, U.S.-Soviet Conference on the Non-Use of Force, October 4–6, 1990.

Corwin, Edward S. *The President: Office and Powers*. New York: New York University Press, 1957.

Crabb, Cecil V., and Holt, Pat M. *Invitation to Struggle: Congress, the President and Foreign Policy*. Washington, D.C.: Congressional Quarterly, 1984.

Cullen, Charles T., ed. *The Papers of John Marshall*. Chapel Hill: University of North Carolina Press, 1974.

Current, Richard N. *Secretary Stimson: A Study in Statecraft*. New Brunswick, N.J.: Rutgers University Press, 1954.

Draper, Theodore. *A Very Thin Line*. New York: Simon & Schuster, 1991.

———. "Presidential Wars." *The New York Review of Books*, September 26, 1991, pp. 64–74.

Eagleton, Thomas M. *War and Presidential Power: A Chronicle of Congressional Surrender*. New York: Liveright, 1974.

Elliot, Jonathan, ed. *The Debates in the Several State Conventions on the Adoption of the Federal Constitution*. 5 vols., 2 ed. (1888). New York: Burt Franklin, 1968.

Emerson, J. Terry. "War Powers Legislation." *West Virginia Law Review* 74 (1972) 73 *ff*.

Fisher, Louis. *Constitutional Conflicts Between Congress and the President*. Princeton, N.J.: Princeton University Press, 1985.

Franck, Thomas M. "Courts and Foreign Policy." *Foreign Policy* 83 (Summer 1991): 66–86.

Georgetown Law Journal. Note. "Self-Defense on Presidential Pretext? The Constitutionality of Unilateral Preemptive Military Action." Vol. 78 (1989), pp. 415–446.

Glennon, Michael J. *Constitutional Diplomacy*. Princeton, N.J.: Princeton University Press, 1990.

———. "Two Views of Presidential Foreign Affairs Powers: *Little v. Barreme* or *Curtiss-Wright*." *Yale Journal of International Law* 13 (1988): 5–32.

———. "War and the Constitution." *Foreign Affairs*, vol. 70, no. 2 (Spring 1991), pp. 84–101.

Harvard Law Review. Note. "Congress, the President, and the Power to Commit Forces to Combat." Vol. 81 (1968): 1771–1805.

Henkin, Louis. *Constitutionalism, Democracy, and Foreign Affairs*. New York: Columbia University Press, 1990.

———. *Foreign Affairs and the Constitution*. New York: W. W. Norton, 1972.

Hodgson, Godfrey. *The Colonel: The Life and Times of Henry Stimson, 1867–1950*. New York: Alfred A. Knopf, 1990.

Holt, Pat. *The War Powers Resolution: The Role of Congress in U.S. Armed Intervention*. Washington, D.C.: American Enterprise Institute, 1978.

Hunt, Gaillard, ed. *The Writings of James Madison*. New York: G. P. Putnam's Sons, 1902.

Johnson, Loch K. *America as a World Power: Foreign Policy in a Constitutional Framework*. New York: McGraw-Hill, 1991.

Kenyon, Cecelia M., ed. *The Antifederalists*. Indianapolis, Ind.: Bobbs-Merrill, 1966.

Koh, Harold Hongju. *The National Security Constitution*. New Haven, Conn.: Yale University Press, 1990.

Kurland, Philip. "The Importance of Reticence." *Duke Law Journal* 1968: 619, 623.

Langer, Robert. *Seizure of Territory: The Stimson Doctrine and Related Principles of Legal Theory and Diplomatic Practice*. Princeton, N.J.: Princeton University Press, 1947.

Levitan, David M. "The Foreign Relations Power: An Analysis of Mr. Justice Sutherland's Theory," *Yale Law Journal* 55 (1946): 467–491.

Lofgren, Charles A. "*United States v. Curtiss-Wright Export Corporation:* A Historical Reassessment." *Yale Law Journal* 83 (1973): 1–46.

——. "War-Making Under the Constitution." *Yale Law Journal* 81 (1972): 672–704.

McDougal, Myres, and Lans, Asher. "Treaties and Congressional-Executive or Presidential Agreements." *Yale Law Journal* 54 (1945): 257–258.

Morison, Elting. *Turmoil and Tradition.* Boston: Houghton Mifflin, 1960.

North, Oliver. *Taking the Stand.* New York: Pocket Books, 1987.

Office of the President. *Weekly Compilation of Presidential Documents,* 1990, 1991. Washington, D.C.: Government Printing Office, 1990–91.

Offutt, Milton. "The Protection Abroad by Armed Forces of the United States." The Johns Hopkins University Studies in History and Political Science, series XLIV, no. 4, 1928.

Patterson, C. Perry. "*In re The United States v. The Curtiss-Wright Corporation*" *Texas Law Review* 22 (1944): 286–314; 445–481.

Quirk, Robert E. *An Affair of Honor: Woodrow Wilson and the Occupation of Vera Cruz.* New York: Norton, 1967.

Reveley, W. Taylor III. "Presidential War-Making: Constitutional Prerogative or Usurpation?" *Virginia Law Review* 55 (1978): 1243–1305.

——. *War Powers of the President and Congress.* Charlottesville: University of Virginia Press, 1981.

Richardson, James D., ed. *Messages and Papers of the President.* Washington, D.C.: Government Printing Office, 1896–99.

Rogers, James Grafton. *World Policing and the Constitution.* Boston: World Peace Foundation, 1945.

Roosevelt, Theodore. *An Autobiography.* New York: Macmillan, 1913.

Schaffter, Dorothy, and Mathews, D. M. "The Power of the President as Commander in Chief." House Doc. 443, 84th Congress, 2nd Session (1956).

Schlesinger, Arthur M., Jr. *The Imperial Presidency*. Boston: Houghton Mifflin, 1973.

Shuman, Howard E., and Thomas, Walter R., eds. *The Constitution and National Security*. Washington, D.C.: National Defense University Press, 1990.

Smith, Jean Edward. *The Constitution and American Foreign Policy*. St. Paul, Minn.: West Publishing Co., 1989.

Sofaer, Abraham D. *War, Foreign Affairs and Constitutional Power*. Cambridge, Mass.: Ballinger, 1976.

Sutherland, George. *Constitutional Power and World Affairs*. New York: Columbia University Press, 1919.

———. "The Internal and External Powers of the National Government." Senate Doc. 417, 61st Congress, 2nd session (1909).

Taft, William Howard. *Our Chief Magistrate and His Powers*. New York: Columbia University Press, 1916.

Tower, John; Muskie, Edmund; and Scowcroft, Brent. *The Tower Commission Report*. New York: Bantam Books, 1987.

Wills, Gary, ed. *The Federalist Papers*. New York: Bantam Books, 1982.

World Peace Foundation. *Documentation on American Foreign Relations*. Boston: World Peace Foundation, 1941.

THE MIDDLE EAST

Abd al-Rahman, Abd al-Jabbar. *A Bibliography of Iraq: A Classified List of Printed Materials on the Land, People*. Baghdad: al-Irshad Press, 1977.

———. *Iraq*. Oxford, England: Clio, 1984.

Abdalla, Ahmed. "Mubarak's Gamble." *Middle East Report*, January–February, 1991.

Abu Jaber, Kemal. *The Arab Baath Socialist Party*. Syracuse, N.Y.: Syracuse University Press, 1966.

Ahmad, Eqbal. "Nightmare Victory?" *Mother Jones*, March–April, 1991.

Ajami, Fouad. *The Arab Predicament: Arab Political Thought and Practice Since 1967*. Cambridge, England: Cambridge University Press, 1981.

_____. "The Summer of Arab Discontent." *Foreign Affairs*, Winter 1990/91.

Assiri Abdul-Reda. *Kuwait's Foreign Policy*. Boulder, Colo.: Westview Press, 1990.

_____. "Kuwait's Political Elites." *Middle East Journal* 42: (1988) 48–58.

Axelgard, Frederick W., ed. *Iraq in Transition: A Political, Economic, and Strategic Perspective*. Boulder, Colo.: Westview Press, 1986.

_____. *A New Iraq? The Gulf War and Implications for U.S. Foreign Policy*. New York: Praeger, 1988.

Batatu, Hanna. *The Old Social Classes and the Revolutionary Movements of Iraq*. Princeton, N.J.: Princeton University Press, 1978.

Bullock, John, and Harvey, Morris. *Saddam's War: The Origins of the Kuwait Conflict and the International Response*. London: Faber and Faber, 1991.

Case Studies in Population: Kuwait. New York: United Nations, 1988.

Cordesman, Anthony H. *The Gulf and the Search for Strategic Stability*. Boulder, Colo.: Westview Press, 1984.

_____. *The Gulf and the West: Strategic Relations and Military Realities*. Boulder, Colo.: Westview Press, 1988.

Crystal, Jill. *Oil and Politics in the Gulf: Rulers and Merchants in Kuwait and Qatar*. Cambridge, England: Cambridge University Press, 1990.

Draper, Theodore. *A Present of Things Past: Selected Essays*. New York: Hill and Wang, 1990.

Foreign Broadcast Information Service. Near Eastern Service, July 1990–February 1991.

Fromkin, David. *A Peace to End All Peace: Creating the Modern Middle East, 1914–1922*. New York: Henry Holt and Company, 1989.

Ghareeb Edmund. *The Kurdish Question in Iraq*. Syracuse, N.Y.: Syracuse University Press, 1981.

Haass, Richard N. "Dealing with Friendly Tyrants." *The National Interest*, Spring 1989, pp. 40–48.

Halliday, Fred. "Gorbachev and the 'Arab Syndrome': Soviet Policy in the Middle East," *World Policy Journal* (London), 1987, 415–441.

Helms, Christine Moss. *Iraq: Eastern Flank of the Arab World*. Washington, D.C.: The Brookings Institution, 1984.

Hewins, Ralph. *A Golden Dream: The Miracle of Kuwait*. London: W. H. Allen, 1963.

Hiro, Dilip. *Holy Wars: The Rise of Islamic Fundamentalism*. New York: Routledge, Chapman and Hall, Inc., 1989.

———. *The Longest War: The Iraq-Iran Military Conflict*. New York: Routledge, Chapman and Hall, Inc., 1991.

Jawad, Saad. *Iraq and the Kurdish Question, 1958–1970*. London: Ithaca Press, 1981.

Kedourie, Elie. "Continuity and Change in Modern Iraqi History," *Asian Affairs* (London), June 1975, 140–146.

———. "Iraq: The Mystery of American Policy." *Commentary* 91 (June 1991): 15–20.

Kelidar, Abbas. *The Integration of Modern Iraq*. New York: St. Martin's Press, 1979.

Khadduri, Majid. *The Gulf War: The Origins and Implications of the Iran-Iraq Conflict*. New York: Oxford University Press, 1988.

———. *Independent Iraq: A Study in Iraqi Politics from 1932 to 1958*. 2nd ed. London: Oxford University Press, 1960.

———. *Republican Iraq: A Study in Iraqi Politics Since the Revolution of 1958*. London: Oxford University Press, 1969.

———. *Socialist Iraq: A Study in Iraqi Politics Since 1968*. Washington, D.C.: The Middle East Institute, 1978.

Khalil, Samir al-. *Republic of Fear: The Politics of Modern Iraq*. Los Angeles and Berkeley: University of California Press, 1989.

Kinsley, Susan. "The Kurds: Persecuted Throughout the Region." *Human Rights Watch* 1, Winter 1991.

Klare, Michael. "Fueling the Fire: How We Armed the Middle East." *Bulletin of the Atomic Scientists*, January–February 1991.

Lewis, Bernard. *The Arabs in History*. 2nd ed. New York: Harper and Row, 1967.

———. *Four Centuries of Modern Iraq*. Farnborough, England: Gregg, 1968.

———. "The Roots of Muslim Rage." *Atlantic Monthly*, September 1990, p. 52.

Longrigg, Stephen, *Iraq, 1900 to 1950*. London: Oxford University Press, 1953.

Luttwak, Edward N. "Saddam and the Agencies of Disorder." *Times Literary Supplement*, January 18, 1991.

Marr, Phoebe. *The Modern History of Iraq*. Boulder, Colo.: Westview Press, 1985.

Matar, Fuad. *Saddam Hussein: The Man, the Cause, the Future*. London: Third World Center for Research and Publishing, 1981.

Metz, Helen Chapin, ed. *Iraq: A Country Study*. Washington, D.C.: Department of the Army, 1990.

Mezerik, Avraham G. "The Kuwait-Iraq Dispute, 1961." *International Review Service*, 1961.

Middle East Watch, *Human Rights in Iraq*. New Haven, Conn.: Yale University Press, 1990.

Miller, Judith, and Mylroie, Laurie. *Saddam Hussein and the Crisis in the Gulf*. New York: Times Books/Random House, 1990.

Monroe, Elizabeth. "The Shaikhdome of Kuwait." *International Affairs* 30 (1954): 271–284.

Mortimer, Edward. "The Thief of Baghdad." *The New York Review of Books*, September 27, 1990, pp. 7–15.

Nonnerman, Gerd. *Iraq, the Gulf States, and the War: A Changing Relationship, 1980–1986 and Beyond*. London: Ithaca Press, 1986.

Nyrop, Richard, ed. *Iraq: A Country Study*. Washington, D.C.: Foreign Area Studies, American University, 1979.

Pelletiere, Stephen C. *The Kurds: An Unstable Element in the Gulf*. Boulder, Colo.: Westview Press, 1984.

Pfaff, William. "Islam and the West." *The New Yorker*, January 28, 1991.

Renfrew, Nita M. "Who Started the War?" *Foreign Policy* 66 (Spring 1987) 98–108.

Sapsted, David. *Modern Kuwait*. London: Macmillan, 1980.

Sciolino, Elaine. "The Big Brother: Iraq Under Saddam Hussein." *New York Times Magazine*, February 3, 1985.

Sherry, Virginia. "Kuwait Before—and After?" *The Nation*, November 5, 1990.

Sluglett, Peter. *Britain in Iraq, 1914–1932*. London: Ithaca Press, 1976.

———, and Farouk-Sluglett, Marion. *Iraq Since 1958: From Revolution to Dictatorship*. Rev. ed. London: I. B. Tauris, 1990.

Sterner, Michael. "Navigating the Gulf." *Foreign Policy*, Winter 1990–91, pp. 39–52.

Viorst, Milton. "The House of Hasham." *The New Yorker*, January 7, 1991.

———. "Iraq at War." *Foreign Affairs* 65 (Winter 1986–87): 349–365.

———. "Out of the Desert: Kuwait." *The New Yorker*, May 16, 1988.

———. "Report from Baghdad." *The New Yorker*, September 24, 1990.

———. "Report from Baghdad." *The New Yorker*, June 24, 1991.

———. "A Reporter At Large: Out of the Desert." *The New Yorker*, May 18, 1988.

Winestone, H.V.F., and Freeth, Zahra. *Kuwait: Prospect and Reality*. London: Allen and Unwin, 1972.

The World Bank. *World Development Report, 1990*. New York: Oxford University Press, 1990.

Yergin, Daniel. *The Prize*. New York: Simon & Schuster, 1991.

Zahlan, Rosemarie Said. *The Making of the Modern Gulf States*. London: Unwin Hyman, 1989.

DESERT SHIELD–DESERT STORM

Adler, Bill. *The Generals: The New American Heroes*. New York: Avon Books, 1991.

Anderson, Jack, and Van Atta, Dale. *Stormin' Norman: An American Hero*. New York: Kensington, 1991.

Antal, Major John F. "The Iraqi Army: Forged in the (Other) Gulf War." *Military Review* 71 (February 1991): 62–72.

Ball, George. "The Gulf Crisis." *The New York Review of Books*, December 6, 1990, pp. 14–17.

Barnes, Edward. "Holding the Line." *Life* magazine, October 1990.

Barnet, Richard J. "The Uses of Force." *The New Yorker*, April 29, 1991.

Blumemthal, Sidney. "April's Bluff." *The New Republic*, August 5, 1991, pp. 8–10.

Bradlee, Ben, Jr. *Guts and Glory: The Rise and Fall of Oliver North*. New York: Donald I. Fine, 1988.

Brown, Lt. Gen. Frederic J. "AirLand Battle Future: The Other Side of the Coin." *Military Review* 71 (February 1991): 13–24.

Bryan, C.D.B. "The Thoughts of General Norm: Conversations with H. Norman Schwarzkopf." *The New Republic*, March 11, 1991, pp. 20–27.

_____. *Friendly Fire*. New York: G. P. Putnam's Sons, 1976.

Bulloch, John and Morris, Harvey. *Saddam's War: The Origins of the Kuwait Conflict and the International Response*. New York: Penguin, 1991.

Bush, George. *Public Report of the Vice President's Task Force on Combatting Terrorism, 1986*. Washington, D.C.: Government Printing Office, 1986.

Chomsky, Noam. "Nefarious Aggression." Z *Magazine*, October 1990.

———. "Oppose the War." Z *Magazine*, February 1991, pp. 49–64.

Cohen, Roger, and Gatti, Claudio. *In the Eye of the Storm: The Life of General H. Norman Schwarzkopf*. New York: Farrar, Straus and Giroux, 1991.

Darwish, Adel, and Alexander, Gregory. *Unholy Babylon: The Secret History of Saddam's War*. Toronto: McClelland & Stewart, 1991.

Dillon, G. M. *The Falklands: Politics and War*. London: Macmillan, 1989.

Drew, Elizabeth. "Letter from Washington." *The New Yorker*, September 24, October 15, December 3, December 31, 1990; February 4, February 25, May 6, May 27, June 17, 1991.

Easterbrook, Gregg. "Operation Desert Shill." *The New Republic*, September 30, 1991, pp. 32–42.

Falk, Richard. "U.N. Being Made a Tool of U.S. Foreign Policy." *Manchester Guardian Weekly*. July 27, 1991, p. 12.

Friedman, Norman. *Desert Victory: The War for Kuwait*. Newport, R.I.: Naval Institute Press, 1991.

Gilbert, Martin. *The Second World War: A Complete History*. New York: Henry Holt and Company, 1989.

Gordon, Michael. "Cracking the Whip." *The New York Times Magazine*, January 27, 1991.

Haass, Richard. *Conflicts Unending*. New Haven, Conn.: Yale University Press, 1990.

Henderson, Simon. *Instant Empire: Saddam Hussein's Ambition for Iraq*. Toronto: Mercury House, 1991.

Hill, Lt. Col. Richard D. "Depot Operations Supporting Desert Shield." *Military Review* 71 (April 1991): 17–28.

Hitchens, Christopher. "Why We Are Stuck in the Sand." *Harpers*, January 1991, pp. 70 ff.

Institute for Strategic Studies. *The Military Balance, 1990–1991*. London: Institute for Strategic Studies, 1990.

Kinsley, Michael. "TRB from Washington." *The New Republic*, November 5, 1990, p. 4.

Lake, Anthony. *The Tar-Baby Option: American Policy Toward Southern Rhodesia*. New York: Columbia University Press, 1976.

Massing, Michael. "The Way to War." *The New York Review of Books*, March 28, 1991.

Morris, Capt. M. E. H. *Norman Schwarzkopf: Road to Triumph*. New York: St. Martin's Paperbacks, 1991.

Myers, Major James E. "Building the Desert Logistics Force." *Military Review* 71 (April 1991): 13–16.

Newhouse, John. "The Diplomatic Round (Iraq)." *The New Yorker*, February 18, 1991, pp. 69–91.

Noonan, Peggy. *What I Saw at the Revolution*. New York: Ballantine, 1990.

Oberdorfer, Don. "Missed Signals in the Middle East." *Washington Post Magazine*, March 17, 1991.

Pogue, Forrest C. *George C. Marshall*, vol. 1. New York: Viking Press, 1963.

Pyle, Richard. *Schwarzkopf in His Own Words*. New York: Signet Books, 1991.

Rocawich, Linda. "The General in Charge." *The Progressive*, January 1991, pp. 18–21.

Salinger, Pierre, and Laurent, Eric. *Secret Dossier: The Hidden Agenda Behind the Gulf War*. New York: Penguin Books, 1991.

Salomon, Lt. Gen. Leon E., and Bankirer, Lt. Col. Harold. "Total Army CSS: Providing the Means for Victory." *Military Review* 71 (April 1991): 3–8.

Sasson, Jean P. *The Rape of Kuwait*. New York: Knightsbridge, 1991.

Schwarzkopf, Lt. Gen. H. Norman. "Deterence and the Constitution: Ability to Fight Surest Way of Providing for 'The Common Defense.' " *Army*, October 1987, pp. 111–132.

_____. "Strategic Role Spawns Flexible, Responsive Force." *Army*, October 1988, pp. 134–153.

————. "Turmoil: Middle East—Business as Usual." *Defense/90*, May–June 1990, pp. 24–30.

Sheehy, Gail. "How Saddam Survived." *Vanity Fair*, August 1991.

Sifry, Micah L., and Cerf, Christopher, eds. *The Gulf War Reader*. New York: Times Books, 1991.

Silvasy, Maj. Gen. Stephen, Jr. "AirLand Battle Future: The Tactical Battlefield." *Military Review* 71 (February 1991): 2–12.

Steel, Ronald. *Walter Lippmann and the American Century*. Boston: Little, Brown, 1980.

Summers, Col. Harry G. "Leadership in Adversity: From Vietnam to Victory in the Gulf." *Military Review* 71 (May 1991): 2–9.

USA Today. Desert Warriors. New York: Pocket Books, 1991.

Viorst, Milton. "A Reporter At Large: After the Liberation." *The New Yorker*, September 30, 1991, pp. 37 ff.

Walker, Martin. "Dateline Washington: Victory and Delusion." *Foreign Policy*, Summer 1991, pp. 160–172.

Wright, Quincy. "The Transfer of Destroyers to Great Britain." *American Journal of International Law* 34 (1940): 680.

Woodward, Bob. *The Commanders*. New York: Simon & Schuster, 1991.

Yant, Martin. *Desert Mirage: The True Story of the Gulf War*. Buffalo, N.Y.: Prometheus, 1991.

ACKNOWLEDGMENTS

I am indebted to many people for reading the manuscript, and for their candid suggestions. These include John Seaman, William Beaney, Linda Rebuck, Lou Pauly, Jeannie Sears, Greg Shirley, Moira Dillon, Cynthia Smith, Arnold Ceballos, David Welch, Lara Friedlander, Julie Rosenthal, Jack McLeod, Katherine Isbester and Janice Stein. The trenchant criticism of my seminar students has been especially helpful.

The manuscript was typed many times, through many drafts, by Brenda Samuels of Erindale College, University of Toronto. The final corrections were typed by Mary Wellman of Erindale College.

Once again, Marian Wood of Henry Holt and Company

did the editing. There is none better. That is also true of John Jusino and of Meg Drislane, who did the copyediting.

Above all, I am indebted to Elizabeth Kaplan of Sterling Lord Literistic. Without her constant advice and encouragement, this book could not have been written.

Jean Edward Smith
Toronto, Canada
August 15, 1991

INDEX